BAD
STRATEGIES

BAD
STRATEGIES

How Major Powers Fail in Counterinsurgency

JAMES S. CORUM

Author of *Fighting the War on Terror*

Foreword by Dennis Showalter
Professor of History, Colorado College

ZENITH PRESS

First published in 2008 by Zenith Press, an imprint of MBI Publishing Company, 400 First Avenue North, Suite 300, Minneapolis, MN 55401 USA

Zenith Press titles are also available at discounts in bulk quantity for industrial or sales-promotional use. For details write to Special Sales Manager at MBI Publishing Company, 400 First Avenue North, Suite 300, Minneapolis, MN 55401 USA.

To find out more about our books, join us online at www.zenithpress.com.

Library of Congress Cataloging-in-Publication Data

Corum, James S.
  Bad strategies : how major powers fail in counterinsurgency / by James S. Corum.
    p. cm.
  Includes bibliographical references and index.
  ISBN-13: 978-0-7603-3080-7 (hbk.)
  ISBN-10: 0-7603-3080-8 (hbk.)
  1. Counterinsurgency. 2. Counterinsurgency—History—20th century—Case studies.
  3. Strategy. I. Title.
U241.C678 2006
355.02'18—dc22
          2007046263

Designer: Helena Shimizu

Printed in the United States of America

CONTENTS

■ ■ ■

FOREWORD

■ ■ ■

by Dennis Showalter

MILITARY WRITING CAN BE APHORISTICALLY described as an enduring dialogue between Whigs and Calvinists. The Whigs interpret warmaking as a contest between progress and obscurantism, with progress—whether represented by technology, doctrine, or reform—emerging triumphant. The Calvinists interpret victory and defeat as judgments on the militarily righteous. The generals, armies, and societies following the straight and narrow path attain victory. The purblind and the contumacious are cast into darkness.

In this volume James Corum firmly aligns with the Calvinists. *Bad Strategies* is a presentation of compound catastrophe. In four scathing case studies it describes the failure of modern democracies in a particular form of asymmetric war. The French in Algeria, the British in Cyprus, the United States in Vietnam and again in Iraq, suffered disaster in counterinsurgencies.

At first glance the chosen case studies appear to resemble not merely apples and oranges but the entire contents of a fruit stand. A case can be made that the examples are so fundamentally different that while they may be juxtaposed, they defy comparison. France was seeking to maintain what its government, its political system, its military, and its public regarded as not an imperial but an organic connection. Algeria was understood as part of France, legally and viscerally. As a point of comparison, one might consider contemporary reactions in the United States to the immediate prospect of the southwest becoming part of a "Republica del Norte." Cyprus, on the other hand, was a classic imperial outpost. Lacking the emotional connotations of India, Singapore, or even Kenya, its perceived value was entirely strategic. The United States entered Vietnam as the ally of a sovereign state threatened by internal subversion and external aggression. Iraq developed in the intellectual context of a war of liberation on the classic World War II model from the Philippines to the Netherlands: destroy the oppressor and allow people to resume normal life.

What might be called the situational awareness of the counterinsurgent powers differed no less fundamentally. French consciousness of Algeria was specific and ran wide and deep, however questionable its accuracy in specific areas. Cyprus was a generic British possession, controlled and administered by the book, not worth the bother of systematic study. American ignorance of both Vietnam and Iraq is best described as comprehensive and spectacular. Different matrices of understanding generated correspondingly different responses, but a common outcome—an outcome Corum presents as predictable, yet avertable.

Corum pulls his discrete examples together under the rubric—the umbrella—of strategy. What makes this work valuable, arguably uniquely valuable, is its complex, sophisticated conceptualization of that concept. Most analyses describe strategy as a balance between ends and means. For Corum it is a synergy among ends, means, and will. The concept of "will" is usually included under "means." In fact it is essentially different, particularly in the "great democracies" presented here. In any conflict, a democracy's policy, strategy, and (increasingly) its tactics—political and military—must be generally supported by the public, the public's representatives, and (increasingly as well) by a public media self-defined as a literal fourth estate: guardian and ombudsman for people and societies otherwise susceptible to deception and manipulation.

Of strategy's three elements, will is the most salient in counterinsurgency. Here the juxtaposition of ends and means is shaped by the significant imbalance of material power between the combatants. This is particularly true for Corum's cases. At the military level the British in Cyprus were far more victims of their own bungling than of inadequacies generated by the overall decline of British power. The success of French armed forces in breaking the military back of the FLN in

Algeria is generally acknowledged. So is American ability to "turn North Vietnam into a parking lot"—or, less drastically, to create Lake Hanoi by demolishing the Red River's dams and dykes. The forces committed to Iraq were indicted from the beginning by military specialists as inadequate, and Corum acerbically depicts the result: coping on the fly with contingencies that too often became emergencies. The ultimate capacity of the United States to increase exponentially its ground strength was nevertheless unquestionable. The numbers deployed have reflected particular decisions—and the political and public will behind them.

Will is additionally significant in shaping this work because the studied counterinsurgencies did not present a mortal threat or a fundamental challenge to the democracies conducting them. Alternative case studies come readily to mind: the struggle for South Korea from 1948 to 1950, the Hukbalahap insurgency in the Philippine Republic during the 1950s, and, not least, Israel's continuing Second Intifada. Each of these situations features stark alternatives and uncompromising adversaries. In each of Corum's cases the counterinsurgents had working room. The Greek Cypriots wanted no more than for the British to go away, and even that finally involved restricting their presence to mutually acceptable base areas. The Algerian rebels' early demands emphasized changing status rather than severing bonds. They were correspondingly susceptible to negotiation, and a major specific strength of this work is Corum's demonstration of the French military's initial recognition of that prospect. In Vietnam, the United States eventually committed itself to a replication of Japan's strategy in World War II: waging an essentially limited war against an adversary committed to total victory. That commitment nevertheless remained incremental, the situation remained a boil rather than a cancer. Corum describes the originally projected endstate of an independent noncommunist South Vietnam as "neither impossible nor unrealistic." A cottage industry of academic, political, and military publication remains devoted to turning points unturned and roads not taken. In contrast to Vietnam, the Iraq counterinsurgency ultimately grew from a single decision: go or no-go. What began as a military-political blitzkrieg built on the concept of a "light footprint" has evolved—or devolved, or collapsed, depending upon perspective—into grass-roots, hands-on involvement in a culture war waged in the context of a religious reformation. At every stage, however, American participation has depended on American will.

Whether in historic or contemporary contexts, will is a product of three factors: time, stress, and visibility. Time is usually considered the most obvious. George C. Marshall's famous aphorism that democracies cannot fight a Seven Years' War became a mantra during the Vietnam years. It has surfaced again in the context of Iraq. It has three usual implications. First, public fortitude weakens and public attention diminishes in proportion to the duration of hostilities. The presumed consequences are best expressed by iconic movie character John Rambo: "do we get to win *this* time?" The second prospect depicts a populist *esprit democratique* emerging red in fang and claw, demanding immediate, presumably apocalyptic, resolution as opposed to the calibrated solutions favored by political, diplomatic, and military professionals. Lyndon Johnson is unlikely ever to be confused with Otto von Bismarck, but among the principles guiding his approach to Vietnam was an expressed reluctance to arouse the American public's warlike impulses by implementing anything resembling national mobilization. A similar thought pattern can be deduced from George W. Bush's early and repeated public insistence that Islam is a religion of peace, and the not-so-subtle concern of various pundits that since 9/11 America is constantly on the verge of anti-Muslim pogroms. Third on the list comes a scenario describing the erosion of democracy by war's Three Horsemen: violence, militarism, and authoritarianism. In the early 1970s, talk of Nixon's possible suspension of presidential elections in the name of national security was current alike in editorial rooms and faculty commons. The alleged comprehensive threat to civil liberties and the rule of law posed by the ill-named Patriot Act, by John Ashcroft, and by "Bushitler" himself remains the major theme of blogs and talk shows. Lest this prospect be dismissed as left-liberal paranoia, France underwent what can legitimately be described as a low-level insurgency by determined opponents of the withdrawal from Algeria.

Time alone does not have a decisive negative impact on will. Stress, broadly defined, is another vital factor. It can reflect situational material and psychological demands. The citizen conscripts France was able to pump into Algeria were a vital factor in the military successes achieved. Increasingly, however, a sense that compulsory service in Algeria challenged the Republic's social contract contributed heavily to metropolitan France's acceptance of de

Gaulle's drastic resolution of the conflict. A major difference between Vietnam and Iraq has involved the sustained morale of a volunteer force drawn (a point usually overlooked) from a significantly larger population. Contributing as well have been internal changes in the armed forces, most notably the abandonment of individual rotation in favor of unit redeployment of both active and reserve components—a policy whose long-term social and political consequences have yet to develop.

Counterinsurgency also nurtures the utopianism endemic to democracies at war. The problem can be defined in terms of a dialectic between clean shields and dirty hands. On one hand, since at least the American and French Revolutions, democratic societies tend toward objectifying enemies as "others," with causes not merely evil but alien. One's own righteousness, in turn, legitimates the means used to achieve victory. At the same time, if the way to win a war is to be as hard, as nasty as the enemy, at what point does a society risk becoming what it fights? Originating in World War II, that question has become central in the democratic response to counterinsurgency.

France in Algeria represents one extreme: *a corsaire, corsaire et demi* (fighting fire with a bigger fire, if you will). Corum depicts a French security system that matched and excelled the FLN in consequent ferocity, to the eventual detriment of the original cause. Since Vietnam, the conventional position in democracies has moved steadily in the direction of separating entirely one's own behavior from one's opponents, with a corresponding tendency to ratchet standards of conduct at all levels of operations ever higher, to a point where no room for mistakes exist, and where "fog and friction" generated by the adversary is dismissed as irrelevant. Osama bin Laden's long-familiar aphorism—"We love death. The U.S. loves life. That is the big difference between us"—invites modification. It is not life democracies love, but righteousness and self-righteousness. Both are difficult to nurture in the murky environment of counterterrorism.

A third element of stress involves the erosion of "cultures of competence." In all societies, but especially in democracies, governments and armed forces depend heavily for their public credibility on a public sense that they have a basic grip on events, that they get most routine things right most of the time. Counterinsurgency, which Corum accurately describes as a more complex process than conventional intrastate war, by its protean nature challenges cultures of competence. What seems solid policy when adopted can metamorphose into catastrophe in a matter of months, often through no generally obvious insurgent reaction. In counterinsurgency Tet Offensives are an exception, not a rule. The usual result is that the counterinsurgent power is left resembling Wile E. Coyote: the cartoon character not merely frustrated but bewildered in his pursuit of the roadrunner.

Applied to Cyprus and Algeria, Vietnam and Iraq, the image is appropriate—and devastating. Democracies have an inherent, and healthy, mistrust of politicians and soldiers. The last thing either can afford is to be embarrassed, to look foolish. The consequences can run from inconvenience for the governing party, as in the case of Cyprus, through what amounts to a particular administration's forfeiting of legitimacy, as in Iraq, to the significant domestic unraveling occasioned by Vietnam and Algeria. In the latter cases the sense of a bungled counterinsurgency acted as a catalyst for a spectrum of other problems. None necessarily critical by themselves (even America's festering racial issues), in critical mass they can alter societies: a consequence to delight aficionados of irony . . .

The final element of stress in a context of will involves the issue of noncombatant immunity. Since World War II, harming civilians by military action has taken center stage. Initially focused on the consequences of using thermonuclear weapons, the question now informs any discussion of counterinsurgency operations. Algeria was the beginning. Vietnam was the tipping point. Coverage of that conflict focused heavily on the harm done to civilians in both the north and the south. The photo of a napalm-seared child fleeing a U.S. air strike is arguably the Vietnam War's defining image. The difficulty of distinguishing between combatants and noncombatants, a central element of the North Vietnamese/NLF doctrine of *dau tranh*, or total struggle, provided a focal point of domestic opposition to the war. Criticism of the U.S. presence in Iraq has consistently sought to make civilian victimization a defining trope of a failing counterinsurgency, albeit with mixed success.

That leads, in turn, to will's third defining element: visibility. Counterinsurgency depends heavily for success on a low domestic profile. By its nature, successes are incremental and long term, challenging facile categorization, and usually involving three steps forward, two back, and one sideways. Anything less congenial to the life cycle of a modern democracy is difficult to imagine. The dichotomy has been exacerbated, when not defined, by the emergence of visual media with a 24-hour communication cycle, highly competitive and heavily dependant on shock effect. "If it bleeds, it leads" is a worldwide journalistic mantra. French television reports, despite being heavily government-controlled, did much to discredit the Algerian counterinsurgency by bringing the consequences of reciprocal violence into French homes. The impact of television on American public opinion during Vietnam is universally acknowledged. It has been suggested, only in part facetiously, that had television existed in the 1860s, the Civil War would have ended after the Battle of Antietam.

Visibility frequently reflects and exacerbates the imbalance of material power mentioned earlier in another context. Arguably the most compelling dramatic theme of the modern era is the struggle of victims against oppressors, their brilliant triumph or heroic defeat. It is particularly powerful in democracies. The mythologies of the American Revolution and the Civil War have alike been shaped by the image of struggle against odds. In particular the enduring cultural triumph of the Confederacy rests far more on stereotypes of ragged, hungry men heroically fending off overwhelming forces in defense of their homes than on nostalgia for slavery or contemporary racism. For Britain the dominant myth of World War II is the Battle of Britain: the victory of "the few." For France it is the Resistance against a brutal occupation.

These conceptions may owe more to the creative imagination than the historical record. They nevertheless contribute significantly to a visceral discomfort at images of armed and helmeted soldiers, backed by the full material panoply of modern warfare, confronting not only men but women and children whose chief weapon is their cause. Insurgencies are correspondingly skilled at presenting themselves in the context of that dichotomy. The case of Mohammed al-Durah, the Palestinian boy whose death at the Israeli army's hands has been convincingly presented as a fiction based on doctored footage, is only one example. In such cases charging the media with culpable carelessness, or with misfeasance for the sake of an agenda, taking sides instead of reporting, may be accurate but is also irrelevant. The "master story" has an independent existence.

The salience of will within democracies engaging in counterinsurgency informs and highlights Corum's recommendations for strategic planning. He emphasizes vision and flexibility: the capacity to develop long-range perspective while modifying endstates to changing circumstances. French aims in Algeria, and Britain's in Cyprus, were initially unrealistic and modified only under the pressure of events. Corum emphasizes, correspondingly, the importance of understanding contexts, of situational awareness. In each of his case studies, the underlying circumstances and potential problems were well known in decision-making circles. The grievances of Cypriots and Algerians, the weaknesses of South Vietnam's government, the underlying internal tensions in Iraq, the absence of any democratic tradition, were not arcane mysteries—except, too often, to those making counterinsurgency policy.

Cluelessness was a consequence of structure. Corum emphasizes functional decision-making processes at government levels as crucial in counterinsurgency. The French Fourth Republic was too divided internally to develop and implement any comprehensive plan of political and economic reform for Algeria. American policies in Vietnam and Iraq were shaped and driven by small circles around the President, fatally susceptible to groupthink and solipsism, not merely unwilling but unable to evaluate alternatives originating outside their boxes. Dysfunctional relationships between military and civilian leaders are no less central to failed counterinsurgencies. Sometimes the dysfunction can be structural. France's colonial army, the cutting edge of the counterinsurgency, had a culture deeply at odds with that of the rest of the army and with France itself. Sometimes, as in Vietnam and Iraq, dysfunction reflects the military's reluctance to dialogue with civilian authority—reluctance that is a product of internecine struggles for power that invite structural gridlock and external manipulation. In either case the outcome is unlikely to be favorable.

Corum's analysis emphasizes appropriate application of resources in counterinsurgency. The most obvious challenge here is calibrating the balance of force and persuasion—no easy task when one eye must be kept on the insurgents, one eye on political authority, and the third on public opinion. States with multiple commitments face an additional problem. Britain and France both saw themselves, however inappropriately, as playing significant, independent international diplomatic and military roles outside the sphere of counterinsurgency. The anonymous—and probably apocryphal—American officer quoted as refusing to destroy the U.S. Army "just to win this lousy war" was more perceptive than blinkered. America's vital interests remained in the Fulda Gap, not the Mekong Delta. The contemporary reconfiguration of U.S. ground forces on a light/medium basis invites the question of just how useful Stryker brigades will be against even a second-class conventional enemy fielding main battle tanks.

Corum stresses the importance in counterinsurgency of seeking political settlements: negotiated compromise solutions designed to convince insurgents to trade guns for politics. But what happens when the dissonance between projected endstates is fundamental? In Cyprus the endstates driving the conflict were close enough to be resolvable by that kind of negotiation. In Algeria and Vietnam, as the counterinsurgency developed the endstates grew sufficiently far apart to generate what amounted to total war in limited contexts. Regarding Iraq, it appears reasonable to suggest that for the United States, deposing Saddam Hussein was seen as both a means and an end in itself. The insurgents had no common endstate, at least not one strong enough to generate a common front. That, in turn, rendered them potentially susceptible not exactly to "divide and conquer," but to "divide and convince"—to seek, essentially, a brokered solution balancing mutual dissatisfaction. The jury is still out on the result.

Corum's major specific recommendations to counterinsurgents reinforce the importance of compromise: maintaining a favorable international profile, training local security forces, maintaining public support at home. Underlying this position is a subtext that might be called "normalizing counterinsurgency." To the extent that success in counterinsurgency is possible in a context of democratic governments and societies, it requires keeping it at the level of "ongoing operations." The red thread of catastrophe emerges when counterinsurgency become a regular subject for question time in Parliament and challenge in the Assembly, when generals speak of "light at the end of the tunnel" and presidents don flight suits to proclaim ephemeral victories.

Strategic analyst Colin Gray recently published *Fighting Talk: Forty Maxims on War, Peace, and Strategy*. On a quick read its ideas appear to challenge and contradict each other at every turn. Certain behavior is wisdom—except when it is folly. Nothing important changes—except when it does. Formulas and preconceptions are signposts to catastrophe. The work's underlying wisdom is Gray's insistence that in "war, peace, and strategy" there may be principles. There are no systems, only situational awareness. That kind of fundamental competence, the competence Corum presents as essential to counterinsurgency, is not beyond the grasp of democratic systems and institutions. A fundamental discontinuity nevertheless persists between Corum's sophisticated, calibrated caution and that "violence of spirit" so often described before and after de Tocqueville as an inherent temptation for democracies. That discontinuity informs this book—and Corum's presentation and analysis of its consequences makes *Bad Strategies* a major contribution to a vital discussion.

INTRODUCTION
What is Strategy?

■ ■ ■

"Poor strategy is expensive, bad strategy can be lethal."[1]
—Colin Gray, *Modern Strategy*

STRATEGY IS INTRINSIC TO ALL forms of conflict. From the earliest organized warfare, perhaps eighty thousand years ago, a group engaging in conflict would have an objective or endstate—essentially a vision of what they wanted to have by the end of the conflict. The British strategist, Colin Gray, argues that "there is an essential unity to all strategic experience in all periods of history because nothing vital to the nature and function of war and strategy changes."[2] Strategy implies an *endstate*, a *ways* (the organization of forces and the agreed upon means to reach the endstate) and applying the *means* (resources to include people, weapons and supplies) to achieve the endstate. One can surmise that eighty thousand years ago warring tribes or clans established clear goals, developed a war organization and plan. They would deploy their warriors, weapons, and supplies to carry out their goals. Judging from what we can document in recorded history, the group or nation that had a good strategy—that is a strategy with clear goals, a good organization and plan to achieve the goals, and adequate resources to support the plan—had a great advantage over opponents with a poor strategy.

17

There are many definitions of strategy. The greatest theorist on conflict, the nineteenth-century Prussian general Carl von Clausewitz, defined strategy in fairly operational military terms. "Strategy is the use of engagements for the object of war."[3] Colin Gray, one of the top contemporary scholars of the subject, defines strategy as "the use that is made of force and the threat of force for the ends of policy."[4] Basil Liddell Hart, another leading theorist of warfare, defined strategy as "the art of distributing and applying military means to fulfill the ends of policy."[5] The above are good definitions of strategy as they pertain to a conventional war, that is, a conflict between two states. But the strategic requirements of a conflict involving non-state entities (namely insurgent groups, factions, militias, mafias, terrorist groups, etc.) are very different and much less oriented on force as a primary solution. Of all the available definitions of strategy, the one from U.S. military doctrine is probably the best suited to a discussion of counterinsurgency: "The art and science of developing, applying, and coordinating the instruments of national power (diplomatic, economic, military, and informational) to achieve objectives that contribute to national security. Also called national strategy or grand strategy."[6] The U.S. military definition of strategy is distinctive because it mentions the non-military resources of the nation in a conflict: diplomatic, informational, and economic.

The other important definition for this book is insurgency, which is an attempt to overthrow an established government by violent means. There are many motivations for insurgency: nationalism, ethnic nationalism, religion, economic and social grievances. Insurgency takes many forms, from coalitions of small groups to a highly centralized Maoist type of insurgency. Insurgents use many different strategies and tactics; from terrorist campaigns designed to intimidate the population, to conventional warfare designed to overthrow the government's army. Yet all insurgents have the same goal— attaining power. It might be autonomy for their region or independence or power for their faction within the government. Most commonly it is the control of the whole nation. Insurgency is also a highly political form of warfare. Insurgent strategies usually start with a program to win as much support among the population as possible. Insurgents wage war through propaganda and organizing the people as much as by military means. And insurgencies, just like the governments they are trying to overthrow, are highly dependent upon winning support among the population.

The U.S. military definition is the most appropriate for discussing strategy in context of counterinsurgency because that definition recognizes that economic, informational, and international aspects of the conflict are just as important—perhaps more important—as the employment of military force. To correctly understand insurgency and counterinsurgency one must see them as forms of warfare that are fundamentally different from conventional state-on-state conflict.

However, for every conflict the strategist can ask the same questions: What is the endstate? What are the resources available? How will the opponents react? What are the geographic and environmental constraints? What is the government's degree of commitment? How will the insurgency affect other interests?

Approaching Counterinsurgency

Insurgency and counterinsurgency have been with us since the start of recorded history. Indeed, several books of the Old Testament record insurgencies such as David against King Saul, or the Maccabees against the Greeks. There is nothing new about rebel groups trying to overthrow the government or gain independence or autonomy. In the modern era insurgency has been the preferred means, often the only practical means, by which a faction or group can confront the power of the government, or confront the forces of a major power. Because insurgency sometimes succeeds, it will continue to be a war of choice for non-state groups mounting challenges against government.

Sometimes we can learn much more from studying failure than studying success. Failure often forces us to ask some very tough questions and conduct a deeper analysis in order to understand the cause and effect of failure. This book is about strategic failure in counterinsurgency. More specifically, it is about how modern great democracies can fail in a fight against insurgents. The great democracies examined in this book are France, Britain, and the United States, and this book centers on four case studies of failed counterinsurgency campaigns: France in Algeria 1954–1962, Britain in Cyprus 1955–1959, and the United States in Vietnam 1950–1975 and Iraq

2003–2007. When faced with an insurgency, modern great democracies have much in common. All such governments are ultimately answerable to the people and therefore must maintain public support for a war outside their homeland. If those governments cannot maintain public support, they will fail in the counterinsurgency campaign. Great democracies have to consider the long term impacts of policy and pay careful attention to the international aspects of counterinsurgency. The great democracies considered in this book all had large, professional armed forces organized, trained, and equipped for conventional state-on-state warfare. Democratic nations all have a tradition of civil-military relations that affects the strategic decision making. Indeed, the style of strategic decision making may vary, but the process is remarkably similar for modern democracies. One of the most important similarities shared by the three nations studied in this work is that all could bring considerable economic and military resources to bear against the insurgencies that they faced. Yet all failed to defeat the insurgents.

Eliot Cohen's book, *Supreme Command*, was one of the inspirations for this book. In *Supreme Command*, Professor Cohen provides four case studies of leadership in great democracies in wartime. In doing so, he did not establish a definitive model of effective strategic leadership per se, but by asking similar questions about great wartime leaders such as Winston Churchill, Abraham Lincoln, Georges Clemenceau, and David Ben Gurion, the author succeeded in developing some valuable insights into the nature of effective wartime leadership. I am taking case study approach similar to Eliot Cohen's model. This book will be looking at strategic failure, and a national civilian and military leadership that got it horribly wrong. It is not my intention to develop an elaborate model of strategic effectiveness, but I do hope that by examining these cases of failure I can come to some insights about how great nations fail to develop effective strategies. The usefulness of such a study is clear—the great democracies will have to deal with insurgencies in the future, and I sincerely hope that they will do better than in the past.

In approaching this subject the first step is to get the history right. To get the history right one must start with a few basic questions about each counterinsurgency campaign: What was the strategy? How did the strategy adapt over time? What was the decision-making process employed by the top civilian and military leaders? How was the military used? What were the essential civilian/ military factors in the campaign? How effective was the intelligence? What were the key assumptions of the leaders? Basically we already know that these campaigns failed. The important issue is to discover why they failed.

As a starting point I try to use original documents to get the most accurate picture of what the government forces knew, and how they understood the contemporary context of the insurgency. When I make some strong critiques of the strategies employed against these insurgencies, I do not do it from the perspective of hindsight but rather from the perspective of the information and advice that was available at the time. This is definitely not a study from the perspective of "We Know Now." In every case of failure there were many people in the government and military who understood the issues, who provided accurate intelligence, and who warned against courses of action. For various reasons, the good advice of senior government officials and military officers was disregarded as the governments embarked upon what would become failed enterprises. In fact, the failed strategies were NOT what seemed to be the most reasonable thing to do at the time. That is what makes these studies so interesting. In every case examined the senior civilian and military leadership had to work very hard to get it so wrong.

Since we are a few decades removed from the insurgencies in Algeria, Vietnam, and Cyprus, many public documents are readily available. In the case of Iraq, only a limited number of unclassified documents are available which outline the decision making of the Bush administration. However, in this case I can base much of my analysis of on my own observation and participation. In 2002 and 2003 I wrote several studies that dealt with the occupation of Iraq for the Army War College group that was developing an outline plan for that occupation. In 2004 I was deployed to Iraq as an Army Reserve lieutenant colonel on a team to develop a strategy to build a new Iraqi armed forces. Since I have been connected to the military as a serving officer and as an academic, I have had close contact with many officers who have served in the Pentagon and in Iraq and have had a close view of the strategic process.

For more than a decade I have taught in U.S. military institutions of higher learning and I believe I can speak with some authority on U.S. military doctrine and the mindset of the U.S. military. In 2005 and 2006 I was part of a small team that wrote the new U.S. Army and Marine Corps counterinsurgency doctrine, FM-3-24, *Counterinsurgency*, which has received considerable attention from around the world.[7] For the last three years most of my students have been army majors who have recently served in Iraq —so I at least have considerable access to people with recent operational experience on the ground. Although I have not had direct involvement with the strategic decision making in the Pentagon and White House, after many years of military service I have a broad range of contacts who have been involved in the Iraq War at the strategic level. I have discussed these issues in some detail and feel confident that my portraits of top leaders in the Defense Department are fair and accurate.

Elements of Strategy

In any strategic process one has to start from the end—what is the objective, or endstate that the government wishes to achieve? From that question one reasons backwards to figure out how to get there, and what kind of problems might be encountered, what resources will be necessary, and so on.

But first the strategist must ask, "Is the desired endstate realistic?"

Absolute victory, à la the surrender on the deck of the Battleship Missouri, is a very rare thing in warfare. When fighting insurgents, governments would like to see the insurgency collapse completely and surrender unconditionally. That is extremely unlikely. In fighting insurgents, most realistic endstates require the government to negotiate a political settlement that makes some concessions to the insurgents.

In addition, the strategic endstate for the government will almost certainly change. Great powers, and great democracies, want victory. But usually they have to settle for something less. Therefore, getting the endstate right is essential. This requires a clear understanding of the national priorities and objectives. It requires understanding when political compromise is likely to work, and what principles cannot be compromised. A good endstate is what Clausewitz would call the aim of any country fighting a war—"A better state of peace." Many insurgencies are settled by political means that allow the government to retain power and preserve its core interests, while allowing the insurgents enough political/economic advantages to win widespread approval.

The negotiated end to the twelve years of civil war in El Salvador in 1992 is a good case in point. The insurgency ended, some reasonable compromises were made, the insurgents became a peaceful democratic political party, and El Salvador has not known political violence since then. In short, most successful counterinsurgency campaigns operations require that the military and national leadership carry on a political dialog in the middle of the conflict.

But setting the endstate is just the first part of a healthy strategic decision-making process. When entering into a conflict a first step of the government and military leaderships is to carry out a thorough strategic estimate of the situation, one that outlines the issues in dispute, the social context, the insurgent groups and ideologies, the insurgent and factional leadership, and so on. Furthermore, the strategic estimate will have to outline the courses of action the insurgents or factions or local governments are most likely to follow. Needless to say, the usefulness of any strategic estimate will be based on the quality of the intelligence available.

The government defending itself against the insurgents must then make specific plans to address the most crucial issues identified in the strategic estimate. A series of branch plans that deals with probable insurgent and factional courses of action must also be developed. While plans are being developed, the government and military agencies tasked to deal with the insurgency also have to determine what personnel and resources (the means of strategy) will be needed to ensure the plan has a chance for success.

Strategic planning implies long-term thinking. That is especially important for dealing with insurgencies because, once they get started, insurgencies tend to last for a long time. Even the model counterinsurgency campaigns took years to achieve their goals. Governments facing insurgencies not only have to think of the resources immediately available, but also the resources that will be needed in two or three years' time. Of course, while allocating personnel and resources the question must always be asked as to the place of the counterinsurgency campaign in the context of a nation's other commitments. Does the priority of defeating the insurgency require too large a commitment of funds and resources, and will combating the insurgency force the government to deny adequate resources to even higher priority issues?

Finally, a counterinsurgency campaign does not exist in a political vacuum. International problems and crises may force a reevaluation of the counterinsurgency strategy in light of other needs. Domestic political events will often force a change in course by the national leaders. With all the variables that affect an insurgency or counterinsurgency campaign, the government strategy must be designed to be flexible.

Strategy for Counterinsurgency

Developing a strategy for fighting an enemy nation is a very complex process. But developing a strategy to deal with a non-state enemy can be even more difficult. First of all, dealing with a non-state enemy is legally complex. Using the military in such operations, where civilians are always in the middle, is far different from the force-on-force fighting of a conventional war. In counterinsurgency one might have to detain large numbers of civilians in a combat zone. What is the right of the military forces to detain civilians? Insurgents might not wear uniforms—so what is their status under the law? Are insurgents legitimate combatants who can be held as prisoners of war or are they criminals? In counterinsurgency, collateral damage is unavoidable. How much collateral damage is acceptable?

In contrast, the rules of a state-on-state conventional war are relatively simple—a combatant nation has the right to target the enemy armed forces and wreck them. In conventional war government infrastructure and war industries are legitimate targets. A nation can legitimately employ sanctions and blockades. Captured enemy soldiers can be legally held until hostilities end. The centers of gravity are straightforward; they are the enemy military forces and their support structure. In conventional war intelligence is geared towards finding enemy units and weapons—not an exceptionally difficult task with modern high tech means of intelligence collection.

Insurgency and counterinsurgency have different centers of gravity than conventional state-on-state warfare. For both the insurgent and the opposing government the center of gravity is the people. Success in such conflicts normally requires winning the support of the population. In conventional war there are legal guidelines for the use of force. But in counterinsurgency force can be constrained by a host of other considerations such as politics and culture. It might be legally acceptable to use force against an insurgent group—but could it backfire politically? Or would it be seen as an acceptable act by the local population? In conflict with non-state forces there are rarely clearly identifiable military centers of gravity to attack. Sanctions and blockades might be employed—but again their use might be more limited than in conventional war.

One of the biggest problems in counterinsurgency is that there is rarely one clear enemy. Normally, various factions take part in an insurgency—and each will probably have its own agenda. Enemies are not clearly delineated. In most cases in counterinsurgency the enemy wears civilian clothes and blends in among the civilian population. Intelligence is especially difficult in counterinsurgency. Defeating an insurgency is much more than a matter of finding the fighters, and success will require that the government break up the civilian support network. Often the insurgents might field just a small number of trained and armed men, but those men are supported by a large underground civilian support network—the people who hide the insurgent fighters; provide money, food, and supplies; run messages; provide intelligence; and so on. At the height of the insurgency in Malaya the insurgents fielded perhaps 10,000 trained fighting men in guerrilla units. But the fighters were supported by over 150,000 active civilian supporters who were organized into cells and supported the insurgent effort through recruiting and propaganda. The British could kill many of the fighting men—but as long as the support groups were there the fighting force could be quickly reconstituted. Breaking up the civilian support network required a vast intelligence effort as well as major initiatives to improve the economy and establish a government infrastructure where there was none before.

Unlike conventional wars, insurgencies often do not end neatly. In many cases an insurgency simply continues for years. Success might mean not the end of the insurgency but the insurgency being reduced to the point that it no longer threatens the government's stability. In conventional war there are clear means to measure success. One can defeat and capture an enemy army and clear a region of enemy forces. But in counterinsurgency you can clear a region—and the rebels will retreat and come back the moment the government forces leave the area. You can hurt the rebel forces by destroying their combat units, but such actions are rarely decisive. Rebels can reconstitute themselves in a way that conventional military forces cannot.

Carl von Clausewitz argued that war was another form of politics. This also applies to insurgency and counterinsurgency. Indeed, insurgencies are all about politics. Unlike conventional war, a very common behavior in insurgency is changing sides. Factions and parties in the population might change their allegiance from the government to the insurgents, and vice versa. The allegiance of the population commonly switches from neutral to either the government or the insurgent. Or it might align with some other factions. Winning the allegiance of the population or of various factions requires a political settlement. Very often insurgencies do not end in straightforward defeat of one side or the other, but with a negotiated settlement. The group that is best placed with the population has the strongest position in the negotiations.

Successful Counterinsurgency

The very complexity of counterinsurgency means that there are a vast number of opportunities to make mistakes. It is extremely difficult to point to a "model" counterinsurgency campaign because even the most successful campaigns involved false starts, major operational mistakes, and, in the end, took years to achieve success. It is no wonder that the conventional soldiers dislike these wars. On the other hand, despite all the problems the defending government faces, it's worse for the insurgent. Most insurgencies fail for good reasons. Governments start with huge advantages: financial resources, international recognition, regular police and military forces. Insurgents rarely possess such things—or if they do, they have them in far smaller quality and degree than the government they are trying to overthrow.

One important thing to remember in crafting an effective strategy against insurgency is that the military side is only one part—and not necessarily the most important part—of a good strategy. When the military is employed in counterinsurgency campaigns it will be doing a great many vital tasks that are outside the normal purview of military operations. Effective counterinsurgency is about nation building and addressing the needs of the population. Thus, the most important military forces might be the civil affairs teams, the engineers, and the medical units. The combat forces, which are the main thing in conventional war, are likely to have a secondary role as security providers. Soldiers who are normally the supporting forces in conventional war (civil affairs, engineers, transport, and so on) are likely to be the main effort in counterinsurgency. In fact, in many instances of counterinsurgency the military is not even the main effort and the primary focus of the counterinsurgency strategy will be on the civilian reconstruction and aid managers. In other instances of successful counterinsurgency campaigns the police, and not the military, have been the main focus of the security effort. In short, an effective counterinsurgency strategy is often a mirror image of a conventional war strategy.

However the counterinsurgency nation approaches the unique aspects of an insurgency, the primary requirement for success is a comprehensive strategy. The counterinsurgency strategy must address ALL the major issues: politics, economics, infrastructure, social problems, security of the population, foreign involvement, and so on. There have been cases—Algeria is one—in which the counterinsurgent nation got the military part of the strategy right but then failed to get the other parts of the strategy right. The result was the failure of the whole strategy. One lesson is very consistent; the counterinsurgent nation has to get the civilian and political side of the effort correct, as well as the military side. This means that the government must be able to employ all of its agencies and assets in a coordinated manner. It is not an easy task—but it is also not impossible if the counterinsurgent nation has good leadership directing the effort.

Conduct of Counterinsurgency by Democracies

Counterinsurgency conflicts are complicated for democracies because winning and maintaining public support for the war is paramount. As long as the conflict continues the government must explain its policies and strategy to the public and answer the questions from a usually critical legislature and press. It is more difficult to explain the nature of the threat from irregular insurgent forces than to point to the armed forces of another nation. In the case of a great power, insurgencies in other countries rarely pose a direct threat to the national interest, or at least a kind of threat that is evident to the average voter. In short, keeping up the public support for counterinsurgency

operations is a difficult task for government. But such support is also a requirement in a democracy.

Democracies, by their nature, must conduct conflicts very differently from
other states. The strategy of democratic states must be broadly supported
by the public and the public's elected representatives. Democracies can only
employ their military forces, indeed, any agency of the government, with the
consent of a majority of the peoples' elected representatives. Democracies
can only conduct wars—even low level ones—in accordance with their own
constitutions and the rule of law. Any widespread violations of the law by
government forces become a public issue and undermine public support.

Even in the absence of clear international law, a modern nation with a
strong democratic tradition is required, by its very nature, to conduct both
conventional and unconventional wars under a basic and recognizable
standard of ethical behavior. Authoritarian states have commonly fought
and defeated insurgencies by the most brutal means. Stalin's Soviet Union
efficiently crushed incipient uprisings by uprooting, deporting, and even
slaughtering whole populations. During World War II the Germans efficiently
suppressed partisan activity in Greece by shooting one hundred hostages for
every German soldier killed by a guerrilla. But no modern democracy can
endorse such methods. While democratic nations might use relatively harsh
measures to control hostile populations—population resettlement, large scale
detentions, martial law declaration, special tribunals for the punishment of
rebels—there are very clear limits to the government's behavior and certain
lines that cannot be crossed. Armies of democracies are required, by law, to
uphold basic ethical standards and to maintain proper discipline of its soldiers
and police. This does not mean that Western democracies do not commit abuses
in fighting insurgents. Unfortunately, such abuses have often occurred when
democracies oppose insurgents. The most dramatic modern instances of abuse
in counterinsurgency include the widespread use of torture by French forces in
Algeria and the exceptionally brutal regime of detention camps established by
the British in Kenya to suppress the Mau Mau rebels.

There are practical, as well as constitutional, reasons for democratic
nations to adhere to legal and proper use of force when confronting
insurgents. In a democratic nation widespread abuse undermines the rule

of law. Tolerating contempt for the law within the military and executive branches of the government actually threatens the foundations of democracy. This was dramatically demonstrated in Algeria in 1961 when some of the French military units in Algeria—including many units that had routinely violated the laws of war while fighting the insurgents—attempted a coup against the French government. On the practical side, routine violations of the law become a scandal that will be exposed by a free press—usually with the result of undermining the public and political support for the government's counterinsurgency strategy. Operating in violation of basic ethical principles is also likely to turn the civilian population, whose support the government requires, against the government.

What is the nature of civil/military relations? One of the primary causes of dysfunction in developing coherent national security strategies has been the decline of a well-functioning model of the military's relationship with the national political leadership and its replacement with a flawed theory of the military's role in the strategic process. As with the other problems in strategic policy that exist today, this is not a recent development, but a trend carried on over several decades.

In the end, I found a surprisingly large number of common elements to strategic failure. If I do not provide a comprehensive model, I can at least provide some useful lessons for the politicians and soldiers who have to deal with these issues. In the four cases examined, failure was not foredoomed from the beginning. In each case a favorable outcome was possible. It was not the serendipitous solution wished for by the counterinsurgent power, but rather an outcome that would have been generally favorable to the national interest of the counterinsurgent power. In this book I will try to outline the major mistakes made by the major powers, and offer some explanations for how these mistakes were made.

For a complete view of the Iraq War we will have to wait for many years. But many of the issues have been discussed already, and a further exploration would seem to be in order. The nineteenth-century German Army General Staff had a useful saying: "The perfect is the enemy of the good." The idea is that a good plan today is of more use than a perfect plan that is somehow never finished. I am very well aware that if I only wait for twenty or thirty years, and more documents become available, I can write a much better book. However, I believe that the problems faced by Western democracies today require some good analysis now rather than perfect analysis produced far in the future. As a soldier and scholar I hope that this book will be of use to military professionals and to strategists of democratic nations, my own nation included. As Colin Gray notes, strategy is truly a life and death issue. A better understanding of strategy can save lives.

CHAPTER 1
France's War in Algeria, 1954–1962

■ ■ ■

"Basically they are a good people. We've gotten along for 130 years.
I don't see why it can't continue."

—A French army staff officer to his divisional commander in the film
The Battle of Algiers, 1967.

FROM 1954 TO 1962 FRANCE carried out a long and bloody campaign to
suppress a nationalist insurgency in Algeria. It was a war that could easily have
been avoided if the social and political inequalities in Algeria had been dealt
with in the decade before the insurgency began. There was certainly plenty of
warning, and many French military and political leaders had for years asserted
the need for fundamental reforms in Algeria. The failure to address the Algerian problems before the start of the war was due to a lack of vision among the
French leadership and an inability of French military and political leaders to
understand the strategic problems facing France in the post–World War II era
and to adjust French policy to new realities.

Algeria is a prime example of winning the military victory and losing
the war. In many respects the French fought a brilliant military campaign in
Algeria, developing some highly successful counterinsurgency techniques that
by 1960 had broken the power of the rebels and effectively secured the country.
In President Charles De Gaulle France had a leader who, for the first time,
understood the need to have both a political and a military strategy for the
war, and he developed a program to end the war by granting concessions to the

rebels while also protecting French interests. Unfortunately, once insurgencies begin they have their own dynamics. By the time De Gaulle came to power in 1958, the passions on both sides had become so inflamed that no reasonable political compromise was possible. In the end, French factions within Algeria sabotaged the progress that De Gaulle had made and forced a rapid and ugly termination of the conflict.

The Strategic Problem

With the end of World War II, France, like Britain, was faced with the fundamental problem of trying to maintain a great colonial empire in a world in which the sentiment of colonial peoples was overwhelmingly in favor of independence for their nations. Britain and France's success as colonial powers was ultimately their undoing. Both great empires had overseen the economic development of their colonies and had helped create an educated indigenous middle class—a class that would provide the leadership for the anti-colonialist movements. Both Britain and France had taught their colonial populations about the benefits of democracy and self-government. Moreover, in the first and second world wars Britain and France had been heavily reliant upon the resources and manpower from their colonies to win victory over the Germans and Japanese. British and French colonies had sent hundreds of thousands of men to the front under the flag of their colonial masters, and the colonial troops had fought with courage and dedication on some of the war's toughest fighting fronts. From the viewpoint of the colonial soldiers, they had earned their right to national independence through their sacrifice in blood. Besides, if World War II had been about defending democracy from the Germans and Japanese, the colonial peoples reasoned, why should they not have a right to govern themselves?

The immediate postwar era saw a rise in nationalist organizations and parties throughout the British and French empires. As armed rebellion against French colonial rule in Indochina, Dutch rule in Indonesia, and British rule in Palestine had already begun, it was clear that the postwar nationalism was more than a passing fad. Britain, bankrupted by the war and facing the huge costs of administering and garrisoning its empire, wisely announced in 1946 that it would divest itself of India, the crown jewel of the British Empire, as well as Burma and Ceylon, within two years. In 1947 Britain also announced that it would give up its mandate in Palestine. The next fifteen years would see the divestment of most of the British Empire, sometimes amicably and sometimes with considerable conflict. As painful as it was, it was an economic and political necessity.

France, facing political, military, and economic problems as severe as Britain's, took a different path in dealing with postwar colonial nationalism. In many respects, giving up the colonial empire was an even greater emotional blow to the French population than it was for the British. Although many in Britain's upper classes and among the military officers had served in the empire and were emotionally bonded to the imperial ideology, most of the British people had little direct contact or interest in the empire. In contrast, the French national identity was far more closely bound to the idea of empire than the British. In Britain, the average Briton saw the Empire as something "other." In France the school texts had for decades emphasized that France constituted not only the mainland but also the colonies. Accurately or not, the North African colonies were referred to as integral to France and "100 million Frenchmen" was a popular slogan that meant the 45 million mainland Frenchmen were intrinsically joined with 55 million North Africans.[1]

Through the Truman and Eisenhower administrations American political leaders were faced with the daunting challenge of trying to build an effective European alliance to meet the threat of the Soviet Union and expansion of communism in the third world. America viewed the European colonial empires as an anachronism in the postwar world. The U.S. administrations were correct in their assessment that attempting to hold on to the colonial empires would simply act as an economic and military drag on Britain and France. The danger was: if the colonial peoples went to war to throw off their European masters, they would naturally turn to the communist nations for help, thus becoming aligned with the communist block—a consequence that the Americans wanted to avoid.

Nevertheless, the U.S. government did not counsel immediate independence for the British and French colonies but rather a controlled process of relinquishing the colonial administration while setting up new governments, moderate and favorable to the west, that would guarantee the economic interests of the former colonial powers. The colonies would have to become independent sooner or later. The best course would be a strategy to control the process while protecting national and Western interests.[2]

The American administrations set forth both the problem and the solution of decolonization to the French government for more than a decade, but successive French governments found the American advice unwelcome. The United States was especially concerned about the future of North Africa, as it rested on the North Atlantic Treaty Organization (NATO) flank. The Americans, moreover, had negotiated the rights to build air bases for the U.S. Air Force's strategic bombers in Morocco. A failed decolonization process resulting in radicalized, anti-Western regimes in Tunisia, Morocco, and Algeria would undermine the security of the whole Mediterranean region. Yet the nineteen successive governments of the French Fourth Republic between 1945 and 1954 refused to accept the American strategic analysis, single-mindedly holding onto the North African colonies. In the minds of the French elites, the loss of empire also meant the reduction of France's status to that of a second-class power. Emotion having overturned sound strategic analysis, France became committed to fighting nationalist movements in Morocco and Tunisia from 1945 until 1956—when those countries were granted independence.

The most difficult conquest of all the French colonies was that of the French protectorate Morocco. In the 1920s the French had faced the brilliant Moroccan leader Abd el Krim who had organized the tribes of Morocco's mountainous interior and proclaimed the "Rif Republic." In 1925 Abd el Krim's forces overran a large part of the French sector of Morocco (Morocco was divided between the Spanish and French protectorates) and delivered a series of sharp defeats to the French army, overrunning many of the French garrisons and advancing to within twenty miles of the French capitol of Fez. To deal with the threat posed by Abd el Krim, France reinforced its sixty-thousand-man garrison in Morocco with fifty battalions of troops supported by additional tanks and aircraft squadrons. In a ruthlessly conducted counteroffensive, Marshal Pétain beat back the rebel forces and forced Abd el Krim to surrender. However, that was not the end of the story, for the French had to carry out desultory campaigns against rebellious tribes until the country was truly pacified in 1932.[3]

Officially ruled by a sultan who was expected to serve as a loyal puppet ruler, the Moroccans remained quiet for a decade. With the French defeat in 1940 and the subsequent American occupation of Morocco in 1942, however, the illusion of French power was broken. The Moroccans, who never forgot their warrior tradition or the effective fight they had made in the 1920s, began to agitate openly for independence. Morocco, like Algeria, had a large community of three hundred thousand French *colons* (colonial settlers) who owned the large farms and Morocco's businesses. However, the French *colons* in Morocco were even more of a minority than their counterparts in Algeria. The three hundred thousand Frenchmen were outnumbered by the eight million Moroccans by a ratio of 26:1 (as opposed to 9:1 in Algeria). Native Moroccans, moreover, had a far stronger sense of national identity with a traditional indigenous leadership. Sultan Sidi Mohammed ben Youssef had cooperated with the French through World War II but saw his chance to assert leadership after the war. As imam (commander of the faithful) he held the position of top religious leader among a people almost 100 percent Islamic. After the war he encouraged the formation of the *Istiqlal* Party (Independence Party) and in 1947 openly spoke in favor of the unity of Islam and an independent Morocco.

Of all the French North African colonies Morocco was economically the most important. Oil was not discovered in Algeria until the mid-1950s, and oil would not be pumped out of the Sahara in 1957. Unlike Algeria, Morocco was rich in minerals, supplying a large proportion of the world's manganese, and one-sixth of the world's phosphates. Morocco's mineral wealth had been the foundation of some great French fortunes. French investment had turned the small fishing village of Casablanca into a modern city of seven hundred thousand people—complete with skyscrapers and modern factories. The *colons* in Morocco had run the colony much like the *colons* in Algeria. Taxes went to infrastructure that benefited the large landowners and French businesses, while there were few schools and benefits for the Moroccans. As in Algeria, many Moroccans lived in dire poverty. Like Algeria, the *colons* in Morocco saw their position threatened and were ready to fight to hold it. When the French ignored Sultan ben Youssef's offer to negotiate, Moroccans turned to forming underground groups and initiating a terrorism campaign against the French settlers.

The French solution was to arrest Sultan ben Youssef in 1953, replacing him with the eighty-year-old, pro-French Pascha of Marrakech to serve as the puppet ruler of Morocco. Sultan ben Youssef was sent into exile in Madagascar. The French soon found that there was virtually no support for their new sultan, and in the mosques in Fez, imams denounced the new leader and demanded the return of ben Youssef. Rather than solving the problem, the French solution had exacerbated it. The anti-French terror campaign increased in intensity. In 1954 Moroccan guerrillas killed two hundred French *colons* and wounded five hundred more. Brutal terror attacks on isolated French settlements brought about brutal retribution, in turn, by French *colon* vigilantes and troops of the Foreign Legion. France sent in a new governor general, Gilbert Grandval, with a mandate to offer reforms to the Moroccans. However, it was too late for a reform program, and in any case the *colons* refused any idea of concessions to the Moroccans and systematically undermined Grandval's reform program. When Grandval appealed to Paris for support, he found that the *colons* had strong backing among some parliamentary parties.[4] With the policy in a shambles, the French government brought Sultan ben Youssef back from exile. Unable to quell the violence in Morocco, France finally agreed to independence in 1956, turning over the reigns of government to ben Youssef, who became king with the title of Mohammed V. Under the independence agreement France was allowed to maintain a military garrison in Morocco for several years in order to protect French citizens.[5]

Until his death in 1961, Mohammed V enacted reforms and followed a moderate path with regard to dealing with the West and with his former colonial masters. Under his leadership, and that of his son, Morocco became a fairly benign authoritarian state that allowed some democratic structures, parties, and elected local governments. The education system was rapidly improved, foreign investment protected, and Morocco maintained a fairly high level of prosperity by the standards of developing nations.

The Tunisian struggle for independence paralleled the Moroccan experience in many ways. Like Morocco, Tunisia was a French protectorate with a small *colon* class dominating the affairs of the three and a half million Tunisians. Like Morocco, post–World War II Tunisia developed a strong independence movement under the leadership of Habib Bourguiba. The Tunisian leader was one of the more moderate third world leaders of the era. From 1950 to 1952, he pushed for a solution that would give Tunisia an autonomous status with internal government in the hands of the Tunisians, while allowing French control of the armed forces and diplomatic affairs.[6] In 1952 anti-French riots broke out in Tunisian cities. Bourguiba and other nationalist leaders were arrested. Bourguiba was exiled in the hope that his removal would quiet the Tunisians. Instead, the violence and anti-French terrorism worsened, and acts of terror against the *colons* provoked a brutal response from the French army and the colonists. The French government under Premier Edgar Faure strongly disapproved of using strong-arm tactics against the Tunisians, but the government had little control over the *colons* and little ability to assert itself. It would be a pattern repeated in Algeria.[7]

After three more years of low-level violence and terrorism, Bourguiba was freed and returned to Tunisia. The Tunisian nationalists negotiated independence from France, which was granted in 1956. The French businessmen were allowed to stay, and France was allowed to maintain a military garrison in the country and occupy the large naval base at Bizerte.

France's poor handling of the independence struggles for Morocco and Tunisia had a major effect on the Algerian dilemma. The Front de Libération Nationale (FLN) rebels were heartened by the fact that the French government could be forced to negotiate. At a critical moment in the Algerian independence struggle, the FLN rebels would have sympathetic regimes on both flanks that could provide political support and even bases for the army the FLN was building.

France's fundamental problem was that of any democracy with an overseas empire. At home a government is clearly answerable to the people. A central part of France's identity as a nation is its heritage from the Enlightenment and French Revolution, a commitment to individual liberty, freedom of the press, and equality of all citizens under the law. The reality of the empire was the sometimes enlightened, but more often heavy-handed rule of a small French minority over the native population. Those in the native population who took the ideals of France seriously and aspired to full citizenship and equality on economic and social terms were usually despised and suppressed by the French settlers. Administrators and soldiers sent out from France usually supported the view of the *colons*. In the meantime, the average Frenchman ignored the reality of Algeria and the fundamental conflict with French ideals versus maintaining a dictatorial system across the sea. When the war in Algeria forced these conflicts into the open, the contrast between ideals and reality worked against colonialism on the stage of French public opinion.

Background to the Conflict

Algeria was the crown jewel of the French colonial empire. Legally speaking Algeria was not a colony but rather a part of Metropolitan France, and Algerian delegates sat in the National Assembly. The reality was that Algeria was ruled and administered as a colony, complete with a governor general and appointed French officials ruling over a population that was overwhelmingly disenfranchised. Virtually all the local power in Algeria was in the hands of the French *colons*. Every adult French male had the franchise and full citizenship rights. On the other hand, only a few thousand Moslems were considered "assimilated"—that is, educated, French-speaking, and possessing considerable property. In the 1947 elections, after a new Algerian assembly was created, 460,000 French citizens along with only 58,000 "assimilated" Moslems voted for the French "college" (half of the legislature), and 1.4 million "unassimilated" Moslems were granted the franchise for the Moslem college. Despite the enlargement of the franchise, only a small minority of Moslems were found qualified to vote at all.[8]

Since the start of the French conquest of Algeria in the 1830s, France had maintained a deep emotional bond with Algeria that was quite different than the relationship with her other colonies. For one thing, out of a population of about ten million people in 1954, approximately one million were French settlers, nicknamed *colons* or *pied noirs* (black feet—probably a reference to the boots the early settlers wore). Most of the *colons* were, in fact, not even ethnically French but the descendents of poor Italians, Spaniards, and Maltese who had emigrated to Algeria in the nineteenth and early twentieth centuries in search of work and better opportunities than could be found in their own countries. The *colons* had done well for themselves. Many were prosperous small farmers, and a few held huge tracts of the best farmland in Algeria, where they grew wheat and fruit and produced wine for the French and European markets. Most of the *colons* were urbanized and constituted the middle class and civil service of Algeria's three main cities: Algiers, Oran, and Constantine. Those three cities were constituted departments of Metropolitan France, and the *colons* elected representatives to the French National Assembly. The nine million Moslem residents of Algeria, mostly ethnic Berbers in the countryside and mountains and ethnic Arabs in the cities, were allowed little say in the affairs of their country.

Prior to 1954 Algeria was a country of the haves and have-nots. It was an agricultural economy that exported wine and food to France while importing manufactured goods from the mother country. In fact, there were two economies in Algeria: the larger, *colon*-owned farms that were highly productive and geared to exporting their produce to France, and the much smaller, Algerian-owned farms, usually on more marginal land, that suffered from low productivity and produced food for local consumption. More than half of the labor force of three million were peasants with tiny plots of land, or else worked as sharecroppers, seasonal workers, or day laborers for the French farms. This class of Algerians were underemployed and commonly on the brink of destitution.

The large landowners and the directors of Algeria's transport firms and industrial concerns effectively controlled the Algerian economy and government through advisory bodies created to help government administrators shape policy. In Algeria most of the government budget went to supporting the road, rail, and port infrastructure that served French business interests. In comparison with France, there was little investment in schools, hospitals, or housing. The average Algerian got very few benefits for the taxes he paid. Despite this, economic growth through the twentieth century had enabled some Algerians to rise to middle-class status. Some Algerians had relatively large farms—in the 1962 land census twenty-five thousand Algerians were listed as having more than fifty hectares of land. An artisan class had arisen, and by the 1950s there were three thousand Algerian-owned businesses that employed twenty or more workers. In addition, some of the French laws had worked to the benefit of the Algerians. A 1917 law required compulsory school attendance for Algerian children who resided within three kilometers of a school. This did little to help the rural Algerians who comprised the bulk of the population as rural schools were rare indeed. However, the law offered a path to education for the urban Algerians. In 1942 more than one hundred thousand Algerian children attended school; by 1954, the figure was seven hundred thousand. Algerian illiteracy was still frighteningly high due to decades of French neglect, but by the 1950s there were more than a million Algerians who could be described as middle class.[9] Despite the increase in Algerian education levels, there were still few opportunities for Algerians to hold management or supervisory positions in business or government. These were reserved for the *colons*. Only 17 percent of the better-paid skilled worker and supervisory positions in the Algerian government were held by Algerians.[10]

The lack of jobs and opportunity in Algeria meant the migration of thirty thousand Algerians a year to France, mainly to the slum districts of Paris and other large cities. Soon, there were Algerian neighborhoods, the sights and smells reminiscent of Algerian towns. The Algerians who migrated to France were desperately poor. Perhaps half were unemployed; most of the others took on the lowest-paid, manual-labor jobs. Despite their misery, they were better off in France than at home. The Paris newspaper *Le Monde* remarked, "Why do they come to France? Simply because they cannot feed themselves and their families in Algeria."[11] As unrest in Algeria grew in the 1940s and early 1950s, the Algerian community in France, numbering over half a million, was a ready-made pool of revolutionary supporters who could provide money and support to the revolution. They also served as a fifth column within France itself.

At the end of World War II, the hundreds of thousands of Algerians and Moroccans who had fought and bled for France rightly expected that they would be rewarded in the form of greater equality with the Europeans and a full share in the governance of their own country. Instead the soldiers who returned home were expected to return to precisely the same status and conditions, as obedient colonial subjects, that they had known before the war. Indeed, many of the Algerians who had served France regarded their treatment as a betrayal—not only a betrayal of the French leadership but also a betrayal of French ideals which proclaimed "Liberty, Equality, and Fraternity" without any qualifications that such rights belonged only to Europeans. Rightfully resenting their postwar treatment, many of the Algerian veterans formed the core of the nationalist resistance to drive the French out. When it came to forming a revolutionary military force against the French there were plenty of Algerians who had been well trained by the French Army who would serve as leaders of the revolution.[12] In 1944 a great part of the Free French forces were composed of soldiers from Algeria, Morocco, and Senegal, with some detachments from other African colonies. While the North African soldiers established a solid reputation on the battlefield, they faced discrimination within the army and sometimes the disdain of their mainland French officers. Toward the close of the war there were several serious mutinies and outbreaks of collective indiscipline within North African units of the French Army, in protest against army policies that treated them as second-class soldiers.[13]

By the end of World War II, unrest among the Arab community of Algeria had been seething under the surface for decades. The Arab and Berber peoples of Algeria had more than proven their loyalty to France by sending a large number of troops to fight for France in both World Wars. Indeed, many Algerians also fought for France in the colonial campaigns in Morocco and Syria in the 1920s, and in Indochina from 1946 to 1954. Before and during World War II, the French governments made promises to reform the politics of Algeria, extend the franchise, allow Arabs to vote, and allow an Arab role in local government. However, the intransigence of the *colons* in Algeria and the volatile and unstable nature of the governments in the Third and Fourth Republics ensured that any real hope for reform in Algeria would be blocked. While the French *colons* enjoyed a high standard of living, good schools, and government services, in 1945 the Algerians were still mostly dirt poor, illiterate, and barely eking out a living working for French landowners and businesses.

The decades of broken promises to reform the country's politics and the state of extreme poverty of the majority of Algerians, exacerbated by a long drought, brought a major explosion on May 8, 1945, during the celebration of V-E Day in the market town of Sétif, eighty miles from the city of Constantine. Political demonstrations quickly turned into spontaneous anti-French riots. The rioting spread out from Sétif into neighboring towns in the Department of Constantine. During the next three days Algerian rioters looted and burned French businesses and town halls, murdering over one hundred French *colons*, mostly French farmers and small business owners, including many women and children. The sheer viciousness of the attacks coming from a traditionally placid Algerian population shocked the French. Women had been raped before being murdered and mutilated. Other victims had been blinded or had limbs cut off, but were left alive. The French military and police quickly retaliated with the utmost violence. Gangs of hastily organized *colon* vigilantes carried out countermassacres of Algerian men, women, and children. American-supplied Douglas Dauntless dive-bombers bombed more than forty of the villages in the area. French ships shelled some villages along the coast as *colon* vigilantes and French troops pacified the Arab community in a manner reminiscent of SS antipartisan operations. Estimates of Arab dead range from the official French figure of 1,020–1,300 to the Algerian estimate of 45,000. A figure of 6,000 Arab dead is considered a fair estimate.[14]

The Sétif uprising ought to have been a wake-up call to the French government about the state of affairs in Algeria and the state of the Moslem majority. General Henry Martin, commander of the French Army 19th Corps that had helped suppress the rebellion, wrote a scathing indictment of French policy in Algeria in his March 1946 report to the Army General Staff on the uprising. General Martin flatly declared that the economic and political conditions in Algeria had caused the uprising. The rebellion, he continued, had not been just an isolated outbreak, but the symptom of a deep dissatisfaction of the Moslem population living under dire economic conditions which he termed "catastrophic." He noted that conditions were ripe for the emergence of a general insurrection in Algeria and argued strongly for a national plan to deal with the economic and political grievances of the Algerians.[15] One of France's top generals Alphonse Juin (he was the son of a *colon* policeman, so he knew Algeria well) in early 1946 wrote a report that argued for major reforms in Algeria. Though he rejected any idea of Algerian independence, he did argue for a complete overhaul of the administrative, economic, and social system. He also argued that all Moslems ought to have full French citizenship, and that elections to the National Assembly ought to include a Moslem list of candidates in proportion to their part of the population. General Duval, the army commander in the Constantine district who had led the efforts to suppress the Sétif rebellion, warned the government, "I have given you peace for ten years. But let us not deceive ourselves. Everything must change in Algeria."[16]

However, the postwar government of France, the Fourth Republic, was in a state of constant turmoil, overwhelmed with France's internal problems. The economy was shattered by the World War, and there was internal disunity caused by the rift between those who had served the collaborationist Vichy regime during the German occupation and those who had joined De Gaulle's Free French or the resistance. War was just beginning in Indochina. Add to that mix of problems the French government's requirement to deal with a large communist party that was staunchly loyal to Josef Stalin and rebuild the French military as a force to occupy Germany and to help the Western powers deter an aggressive Soviet Union. The France of 1945–1946 was a nation divided into dozens of political parties. These, in turn, constituted several major political blocks that constantly jockeyed for position in forming governments. Indeed, during the tenure of the Fourth Republic from 1945–1958, the average lifespan of a government was six months and France twice went through periods of several weeks without a government. Given the domestic political situation, it is no wonder that the problems of Algeria went largely overlooked until a major insurrection broke out.

But the Sétif massacre had alarmed the French government and the *colons*, and a few minor reforms were introduced into the Algerian political system in 1947. The direct rule of Algeria by Paris was abolished and an elected Algerian Assembly was created which allowed Algerians to modify French metropolitan laws for Algeria and to vote on a budget and financial issues. The Algerian Assembly was organized into two colleges of sixty delegates each, one college elected by the one million French *colons*, and the other elected by the 9 million Arabs. Other fundamental reforms demanded by the Algerians, however, such as the recognition of Arabic as an official language, the franchise for women, and ending military government in the Sahara, were all tabled by the French National Assembly which was afraid of offending the *pied noir* delegates. Unfortunately, the creation of the Algerian Assembly actually increased, rather than mollified, the Algerians' grievances with France. The *colon* administration ruthlessly suppressed the more vocal nationalistic Algerian political movements, jailing their leaders and banning some groups. To represent the Algerians the *colons* hand-picked Algerians known for their loyalty to France, nicknamed "Beni Oiu Oius" (Beni Yes-Men) by Algerians and *colons* alike. For their part, the loyal Algerians were rewarded with local leadership positions and the chance to rake in a bit of the graft that such positions enabled. Just to ensure that Algerians elected the kind of government the *colons* wanted, the *colons* resorted to blatant election fraud. In the 1947 municipal elections, in some districts the pro-government Algerian candidates received more votes than there were registered voters. In fact, elections in Algeria became something of a national joke in France, serving to radicalize the Algerian middle class who now understood that there would be no peaceful means of obtaining their promised rights as Frenchmen.[17]

The growing Algerian community in France assumed more and more the radical anti-French attitudes of their relations back home and formed a willing group that the FLN revolutionaries and other nationalists could draw support from. In July 1953 the state of the Algerians in France provided the French capital a preview of the nationalist violence that was lying just below the surface. During Paris' annual Bastille Day parade, two thousand well-organized Algerians carrying signs demanding the release of nationalist leader Messali Hadj marched in close formation at the tail end of the Communist Party marchers. At the Place de la Nation the Algerians clashed with the French riot police, and the violence escalated in central Paris. Algerians attacked the police with stones and improvised clubs, and soon the police opened fire on the Algerians. By evening six Algerians and a French trade union leader lay dead, and 130 people, including 82 policemen, were injured.[18]

The Insurgents

In the 1930s Algerian intellectuals began organizing and agitating for Algerian rights. Several important figures emerged, who can be counted as the founders of modern Algerian nationalism. Most prominent among them was Messali Hadj, who founded the Mouvement pour le Triomphe des Libertés Démocratiques (MTLD) in 1937 as an Algerian nationalist party demanding full citizenship for Moslems and an autonomous status for Algeria. Another well-known Algerian nationalist leader was Ferhat Abbas, who founded the Union Démocratique du Manifeste Algérien (UDMA) after 1945. Messali Hadj, Ferhat Abbas, and their supporters were put under close observation by the police, and the party leaders spent considerable time in French jails. At this point the Algerian nationalists were not agitating for full independence, but in a short time the old leaders would be surpassed by a new generation. What the postwar Algerian parties did provide was a venue for Algerian intellectuals to meet each other and refine their knowledge of politics and organization. When the time for insurrection came, the Algerians were intellectually well prepared.[19]

When meaningful changes failed to come out of the 1947 reform laws, an underground group called the Organisation Spéciale (OS) was recruited from MTLD members by Hocine Air Ahmed to conduct anti-French terrorism. The OS grew to two thousand members before being broken up by the French police in 1950. Some leading Algerian nationalists such as Ben Bella fled to the protection of Nasser's Egypt, and others went underground.

A new group, the Comité Révolutionnaire d'Unité et d'Action, "Revolutionary Committee of Unity and Action" (CRUA), was formed in early 1954 in Cairo from the remnants of the OS and from MTLD activists. The nine nationalist activists were young men (average age thirty-two) intent on carrying on a war with the French with an objective of nothing less than full independence for Algeria. The nine original leaders, who came to be known as the *chefs historiques* (Ben Bella, Ait Ahmed, Mohamed Boudiaf, Belkacem Krim, Rabah Bitat, Larbi Ben M'Hidi, Mourad Didouch, Moustafa Ben Boulaid, and Mohamed Khider), had a long history of anti-French agitation, and most had spent time in French jails. Some were army veterans. Ben Bella had served in World War II as a French army NCO and had been decorated for bravery in the Italian campaign. Their ideology was a mixture of nationalism and Islamic fundamentalism with a bit of Marxism thrown in. The long-term program of the revolutionaries was to build up an organization throughout the country, organize guerrilla forces to liberate areas, and finally to build a conventional army that would defeat the French in battle in a replay of the Vietnamese victory over the French at Dien Bien Phu. CRUA's founders put considerable hope in receiving both political support and military support, in the forms of arms and equipment, from the Arab nations—most importantly from the anti-Western regime of Nasser in Egypt.

In October the CRUA renamed itself the Front de Libération Nationale (FLN) and prepared a national revolution. The military arm of the FLN was called the Armée de Libération Nationale, "National Liberation Army" (ALN). What distinguished the FLN from the other Algerian nationalist groups was their single-minded focus on the goal of independence, rather than reform, and their considerable talent in planning and organization. The ALN had a proper central staff and was organized into six districts (*wilayas*), each with a commander and staff. The fighting forces were organized into 11-man sections (*faoudj*), 110-man companies (*katiba*), and 350-man battalions (*failek*). In the course of the war, the shortage of arms and lack of trained guerrillas meant that the largest force normally employed by the FLN inside Algeria would be the *faoudj* or *katiba*.

The FLN established a leadership council and a political staff who could represent the Algerian national movement to the Arab World and to the West. The leaders and staff would coordinate the operations of underground operatives, who would organize and collect funds from the Algerian exiles in France and carry out clandestine arms buying overseas. The FLN also had a propaganda branch to make broadcasts to the Algerians and Arab world, and to distribute revolutionary pamphlets and newspapers to the Algerian public. Egypt and other Arab nations were approached for support by the FLN. The Egyptians and other Arabs were encouraging but cautious in their dealings with the FLN and initially provided no arms. Their view was that the FLN should start the war first and, if the movement showed promise, then arms and aid would be forthcoming.

The FLN's national military offensive began on November 1, 1954, with no more than 1,700 guerrillas and auxiliaries and armed with a few hundred small arms including old shotguns and hunting rifles. In small towns near Oran, in the Aures Mountains and Constantine region, there was a spate of bombings, arson, and the shooting of some French settlers and pro-French Algerians. At the end of the first day of the rebellion the FLN had killed only eight Frenchmen and wounded 30 others. The FLN broadcast a message from Cairo calling for the Moslems in Algeria to join the struggle for the "restoration of the Algerian state, sovereign, democratic, and social, within the framework of the principles of Islam."

Given the troubles the French were facing in Morocco and Tunisia in 1954, the beginning of the Algerian insurgency seemed more like just another minor outbreak of trouble than the start of a major nationalist revolution. The first French move was much like Police Commissioner Claude Rain's order in the film *Casablanca* to "round up the usual suspects." Nationalist clubs in Algiers, Oran, and Constantine were raided by police and 175 suspects jailed. The initial dragnet failed to catch any of the FLN leaders. As the French army had fewer than fifty thousand troops in the country in 1954, reinforcements were quickly sent, most notably the 25th Paratroop Division. Speaking before the National Assembly, Socialist Deputy and Interior Minister François Mitterrand insisted that "the only possible negotiation is war."[20] Premier Pierre Mendes-France also called for a military solution, rejecting any talk of compromise with Algerian rebels. During the winter of 1954–1955, the French army began an aggressive campaign in the Aures Mountains, the most active military region of the FLN, and managed to track down and kill some of the top leaders in the *wilaya* and disperse several guerrilla bands. The French newsreels of late 1954 presented an optimistic picture of operations in the Aures, complete with films of French infantry and armored units driving about the countryside in American-made halftracks and armored cars (World War II lend-lease equipment provided to France). Military spokesmen talked confidently of "rounding up the bandits" and anticipated a rapid "end of the crisis."[21]

Despite years of explicit warnings from Algerian military commanders and the more liberal *colons* who criticized the heavy-handed French rule of the Moslems, the outbreak of rebellion in Algeria caught the French government and political establishment by surprise. Misunderstanding the new form Algerian nationalism had taken, the French government blamed the violence on three causes: Tunisian bandits who had been driven out of their own country; Radio Cairo, for inciting Arab nationalism; and Messali Hadj's MTLD Party. That the MTLD had been surpassed by the more radical FLN as the flag bearer of Algerian nationalism had apparently escaped the notice of a government in Paris that was occupied with other crises.

The Insurgency Grows 1955–1957

From the start, the French government had grossly underestimated the ability of the FLN and the new and very ruthless style that they brought to their guerrilla war. During 1955 the level of violence—still mostly individual assassinations, sabotage of public works, and small raids on the police and military—steadily escalated. The FLN, recognizing its military weakness, carried out its war by means of a large-scale terrorist campaign that targeted first the French *colons* in order to drive them out. Isolated French farms were attacked, and French civilians killed; French businesses were bombed and torched. The second part of the campaign was much more extensive. Pro-French Algerians, such as French-appointed village leaders and their families, were specifically targeted for assassination. Indeed, the largest number of casualties inflicted by the FLN were upon fellow Algerians. By means of terror, the FLN ensured that there were no neutrals in the war; Algerians had to decide either to support independence and the FLN or the French. An order from Ben Bella to ALN field commanders, issued early in the war, outlined the intent of the FLN's

47

terror policy. The FLN was committed to nothing less than full independence. Any Algerians, staunch nationalists or not, who were willing to accept anything less than that goal were to be eliminated: "Liquidate all personalities who might act as valid intermediaries (between the French and Algerians)."[22]

An integral part of the FLN strategy was the destruction or absorption of other Algerian nationalist groups and parties. Whatever its revolutionary myths, the FLN of 1954–1955 did not represent the average Algerian, who resented the French but was more likely to prefer Algerian autonomy and a peaceful solution to outright war. Whether from motives of idealism or of pure self-interest, many more Algerians fought for France than for the FLN. Through a program of terrorism and assassination, other nationalist groups were crippled and absorbed into the FLN. Since the FLN's leadership did not allow for sharing power, if a group wanted to ally with the FLN it would be on the FLN terms. One of the consistent strengths of the FLN versus other nationalist groups was its strong party organization. During the war the FLN maintained a permanent headquarters outside Algeria and held underground party congresses within Algeria to coordinate the military and political strategy.[23] As the FLN's political clout grew, some well known nationalist leaders came over. In 1956 Ferhat Abbas flew to Cairo and formally joined the FLN. This action brought in former UDMA supporters and undercut the moderates who favored mediation with the French.

The FLN leadership feared that the French would pit Algerian against Algerian, and they were right. In 1954 the French authorized some Algerian nationalist leaders to recruit their own militia forces to fight the FLN. One force under Ben Hadj fought successfully against the local FLN for a while, but the ranks of his private army were infiltrated by FLN supporters, who assassinated Ben Hadj and led a portion of his force off to join the FLN. Messali Hadj, who had split with the FLN, was allowed to raise a personal force of 3,300 men and was armed by the French. Messali Hadj's own political ambitions later became evident when he set up his own political network, and the French began to view him as untrustworthy. He was killed by French forces in 1958, with the result that most of his well-armed troops went over to the FLN.[24]

Since Algeria was part of Metropolitan France, the effort against the Algerian insurgents did not lack for troops or resources. Since Algeria was not a colony, there were no restrictions on employing conscripts and reservists in the war. As violence escalated in 1955 and 1956, France doubled its force in Algeria by calling up reservists and extending military service obligations from eighteen to twenty-seven months. By the end of 1956 there were about four hundred thousand French troops in Algeria, a strength that was maintained until the end of the war in 1962.[25] France had a further one hundred thousand local reserve and militia forces in Algeria as well as the paramilitary Gendarmerie. Altogether, France had five hundred thousand well-trained, well-equipped soldiers and policemen to control a population of approximately ten million people. By any standard of counterinsurgency, this was certainly a force adequate to carry out an ambitious military and civil campaign.

With enough troops and resources for the mission, the French were able to saturate the Algerian cities and countryside with a large number of troops. For most of the French soldiers in Algeria, the war meant guard duty, manning small garrisons and patrolling the local areas. However, the French high command was able to assemble task forces composed of elite troops such as paratroops (all volunteers) and Foreign Legion units to search out and track down the insurgent units in the mountains and rural areas. The Algerian War featured few large actions, for the ALN could rarely assemble more than a *katiba* (company) for an operation. Therefore, the ALN stuck to a hit and run warfare, ambushing small French patrols and carrying out small-scale attacks. Rarely did the FLN try to fight any defensive battles—unless they were cornered and had little choice. In such cases, French firepower usually won the day. The French Air Force and army dramatically enlarged their aviation forces in Algeria from 197 aircraft at the start of 1955 to 686 airplanes and 82 helicopters by November 1957.[26] With ample airpower the French Air Force was able to patrol the borders and mountains and to spot guerrilla movements. If a firefight developed, fighter bomber and light bomber squadrons were on call to support the ground troops.

The early French strategy was oriented simply towards military victory, and the approach to the war was heavy-handed. When the FLN carried out atrocities and terror attacks on French civilians or isolated army patrols, the army responded with the doctrine of collective punishment, carrying out reprisals against the closest Algerian village on the suspicion that the locals would have known of the attacks beforehand and had failed to warn the French. Most of the Algerian victims of French reprisals were innocent civilians since the perpetrators of terror attacks were usually far away by the time the French military and police forces arrived at the scene. The doctrine of "collective responsibility" in fighting Algerian guerrillas was reminiscent of the German doctrine of fighting partisans during World War II. For example, if sabotage occurred then all of the males of the nearest village would be held accountable and rounded up and shipped to internment camps. French reprisals for egregious terror attacks by the FLN could be especially violent. When thirty-seven French civilians were brutally massacred by Algerians in the mining town of Philippeville in August 1955, French army forces went berserk, slaughtering more than a thousand local Algerian villagers and giving no quarter to women or children.[27] Again, most of the Arabs killed were innocent of any wrongdoing. The FLN was pleased when the French were provoked to respond with brutality. In the words of one FLN leader, "The people will now hate the French more."

Still, the French had considerable success against the guerrillas thanks to the massive deployment of military and police forces in Algeria. Offensive operations inflicted heavy casualties on the FLN in several districts. Still, the guerrilla numbers continued to increase and the number of attacks and terrorist incidents continued to climb throughout 1956. Despite the doctrine of "Revolutionary Warfare" that the French army had developed in fighting insurgents in Indochina, the French army was slow in developing the psychological operations and civic action side of the campaign. Some officers understood that one needed more than brute force to turn the rural population away from the FLN and win them over to the French side.

In 1956, two years after the start of the insurgency, the French began to deploy small groups of Arabic-speaking, culturally sensitive French soldiers and civilians known as the "Sections Administratives Spécialisées" (Special Administrative Sections—SAS). These detachments, along with their urban counterparts, the Sections Administratives Urbaines (SAU), were responsible for organizing and directing government relief and jobs programs as well as manning new schools and clinics for the benefit of the Algerian rural population, most of whom were desperately poor and illiterate. In order to deal with the Algerian Moslem women, the French also deployed Arabic-speaking French Army women as part of the SAS detachments. Colonel Argoud, one of the counterinsurgency theorists, pointed out that to win the support of the undecided population it was necessary to "Protect Them, Involve Them, and Control Them."[28]

By 1957 the ALN had an estimated fifteen thousand to twenty thousand "regular" guerilla forces in the interior of Algeria supported by an equal number of part-time guerrillas.[29] The ALN desperately wished to expand its guerrilla forces in the countryside in order to fight the French army more aggressively. With enough trained and equipped guerrillas in the mountains, the ALN hoped to destroy whole French units in battle, thereby proving to the Algerian people that the FLN was the superior force and further eroding morale in mainland France. To meet the increase of violence in the countryside between 1955 and 1957, the army developed pacification tactics designed to saturate the countryside with troops, each unit assigned a particular sector to secure. The French also built a reserve force consisting of the elite 10th and 25th Paratroop divisions that could be quickly shifted around the country to meet any major ALN threats.

For the French the Algerian War was a high-tech war. It was the first war in which helicopters played a major tactical role, both in the troop lift role and as gunships. French light infantry, carried by helicopters, could easily be deployed in terrain thought impassible by the rebels. By 1958 the French had become proficient in using the helicopter in battle.[30] By 1960 the French armed forces had deployed more than four hundred helicopters to Algeria, ranging from the French-made Alouette light reconnaissance helicopters to the heavy U.S.-built Sikorsky H-19s and H-34, which could carry twelve or more soldiers into battle.[31] When the rebels engaged army troops, a mobile reserve could be brought by helicopter to block the rebel's route of retreat. An extensive system of small airfields was built throughout Algeria, and fighter bombers and light bombers were distributed around the country so that every French unit could expect rapid support if it encountered the ALN.[32]

The French set up a sound organizational model that divided the country into districts that paralleled the civil government districts. Each district or regional commander had a mix of forces at his disposal with a strategic reserve available for rapid deployment to support specific operations. A joint command system and modern communications net enabled the very effective joint operations and effective air support for the army. Joint operations centers were established to coordinate service efforts and logistics support.[33]

With the army now conducting large scale operations in the interior as well as saturating the countryside with troops, the ALN was hard pressed to hold onto its position in rural Algeria. By 1956 the ALN was in desperate need of more men, arms, and supplies. The terror campaign by the FLN to intimidate the Moslem population often backfired, inspiring many in the countryside, especially the ethnic Berbers, to turn away from the FLN and join the French-sponsored home defense groups. The FLN remained a highly factionalized organization, plagued by disputes within the leadership. In July 1957 one of the top ALN commanders in central Algeria, Si Cherif, defected to the French and brought 330 of his men with him.[34] In Algiers the French army broke the urban insurgent organization by the most ruthless methods and put an end to the FLN terror campaign against the *colons*. By late 1957 the ALN forces in the countryside were reduced to small, scattered and poorly-armed bands, scarcely a real threat to French control. The French strategy was making noticeable progress, and the FLN needed to do something to turn the situation around.

Using Tunisia and Morocco as sanctuaries, the FLN planned to move trained units, weapons, and supplies into the interior of the country, especially the Aures Mountains where there was already a strong FLN presence. The FLN hoped to change the dynamic of the war with the thousands of men being trained in the sanctuaries. If the French could interdict support from reaching the interior, the guerrilla forces there would wither. The ALN had more than thirty thousand guerrilla soldiers who had left Algeria and, now trained and equipped in ALN camps tolerated by the Tunisian government, were ready to get back to Algeria and fight.

In late 1957 General Raoul Salan took over as military commander in Algeria and focused a great part of his effort on defeating the FLN strategy of infiltrating large military units from the newly independent sanctuaries of Tunisia and Morocco. Aware of the large ALN forces being trained and equipped by Egyptian advisors in the Tunisian camps, the French worked on developing an elaborate defense line on the Moroccan and Tunisian borders complete with minefields, electrified fences, and numerous observation posts. The civilian population was cleared out of the border regions so that the FLN troops could not get local support or blend in with the population. The whole area was made a free-fire zone. The key to holding the defense lines and preventing the infiltration of large numbers of FLN troops or large quantities of supplies was a highly mobile force stationed at key intervals to respond quickly to any attempt of the FLN to rush through the barrier lines. The most elaborate of the defense zones was the one along the Tunisian border, which ran south from the Mediterranean for two hundred miles and ended with the dunes of the Sahara. The area south of the line was covered by air patrols which could easily spot infiltrators in the barren country.

By late 1957 Salan had committed more than eighty thousand French troops to the border regions where the elaborate defense lines were now ready for a major test. The period from late 1957 through the first half of 1958, known as the "battle of the frontiers," saw the only large battles of the war as the ALN tried to infiltrate battalion-sized forces through the Morice Line to reach the interior. French firepower and technology worked. In February 1958 the ALN lost 3,400 killed on the Tunisian border with another 500 captured. Total French losses for that month were 360 dead. In March another 3,000 ALN soldiers were killed on the frontiers and more than 700 captured. In April the ALN lost more than 3,700 dead and more than 700 captured. French losses remained low. A few ALN fighters survived the encounters to reach the interior,[35] but an estimated 70 percent of all reinforcements and supplies were interdicted at the borders. By mid-year the ALN ended the destructive strategy of attacking the frontier defenses. From that point the ALN would continue to build a well-trained and disciplined army in Tunisia and Morocco under the command of Colonel Houari Boumédienne and complete with a general staff. By 1962 the ALN force in Tunisia was forty-five thousand men strong. It remained ready to intervene in Algeria to uphold the power of the FLN once the French were forced to leave through a combination of guerrilla war and international pressure.

Understanding the Enemy

When the insurgency broke out, the French had the advantage of a capable police force in Algeria as well as an intelligence service, the Deuxième Bureau, effective in foreign as well as domestic intelligence. To back up the police was the Gendarmerie (a national, paramilitary police force) with more than 2,300 men stationed in Algeria.[36] The French had long maintained a network of informers and agents within the Algerian nationalist circles, so it is a remarkable testimony to the security and efficiency of the FLN that the French knew so little about it when the insurgency began.

Despite a long and close connection with the Algerian people, most of the French—and certainly most of the *pied noirs*, who thought they knew the Algerians, in fact had little real understanding of the people they were dealing with. One common saying of the *pied noirs* was that the Moslems did not want political power but only wished to be ruled justly.[37] It was the kind of statement that Rhodesians and South Africans would later say about their native workers.

The French failure to understand the extent of the FLN's organization in the first months of the insurgency gave the FLN a good chance to organize, grow, and increase their forces. By the time the French realized that the FLN attacks were more than an isolated rebellion, the FLN and its military arm had a good hold on large parts of the Algerian countryside. A special parliamentary commission set up by the National Assembly in June 1955 to study the Algerian crisis consisted of socialist, right wing, and Gaullist deputies to ensure that the commission's report would not be interpreted as the views of one political block. The report, issued in July 1955, provided accurate insights into the causes and nature of the rebellion and was scathing in its criticism of the Algerian administration which, in the last decade, "seemed to have lost contact with the native population." The report went on to question the strong-arm tactics employed by the police and military to quell the rebellion, pointing out that methods such as collective punishment and torture were ultimately counterproductive: "Our experience in Indo-China has shown that such methods breed hatred far more than fear, and play, in the end, into the hands of the rebels."[38]

Throughout the war French tactical and operational intelligence was often outstanding. The French had the advantage of a well-established police and intelligence force at the outbreak of the war. In the field, the army, police, and Gendarmerie had many Moslem North African servicemen (the French army had twenty thousand North African troops at the outbreak of the conflict), and the regular officers of the French army who served with North African troops had to learn Arabic, much like British officers of the Indian Army who were required to learn Indian languages. In addition, many of the *pied noirs* who served as reservists knew Arabic. In short, the French had plenty of people knowledgeable in Arabic and in the Algerian Moslem culture. Once the French got over their initial shock at the rebellion, the army was able to put together some first-rate human intelligence teams to develop a detailed tactical analysis of the FLN organization, leadership, and military forces. Of especial importance was the work of the Deuxième Bureau in France and in Europe, waging a clandestine war to break up the FLN support network among the Algerians in France and to break up the FLN's weapons buying and smuggling organization.

Part of the revolutionary war doctrine espoused by the colonial French army was the use of torture as a standard means to elicit information. Colonel Trinquier, in his highly popular book on counterinsurgency, argued frankly that torture was a valid and necessary means of interrogation—but should only be used by skilled professionals who would take care to use methods that would not permanently injure the prisoner either physically or mentally.[39] Unfortunately, few followed Trinquier's rules for regulating torture. From the start of the campaign the French army used torture as a normal interrogation technique, commonly using methods that permanently crippled or even killed their prisoners. Once information had been elicited, a quiet summary execution would prevent complaints from being made. In the course of the war, several thousand Algerians simply "disappeared" while in the custody of French forces.

On the other hand, many French officers refused to employ abusive methods against the Algerians. Some French commanders of rural districts worked closely with the SAS, insisting that their forces respect the local Algerian leaders and their customs. When treated decently by the French, many rural villages responded positively and raised very effective local home guard units, willingly helping the French track down ALN guerrillas.[40]

In addition to one of the largest and most efficient human intelligence networks in modern counterinsurgency, the French also employed the most modern technical methods to glean intelligence. The French Army Signal Corps deployed special detachments to Algeria that set up an elaborate system of radio direction finders to monitor and locate rebel radio transmissions. Once these had been identified the French could establish a fix on FLN headquarters for attack by air force bombers and by heliborne commando troops. French intelligence specialists recorded and deciphered FLN radio transmissions to the FLN headquarters in Tunis.[41]

The most famous campaign of the Algerian War took place in the city of Algiers, where the army carried out an urban counterinsurgency campaign from January to October 1957. In response to a series of terrorist attacks aimed at *pied noir* civilians in Algiers in late 1956 and early 1957, the French Army sent the 10th Paratroop Division into the city and gave its commander, General Massu, a virtual blank check to destroy the FLN terrorist network by any means necessary.

The FLN in Algiers consisted of approximately 1,200 supporters and a small cadre of fighters hidden among the four hundred thousand Moslem residents of the city. The French were able to deploy approximately forty thousand military and police personnel in Algiers, among them the regular police, Gendarmerie companies, *pied noir* army reservists, and army garrison units, in addition to the 10th Paratroop Division. The French army was especially strong in its intelligence capabilities—an absolute requirement for success when facing small groups of urban guerrillas hidden within a sympathetic civilian population. Many of the French officers and NCOs spoke Arabic and had long experience in Algeria. The French army also deployed a team of crack intelligence specialists to help General Massu's staff sift through the vast amount of information gleaned from interrogations and captured documents, and to develop a detailed analysis of the FLN organization and membership in Algiers. Ignoring normal judicial procedures, the army conducted mass roundups of Moslems, detaining any person whose papers or story seemed even slightly out of order. In the army detention centers, torture and abuse of Algerian suspects was commonplace. Using a very methodical system, the French army sectioned off the neighborhoods of the Casbah (Arab section of the city) and restricted communication between neighborhoods. Step by step, Massu's forces tracked down, captured, or killed FLN leaders, who were well hidden in the city. Yet, despite an excellent intelligence service and a troop ratio of one soldier to every ten Moslem inhabitants, it took Massu's force ten months to eliminate the FLN terrorist cells in Algiers and end the attacks upon French civilians.[42]

The methods of the Battle of Algiers and the use of torture throughout the Algerian War was often justified as necessary to end a terrorist campaign that was murdering civilians. Certainly there was a broad belief in the French army at the time that the ends justified the means. However, the moral issue caused a serious rift in the French officer corps at the time.[43]

There is no doubt that the highly effective French tactical intelligence system helped break the FLN forces in the field. By 1958 the ALN had not only been beaten in Algiers but was in serious decline in the rural areas. The next year would see the ALN almost destroyed in the field. The question is whether it was necessary to employ torture to obtain good intelligence on the FLN. The fact that many SAS detachments and field units obtained excellent intelligence and cooperation from Algerians by treating them with respect and studiously avoiding abusive behavior indicates that torture was not a necessary means of obtaining intelligence. The employment of abusive methods largely seems to be symptomatic of the culture of the French colonial army which acted as a law unto itself. The belief of the *pied noir* "ultras" that the Algerians could be intimidated through a French brand of terrorism also encouraged the colonial French army to go far beyond the bounds of military behavior.

Of course, even the best intelligence analysis cannot overcome assumptions made by the senior leadership. The greatest mistake of the French leadership in understanding their opponents was the assumption that Nasser and the Egyptians had inspired the Algerian rebellion, and without Nasser's support the revolution would quickly collapse. The comforting view that there was one, simple external cause of the Algerian revolution—Nasser—was accepted uncritically in the top ranks of the French government and military in 1955–1956. Pierre Lactose, who served in several cabinets and would later be De Gaulle's minister for Algeria, remarked in 1956 that the real enemy was in Egypt, not Algeria, and "one French division in Egypt is worth four in Algeria."[44]

That belief about Egypt helped drive the French leadership to commit their forces, alongside those of Britain, in attacking Egypt in October 1956 to regain control of the Suez Canal. The British and French leaders generally believed that if their troops landed, Nasser would fall and then all of their problems in North Africa and the Middle East would be solved.[45] Instead, the Egyptian military defeat was hailed throughout the Arab world as valiant resistance to the aggressive colonial powers, and Nasser's power and prestige were actually enhanced by the British-French invasion. The whole affair had been a fiasco. When the French were forced by great power diplomacy to withdraw from the Suez Canal Zone in early 1957, Nasser was in a stronger position than ever. Egyptian and Arab aid to the Algerian rebels would subsequently be stepped up.

French Strategy and Decision Making

Although many deputies of the National Assembly were willing to work with other political blocks to resolve the Algerian crisis, for the most part the sharp divisions on the domestic policies of the Fourth Republic resulted in coalition cabinets unable to establish a clear policy.[46] For the French, Algeria was especially complicated. Legally, Algeria was a domestic issue, since Algeria constituted three departments of Metropolitan France. The French judicial system operated in Algeria, and even with the emergency regulations in effect, the police still came under the jurisdiction of the French interior ministry. Most important of all, the small *colon* community in Algeria elected more than thirty delegates to the National Assembly, an important block of votes in a political system composed of dozens of parties organized into several blocks. Voting as a group, the *pied noirs* carried a political influence that far outweighed the size of their population.

The Fourth Republic contained some very able political leaders, but it was not in the nature of a weak system built on shifting party coalitions to enact the major reforms of the Algerian government system that the senior military officers and political leaders in France knew were necessary. Until the Fourth Republic had collapsed and the new constitution of the Fifth Republic was established in 1958, the successive French governments were locked into a position of maintaining the status quo: keeping Algeria as it was and sending more troops to suppress the insurgency.

The accession of Charles De Gaulle to power in 1958, with a new constitution that allowed for a strong presidency, broke the logjam in strategic policy over Algeria. With a strong mandate De Gaulle had the option of negotiating with the rebels and openly discussing reform programs and even major changes in Algeria's status. De Gaulle made it a point to discuss a variety of ideas for Algeria while being careful not to commit himself to any of them. His speeches and policy statements on Algeria from 1958 and 1959 were carefully couched in vague terms, which could be interpreted by the Algerians as favoring fundamental reforms and granting political power to the Moslems, while the *pied noirs* were reassured that Algeria would remain French.

While De Gaulle entertained a variety of ideas for reform in Algeria, he also insisted on a new military strategy to crush the rebellion. At the start of his tenure as the first president of the Fifth Republic, De Gaulle probably had no clear plan other than to break the insurgent forces and then, from a position of strength, to negotiate a deal with the FLN and other nationalist leaders over the future status of Algeria. While De Gaulle may have considered independence for Algeria in 1958, any form of independence that De Gaulle envisioned would have been an Algeria with home rule: a legislature elected by all the Algerians, *colon* and Moslem, but bound to France on defense, diplomatic, and trade issues. Whatever course De Gaulle preferred, it was certainly not going to be to the liking of the *pied noirs*, who earnestly clung to the status quo.

One of the most serious obstacles in crafting a political solution to the Algerian War was the mindset of the French military and a great part of its leadership. After the debacle of 1940, the French army rebuilt itself under De Gaulle's leadership and from 1943 to 1945 again proved it was a first-rate fighting force in Italy, France, and Germany. After World War II France looked to rebuild itself. Neither the French government nor the military were eager to become involved in a major colonial war. After De Gaulle's departure from power in 1946, however, the successive governments of the Fourth Republic blundered into a disastrous war in Indochina which ended with the defeat of a French army at Dien Bien Phu in 1954. The war in Indochina had little impact on the French people at home, as the war was largely financed by the United States and fought with colonial troops, not the main French army.

By law France essentially had two armies, and this arrangement would be at the core of the later conflicts between the army and the government. The main force of the French regular army was manned by conscripts, who by law could not be committed to fight in the colonies. France's other army, the colonial army, was a mix of volunteer soldiers, locally raised forces, and the Foreign Legion. This was the force that fought in Indochina and the counterinsurgency campaigns in Morocco and Tunisia. It was an exceptionally tough and capable army. The Foreign Legion in this period, by any reckoning one of the most elite military forces in the world, was largely recruited from former Wehrmacht veterans. The officers of the French colonial army had seen almost two decades of warfare, from Europe to Indochina to North Africa, and were among the most experienced combat commanders in the world. Their view of combat was not the big conventional war in Europe envisioned by the NATO planners, but a small unit war, fought in the jungles and deserts against lightly-armed guerrillas who could blend into the civilian population at will. Although aircraft, paratroops, and tanks featured in these campaigns, the war that the colonial army understood was the light infantry war. In addition to fighting, the colonial soldiers often served as the de facto government in the colonial countryside, where French administration sometimes scarcely existed. While fighting in Indochina and Morocco, the colonial soldiers had been forced to think through many of the problems of modern counterinsurgency warfare, including methods of controlling and securing the population, and of mounting propaganda campaigns to win over the colonial subjects and undermine the appeal of the insurgents. The colonial soldiers had a long habit of being largely on their own and holding vast authority over the colonial peoples they were trying to simultaneously protect and subjugate.

From the postwar experience the colonial army officers had developed their own doctrine of war, essentially a counterinsurgency doctrine designed to deal with the political and psychological aspects of conflict as well as the military tactics. The *Guerre Révolutionaire* "Revolutionary Warfare" theory was meant to counter what the colonial officers understood to be the primary threat to the West: not the big conventional war, but a war of subversion and insurgency inspired and supported by the communist nations. Although the French colonial army had failed to defeat the communists in Indochina, they also believed they had learned lessons from that war and had the right theory and doctrine to defeat guerrilla and nationalist enemies. When conflict came to Algeria, they knew what to do.

However, France also had her other army, the regular armed forces, whose officers dominated the top military command and staff positions. In the aftermath of World War II, at the beginning of the Cold War, the top priority of France's military high command, and of the French government, was to rebuild and modernize the French armed forces to serve as a large conventional force to protect France and Western Europe from the Soviet threat. General Charles Léchères, chief of staff of the air force from February 1948 to 1953, saw the buildup of NATO, rearmament, and modernization as the primary interests of his service.[47] It was much the same for the army and navy. Though colonial soldiers had seen most of the toughest combat, they were often snubbed by a mainstream military leadership that was focused on building a force capable of fighting the Soviets. France's military forces stationed in Europe would get the new tanks, airplanes, missiles, and vehicles being developed by French engineers in the late 1950s and early 1960s, while the colonial forces would have to make do with minimum budgets and worn out equipment left over from World War II—a great part supplied by the Americans through the wartime Lend-Lease program. Newsreels from the Algerian War invariably show the French army equipped with old American halftracks, armored cars, Sherman tanks, and 105mm howitzers.

When the two armies served in separate spheres, as in the Indochina War (which did not involve any of France's regular forces), the split between the two forces was not too evident. But in Algeria the two armies would have to fight side by side, the colonial commanders propelled to take a leading role. In Algeria the culture clash of the two armies would lead to distrust within the top ranks of the military and the eventual rebellion of colonial forces. Success against the insurgents in Algeria would require a clear political strategy by the civilian government. This, however, was generally absent from 1954 to 1958. In the absence of strategy or policy, the French commanders in the field would create their own—often with disastrous results for French foreign policy. The officers of the colonial army had long been in the habit of disregarding their civilian leaders when it suited them. This habit was taken to the Algerian War where it would eventually divide the army.

French Public Opinion and the War

When the FLN began the insurgency in November 1954, public opinion in France was overwhelmingly in favor of crushing the uprising. Although France had a left-liberal government at the time under Prime Minister Mendes-France, even the French left had no sympathy for any independence movement in Algeria. Even the powerful French Communist Party refused to support an Algerian independence movement in 1954, having argued for two decades that the Algerians ought to instead be assimilated as full French citizens. French newspapers, from right to left, called on the government to take stern measures to restore order in Algeria. Almost no one in France, aside from the Algerians living there, could conceive of France abandoning Algeria.

For the average Frenchman Algeria was not a foreign country, but an integral part of France. Emotions on the issue ran very high.

By 1956, after the conflict had widened and showed no signs of letting up, public opinion was still strongly in favor of retaining Algeria with opinion polls showing 49 percent of the public wishing to retain Algeria as a department of Metropolitan France versus 25 percent who favored a looser connection between France and Algeria with more autonomy for Algeria. That year Jacques Soustelle, who had served as governor general of Algeria in 1955, summed up the French government's view in the National Assembly where he argued that the loss of Algeria was equivalent to the French defeat at Sedan in 1870 or France's defeat at Germany's hands in 1940.[48]

The French Army was certainly not blind to the importance of a war for the hearts and minds of the population. The *Guerre Révolutionaire* theory stressed the importance of psychological warfare. In 1955 the French high command set up a special psychological warfare organization to orchestrate media and propaganda operations. The new organization was placed under the direct control of the defense minister, and several companies of psychological operations soldiers were organized and equipped with printing presses and loudspeakers and staffed by French soldiers fluent in Arabic and knowledgeable about Algeria. The new psychological organization was given a high priority and manned by some top staff officers. The French psychological warfare efforts were two-pronged, one dealing with the education of France's own soldiers to convince them of the rightness of French policy in Algeria, and the other aimed at convincing the Algerians to stay loyal to France.

One of the major efforts of the psychological warfare branch was the establishment of ten large "reeducation centers" in Algeria where Algerian prisoners were screened under categories of "incorrigible" (convinced FLN supporter) and "reformable" (a weak commitment to the FLN). Once sorted out, the prisoners most susceptible to indoctrination were sent to a relatively comfortable camp where they were given some education and job training mixed with a daily dose of pro-French propaganda including classes on the French way of life. After a few months of such treatment many of the detainees were considered reeducated and set free. It was, in fact, doubtful whether the treatment really won over any Algerians to the French cause or had any lasting effect.

The French military employed every means to support its psychological warfare campaign. Air force leaflet drops over the isolated villages encouraged FLN members to come in and surrender. Other leaflets promoted the civic action program of the French government and told the villages of the benefits to be gained by denouncing the FLN supporters in their midst.[49] One leaflet designed for the nomadic tribesmen of the Sahara Desert consisted of simple pictures warning the rebels that if they killed French soldiers, French aircraft and heavy weapons would kill them all. The final message in large print said "Crime Does Not Pay."[50]

The French psychological warfare efforts in the villages that were carried out by the SAS from 1958 to 1960 were demonstrably more successful in winning the Algerian hearts and minds than the leaflet drops and indoctrination centers. The civic action units in the countryside backed up their words with deeds, and their efforts were carried out by officers, NCOs, and civilians who understood the local language and culture. One must not forget that a large proportion of the Algerians stayed loyal to France, and far more Algerians fought against the FLN than for it. The SAS efforts in the countryside deserve the credit.

On France's home front successive governments from 1954 to 1957 managed to maintain strong support for the government's policy of suppressing the insurgency. Soon after the start of the insurgency, the government put forward an "emergency powers law" suspending all representative bodies in Algeria until 1958 and creating "emergency zones" which allowed for special population controls and regulations. This allowed the government to put tight restrictions on travel. There were some complaints in the National Assembly about the threat to civil liberties that the law entailed, but the bill was quickly passed with a 379 to 219 majority.[51]

Yet, as the war entered its third year with no sign of letting up, the support of the French public became impossible to maintain. French reservists and conscripts returning from the war talked about the widespread use of torture and the readiness of French soldiers to abuse the Moslem population. By 1957, despite government efforts to suppress such accounts, stories of arbitrary arrests and deaths of Algerians under torture were published. In that year the French leftist intellectuals who had not supported Algerian independence, such as

Jean-Paul Sartre, changed their position and came out for independence arguing that France had lost its moral right to stay in Algeria.

Criticism of the French military's behavior also came under sharp attack from the right in the form of denunciations of torture and human rights abuses by French bishops.[52] In 1957 and 1958 the moral issue of France's policy came to the forefront. Because the charges were essentially true, public support for the war began to fall across all the French political parties, including those of the right. Catholic army officers—certainly not known for sympathy to the left—also joined the chorus of protest. In April 1959 a letter to some French bishops, signed by thirty-five army officers who had served in Algeria, denounced the standard behavior of the army and police in Algeria. They wrote that "arbitrary arrests and detentions are numerous . . . interrogations are conducted only too normally by methods that we must call torture. Summary executions of prisoners, civilian and military . . . are not exceptional. Finally, it is not unusual during operations for wounded to be finished off."[53]

Though they won on the battlefield, the French lost the media and propaganda war. The excessive use of force against Algerian rebels played into the hands of the French and world media. On the other hand, while the French media and propaganda efforts had some success within Algeria, the message that France was fighting Algerian rebels as the Free World's first line of defense against communism fell flat. The ongoing crisis in Algeria and the public's lack of faith in the government to deal with the issue were central to the downfall of the Fourth Republic and the accession of Charles De Gaulle to power. When De Gaulle came to power in 1958 everyone, Algerians and Frenchmen, was tired of the war. By that time the French public was more than ready to accept the idea of autonomy for Algeria—an idea that would have been rejected out of hand four years before. De Gaulle did the popular and necessary thing by broaching the idea of some form of independence for Algeria when he came into office. However, as the *colons* feared, once the idea of even limited independence was publicly endorsed it could not be revoked. Whatever the results on the battlefield, public opinion was overwhelmingly in favor of some form of negotiated solution.

In contrast to the French government, the FLN started the conflict with only a small minority of the Algerian population on their side. For one thing, illiteracy in Algeria was high, as was the poverty level. For farm workers, day laborers, and lower level employees—essentially the majority of Algerian men—the main daily concern was simply the struggle to stay alive and feed one's family. There was little time or inclination for taking an interest in politics or studying revolutionary ideology. Given such a situation, the FLN employed the radio as a primary means of reaching and educating the Algerian populace and also spreading their position to a broad audience in the Arab-speaking world. Starting early in the insurrection, Radio Cairo took up the FLN cause and broadcast FLN proclamations and information bulletins to the Algerians and throughout the Middle East. After Morocco became independent in early 1956, the FLN used that country as a base for broadcasting "Voice of the Arabs" into Algeria.[54] The broadcasts to the Algerians were made in fairly simple language, describing—in fact, grossly overestimating—the strength and numbers of the FLN fighters, and portraying minor military actions as victorious battles. At the same time, French abuses, of which there were plenty of genuine cases, were also exaggerated as the FLN built a sense of grievance against the French among the Algerians.

One of the most important missions of the FLN leadership and propaganda specialists was to build a sense of national identity among the Algerians. The French claim, that there really was no Algerian nation, per se, when the colonization effort began in the 1830s, was essentially true. What became Algeria was at that time a collection of city-states and tribal territories. What the French did in the nineteenth century was tear down the tribal system in Algeria. By doing so they helped the insurgents of the 1950s. The FLN manufactured a romanticized version of an Algerian nation before the French conquest and put it forward in broadcasts and underground publications. The FLN claimed that they were reviving this idealized Algerian nation through the anticolonial struggle. Accurate or not, this national myth had a powerful effect upon the Algerians, and the struggle against the French did, to a large degree, build a foundation for unity among the Algerians.

Beginning in 1956 the FLN produced a bimonthly journal, *El Moudjahid*, for the educated Algerian. Three to ten thousand copies of the journal were produced and circulated secretly. Written in both Arabic and French, *El Moudjahid* concentrated on four major themes: popularizing the ALN and its accomplishments, attacking the policies and behavior of the French government and military, describing the international aspects of the struggle, and discussing economic issues including the ideas of the FLN for a post-independence economic structure. *El Moudjahid* answered the need for a more intellectual form of propaganda capable of convincing a largely skeptical Algerian middle class of the FLN's program.[55]

FLN organizers among the Algerian community in France quietly raised funds for the FLN propaganda effort and worked on spreading the FLN message among the Algerians outside of the country. Key to all the FLN propaganda efforts was the support of President Nasser of Egypt. Not only was Cairo a home for FLN leaders serving as a government in exile, but Nasser's Radio Cairo was also a primary means of popularizing the FLN through the Arab world. Nasser saw in the independence movement in Algeria the type of revolutionary nationalism akin to his own ideology. More importantly, Nasser initiated a major press and media campaign in favor of the Algerian nationalists and led the other Arab states to bring the cause of Algerian independence before the United Nations.[56]

As a member of the United Nations and a leading member of the nonaligned block of third world countries, Egypt was able to bring the Algerian independence issues before the United Nations. France, with its veto on the Security Council and with the reluctant support of America, was able to repeatedly block any real UN action on Algeria. But simply raising the Algeria issue in international forums worked to publicize the FLN cause and legitimize the FLN in the eyes of Arab and third-world nations. The recognition of an FLN delegation in the meeting of the nonaligned block of nations was further proof of the legitimacy of the FLN as the true representatives of the Algerians. Although the FLN's support among the Algerians was, at first, very thin, the breadth and sophistication of its propaganda efforts worked to undermine rival Algerian nationalist groups and to establish the FLN as the undisputed torchbearers and representatives of the Algerian national movement. By 1956 rival Algerian parties and factions were marginalized. From that point the only major nationalist movement that the French could negotiate with would be the FLN.

International Aspects of the Algerian War

The international support that France obtained for its Algeria policy before the accession of De Gaulle to power is easy to describe—none. The Algerian War was a major friction point between the United States and France from 1954 to 1962. Increasing the friction was France's dependence upon large loans and grants from the United States to rebuild the postwar economy and to enable France to play a major role in NATO.

While the United States was privately very critical of French policy, publicly the U.S. government under Eisenhower avoided an open rift because the United States needed France's contribution to NATO. However, the war in Algeria soon became the main effort of the French armed forces, which interfered with NATO plans for building a capable conventional shield in Europe. In 1957 French defense minister André Morice declared that the French forces in Algeria had "an absolute priority" for equipment and personnel over NATO and other French commitments. In Algeria, he declared, France was developing the equipment and tactics to fight communist subversion."[57] In fact, although the French military leadership seems to have largely believed this, neither the U.S. government nor the governments of France's other NATO allies bought this line of reasoning. Indeed, the vast commitment of French military resources to Algeria was especially damaging to NATO strategy for several years.

Remaining true to his word, Nasser began to provide economic and military aid to the Algerian rebels after the start of the revolution. Nasser initiated a major press and media campaign in favor of the Algerian nationalists and led the other Arab states in bringing the cause of Algerian independence before the United Nations.[58] Cairo served from 1954 to 1956 as a safe haven for the FLN external leadership to mount an international and diplomatic campaign. Egypt put together the support from the Arab states in 1956 to have the Algerian issue brought before the UN General Assembly. This act caused the French ambassador to walk out in protest, insisting that Algeria was a French domestic issue.[59] The Soviet block, trying to broaden its links to the emerging third world states, also provided military and financial aid.

Most important for the Algerian rebels was the independence of Morocco and Tunisia in 1956. The ugly and violent process that led to independence from France in both countries made the two newly independent states ready partners in supporting the Algerians. The FLN was able to constitute a government in exile in Tunis in 1956. With aid and equipment flowing in from the Soviet block and Egypt, the Algerians began building a professional army in camps inside Tunisia and Morocco. Tunisia became the main base for the FLN, and there were an estimated thirty-five thousand well-trained and equipped ALN soldiers in Tunisia by 1959. A smaller ALN force, perhaps ten thousand men, was stationed in camps inside Morocco. With sanctuaries to build forces, the ALN formed and trained a general staff.

At several points in the conflict, actions by the French military set off crises that threatened to broaden the war. In the fall of 1956, an aircraft carrying Ben Bella and four top FLN leaders from Rabat in Morocco to Tunis was forced to divert into French airspace and land at Algiers. There was an international outcry at this open violation of international airspace rules as Ben Bella and the FLN leaders were put into French jails. Freed in 1962, Ben Bella became the first president of Algeria. The incident raised the level of anti-French passion in both Morocco and Tunisia and served as an incentive to provide increased support to the Algerian rebels.

The French military's desire to strike a decisive blow against the ALN force being trained in Tunisia led to an international incident that was one of the greatest French blunders of the war. In February 1958 the French handed the FLN a huge moral victory by bombing the Tunisian border village of Sakiet with a squadron of B-26 bombers. Sakiet was a known base for FLN rebels trying to infiltrate into Algeria and might be considered a legitimate target, but the bombing took place on market day when a large number of civilians were present. The French managed to hit a school during the bombing run. At least eighty civilians, including many women and children, were killed and hundreds more wounded. The French action seems to have been the idea of the military high command in Algeria, for the premier had not been informed beforehand about the attack on another country.[60] This French action became world news as dramatic pictures of the wrecked school and injured children were published. The action of the French in bombing a target in another country became an issue in the United Nations and helped mobilize international efforts to provide political support for the FLN.[61] It was a blunder that received worldwide condemnation.

The Sakiet attack brought France and Tunisia to the brink of war. President Bourguiba tolerated the Algerians in his country partly because he had no choice. If he had ordered the ALN forces out of the country, he would have been deposed by his own people as a stooge of the French. The Tunisians reacted to the French attack by demanding a large indemnity and beginning the expulsion of French estate owners and businessmen from their country.[62] Tunisia demanded the withdrawal of the French garrisons that remained in the country, and several skirmishes erupted between French Marines defending their bases and Tunisian mobs. Although the French-Tunisian tensions were brought under control, partly by a U.S. diplomatic effort, from that point the Tunisians were more open in their support to the FLN.

After the FLN military effort largely collapsed between 1959 and 1960, the insurgency was kept alive by the international political support and the existence of its government and army in exile. If the FLN was a broken force inside Algeria, it still had the trappings of a legitimate government and movement outside the country. That the FLN received such strong support from the Arab world and from Morocco and Tunisia is largely due to the incredibly clumsy French foreign policy from 1954 to 1958.

De Gaulle Steps In: New Strategies 1958–1961

By early 1958 Algeria had become a millstone for the French public. Reservists and conscripts brought back tales of brutality and torture by the French and the Algerians. The war was costing France a vast sum of money, and it had dragged on interminably with no end in sight. Although France was prosperous on the surface, inflation was running high. The government was deeply in debt and only able to survive through American loans. By April 1958, none of the political blocks in France could reach agreement. Starting on April 16, France was without a government for thirty-seven days. The supporters of Charles De Gaulle saw a golden opportunity to bring him back to power and worked tirelessly behind the scenes to have him named premier. De Gaulle was helped by the *pied noir* leaders in Algiers and the military commanders, who took over the city hall of Algiers in May 1958. They declared themselves to be a committee of public safety and called for De Gaulle's return to power. As the crisis worsened the National Assembly agreed by 329 to 224 votes to make De Gaulle the premier with full powers for six months and special authority to reform the French constitution.[63] Within weeks De Gaulle's staff had drafted a new constitution for France which would establish a strong presidency and give Algeria a new status as associated with France, but no longer legally a part of Metropolitan France.

69

Although initially inclined to win the war and keep Algeria a French possession, De Gaulle also understood that the war in Algeria was hurting the French economy and tearing the political fabric of the nation apart. For the first few months in office he made several speeches that promised that Algeria would remain French, but also promised that Moslem Algerians would have full rights and a degree of autonomy under a new system to be negotiated. One of his first acts as premier was to visit Algiers, where he was greeted with wild enthusiasm by the *colons* and the Moslems. Both sides were looking for a leader who could break the impasse over Algeria. Moslems and *pied noirs* saw De Gaulle as the answer.

A core element of De Gaulle's effort to build support for his policies was to include all the Algerians in the national referendum in September 1958 to approve the draft of a constitution for the Fifth Republic. It was a first step towards autonomy and, for the first time in Algeria's history, all Moslems—including women—were registered with Europeans on a common electoral roll. Rightly fearing that the public would support a new constitution that provided Algerians with something less than full independence, the FLN mounted a terror campaign to intimidate the Moslem population into boycotting the election. The FLN failed. Some 80 percent of the Moslems turned out to vote, and 96 percent supported the new constitution. In February 1959 De Gaulle became the first president of the Fifth Republic. In October of that year, with terrorism diminished and General Maurice Challe's plan to break the FLN in the field working, De Gaulle visited Algeria to announce a plan to end the war and create a semi-independent Algeria with partnership between Moslems and *colons*. The FLN leaders, again fearing that the Moslem population would support De Gaulle's plan, refused to negotiate and vowed to carry on the fight. However, the defeat of the ALN in the field and the inability to bring new fighters into Algeria had greatly weakened the FLN.

De Gaulle's strategy to settle the war was crafted around a political and military program. On the political side the French government would reach out to the Algerians, raise their status and standard of living, and grant them considerable political power and some form of autonomy without granting full independence. In 1958 De Gaulle initiated a broad social and economic reform program for the Algerians called the Constantine Plan. De Gaulle's idea was to create a moderate Algerian governing class that would be prosperous and also loyal to France. Under the plan twenty-three thousand Algerians would be trained in administration, business, engineering, and professions. The training program addressed the obvious problem of a lack of Moslem Algerians in supervisory or management jobs. DeGaulle hoped that this new class of French-trained professionals would form a leadership corps for an autonomous or independent Algeria.[64] The problems of endemic poverty and unemployment also had to be addressed. Under the Constantine Plan the French government would provide $600 million a year to be invested in public works, schools, housing, and industry. The oil revenues that were just beginning to flow from the Sahara (the Saharan wells only started to pump oil in 1957) would cover much of the cost of the plan. It was a very sound strategy that addressed many of the fundamental problems that had driven the insurgency. If a similar plan had been proposed ten years before, the insurgency would never have gotten off the ground.

The other side of the strategy was a program to win a military victory over the FLN and secure the countryside against the rebels. Dealing from a position of political and military strength, De Gaulle could then negotiate a deal with the FLN, offering amnesty and some form of autonomy while protecting French sovereignty and economic interests. To assure the success of the military plan, De Gaulle brought in General Maurice Challe, an air force general, who was told that he had a year to defeat the FLN. After that time France would be entering the demographically "hollow years"—the birth years from 1940 to 1944—when there would be far fewer conscripts available for the French army.

Challe demonstrated a high level of imagination and leadership in reorganizing his forces for a grand offensive to break the FLN. Challe built upon the tactics and programs that General Salan had developed. Salan's battle on the frontiers had been very successful; through 1958 and 1959 only a trickle of arms and reinforcements had managed to get into Algeria to support the FLN fighters. Other successful programs were the work of the SAS in the rural areas and the formation of Algerian home guards, known as the *harkis*. The self-defense program in the villages increased from 9,100 Algerians under arms in January 1957, to 85,000 villagers enrolled by June 1960.[65] Under the home guard program much of the countryside became a more hostile place for the insurgent fighters. Under Challe the home guards programs were vastly expanded, and the SAS given more personnel and resources. Although it started

71

relatively late, the combination of civic action programs and self-defense forces was remarkably successful. By 1959 4,868 French officers, NCOs, and civilians were part of the civic action program. By a decree in September 1959, they were made responsible for coordination between the local Algerian officials and the French government.[66]

Challe built on General Salan's program of creating special task forces to hunt down the ALN guerrilla units. The increase in the home guard force of *harkis* ensured that the villages loyal to the French were protected, while freeing up a large number of troops who had been holding static posts for offensive operations. The successful operations along the frontiers had largely ended the attempt of the ALN to infiltrate large forces into the interior, so thousands more of the best combat troops in the army were made available for offensive operations. Challe reorganized the military forces in Algeria so that he would have three divisions: the 10th and 25th Parachute Divisions and the 11th Infantry Division, to serve as a general reserve that he could rapidly deploy as a concentrated force.

In a series of nine large operations over the first seven months of 1959, large French task forces systematically pacified the Algerian countryside starting in the west and moving east. The *harkis*, who knew the countryside as well as the ALN guerrilla fighters, played a central role as scouts for the army units in these operations. Each major operation was backed by aircraft and helicopter units to provide rapid mobility and overwhelming firepower. Challe's offensive plan worked brilliantly, and an estimated 40 percent of the ALN forces were killed or captured. The French forces also killed two of the six *wilaya* commanders. As areas were systematically cleared, the SAS units would go to work organizing civic action programs and organizing the loyal members of the population into home guards. The combination of military operations, civic action, and Algerian home guards broke the ALN as an effective military force.[67] By early 1960 most of the FLN bands were on the run and the morale of the revolutionaries hit rock bottom.[68]

With a military victory and a successful civic action program, Algeria became a much more secure place. By February 1960 there were only 1,200 insurgent actions (attacks upon French military and civilian targets and pro-French Algerians) throughout all of Algeria—less than half the level of activity of mid-1956, when the FLN had carried out 2,500 attacks. Now in a position of strength to open negotiations, De Gaulle cut a deal that would allow more democracy and a form of independence to the Algerians while protecting the French *colons* and interests there. From 1959 to1961, several plans for a political settlement for Algeria were floated. Most of the plans considered some form of autonomy for Algeria along with programs to grant land to Algerian peasants and reorganize the local governments to allow Algerian majority rule. Algeria would join the French Union under a commonwealth status, while the *colons* would retain dual citizenship. One plan was to grant Algeria full independence while retaining a *colon* enclave along the coast near Constantine as fully French, and to keep an overland strip of territory in the Sahara, which would also remain French along with its oil reserves.

However, the *colon* community had been radicalized by the war, and a major faction was now violently opposed to any plan for equal rights for Moslems or autonomy for Algeria. Now Frenchmen fired on Frenchmen as *pied noir* militants organized themselves and began a series of violent protests in January 1960 against De Gaulle's conciliatory policies. That month rioting between the *colons* and Gendarmerie left 19 dead and 146 wounded. In February 1960 *pied noir* protests in Algiers crossed the line into open rebellion as twenty thousand *pied noir* militants, including militiamen, students, and city workers, erected barricades in the streets and fortified the city center of Algiers. General Challe brought troops in from the interior to reinforce the Algiers garrison, but for days the troops mingled with the *colons* as the leaders tried to negotiate out of the confrontation. De Gaulle finally spoke to the nation, condemning the *colon* attempt to intimidate the government. He followed up his speech by relieving the commander of the 10th Paratroop Division, who had been reluctant to act against the rebels. The army troops in Algiers became tougher about sealing off the city, and *colon* reservists were given military orders to report to their unit depots. With little sympathy outside Algiers, the *pied noir* military leaders surrendered and the barricades came down.[69]

The violent dissention in the French ranks was a godsend that encouraged the weakened FLN to maintain the fight. While part of the army—namely the Foreign Legion, the paratroops, and the colonial troops—had shown themselves to be sympathetic to the *colons*, there was little sympathy for the *colons* in mainland France or among the regular French army. The war was costing France a lot of money, and the overwhelming majority of Frenchmen stood behind De Gaulle's attempts to reach a negotiated solution with the Algerians. The behavior of the Algiers *pied noirs* was a serious warning of just how things might get out of hand. The surrender of the *colon* militant leaders without further violence and the refusal of the *colon* reservists to disobey military orders also signified that the average *colon* was still willing to accept the proper authority of the government.

Collapse of the French Position, 1961–1962

With FLN activity within Algeria still declining through 1960, De Gaulle decided to break the impasse by pushing through a political deal. On September 16, 1960, De Gaulle announced a referendum to allow the Algerians to determine their future. Despite widespread opposition by the *pieds noirs*, the vote occurred on January 8, 1961, with most non-Europeans voting for some form of independence.[70] De Gaulle hoped that the referendum would form the basis for a negotiated political settlement by all the parties. What he got was another war. De Gaulle's perceived betrayal of the sacred cause of French Algeria provoked a decision by the *pied noir* "ultras" and some factions of the military to not just protest the government's action, but actively overthrow De Gaulle and put into power a government that would keep Algeria French.

Within weeks of the 1961 referendum on independence, a group of *pied noir* "ultras" and some former military men formed a secret society called the *Organisation Armée Secrète* (Secret Army Organization, OAS). The OAS, with its headquarters in Madrid, initiated a program of major terrorist attacks designed to cow the Moslem population. Even more radically, the OAS carried out assassinations and terror attacks against *colons* who favored De Gaulle's vision of compromise. The *pied noirs* of the OAS quickly proved to be just as ruthless and effective as terrorists as the FLN. Throughout France and Algeria OAS bombings and terror attacks killed hundreds. In France Algerians suspected of supporting the FLN were killed. In Algeria the primary victims of the OAS were Moslems, but *colons* who favored a liberal policy towards the Moslems were also targeted for assassination. The OAS would be difficult to crack because the police and Gendarmerie in Algeria were largely sympathetic to the OAS and its aims. During the next year the OAS waged a violent terror campaign in France and Algeria that made the conflict, which seemed ready to end in 1960, front page news again. The OAS actions further deepened the divisions in the French military and society over the Algeria issue. Because so many Algerian police and Gendarmerie supported the OAS, De Gaulle's government had to create a special police unit of detectives from Metropolitan France to break the OAS. After months of hard work, De Gaulle's special police unit began to crack the OAS organization and to arrest its members and send others into hiding.[71]

De Gaulle faced the greatest crisis of his presidency on April 21, 1961, when two of his former commanders in Algeria, Generals Raoul Salan and Maurice Challe, seized power in Algiers and declared an open coup against the government. They hoped that they could reproduce the 1958 crisis that had brought De Gaulle to power, but in this case they wanted to force De Gaulle out of power. Supported by some units of the colonial army, notably the 1st Foreign Legion Parachute Regiment, the coup leaders quickly proclaimed a new military government to the acclaim of the *colon* population of Algiers. By the end of the first day part of the Oran garrison had joined the rebellion. But Challe and Salan had been much better at fighting wars than in planning coups. De Gaulle's appointed civil leaders refused to cooperate. The vast majority of the French troops in Algeria stood by and also refused orders from the coup leaders who had recently been their commanders.

The coup leaders and the *pied noir* "ultras" completely misjudged De Gaulle and public opinion in France. With the military in Metropolitan France on full alert in case the plotters attempted to spread the rebellion to the mainland, De Gaulle addressed the nation on television and radio on April 23. Many regard De Gaulle's speech that day as the best speech of his career. The president derided the rebellious generals and described the result of the rebellion: "the nation defied, our strength shaken, our international prestige debased, our position and our role in Africa compromised." Then De Gaulle issued a stern order, "I forbid every Frenchman, and above all any soldier, to execute any of their orders."[72] The speech broke the coup, as most army units in Algeria steadfastly refused to obey orders from rebellious officers. Two days later the coup collapsed as Challe surrendered and other senior officers who had supported it fled or went into hiding.

The attempted coup served to lower French morale. The army was torn about by the coup as an estimated fourteen thousand soldiers had been implicated in the rebellion. Five generals and two hundred other officers were arrested. The 1st Paratroop Regiment of the Foreign Legion was disbanded in disgrace. The attempted coup was the final straw for the French people, and for De Gaulle. One month after the coup De Gaulle opened formal negotiations with the FLN. The FLN, which had been in a terrible state a few months before, could now negotiate from a position of strength. The talks broke down quickly when the FLN took an uncompromising position on independence.

During 1961 the political atmosphere in France worsened. The failure of the coup enraged the OAS, who stepped up their terror campaign in Algeria and in France. In September 1961 a group affiliated with the OAS led by Lieutenant Colonel Jean Bastien-Thiry attempted to kill De Gaulle near Paris. The would-be assassins were foiled, and Bastien-Thiry was executed.[73] An exasperated De Gaulle now began to speak of "Algeria for the Algerians." Simply to free France of an impossible burden and to repair the fabric of the country and the armed forces, De Gaulle was determined to end the war. If the price to end the war were now full independence for Algeria, then De Gaulle and the majority of the French people were willing to pay that price. There were certainly personal factors that pushed De Gaulle to sacrifice the *pied noirs*. The *colon* community in Algeria had been staunchly pro-Vichy and anti-Free French during the fist half of World War II, and after the Allied landings in 1943 the *colons* had intrigued to keep De Gaulle out of power. Charles De Gaulle was not one to forget such actions, and at the end of war in Algeria refused to express any sympathy for the *colons* who had brought the disaster upon themselves. One might wonder how De Gaulle might have reacted if the *pied noirs* had supported him in 1942–1943. History turns on such personal issues, and one must not forget that the prejudices of leaders affect national strategy.

The negotiations with the FLN went on sporadically as the French tried to find some compromise to protect the *pied noirs* and their property. The French proposed a duel citizenship scheme for the *colons*, but the FLN rejected this offer as they stuck to the goal of nothing less than full independence. In March 1962 at Evian, France, the French government and the FLN reached an agreement to end the war and to grant Algeria full independence in July of that year.

The last months of French Algeria were as ugly as the direst predictions of the *colons*. Rather than live at the mercy of the FLN in a post-independent Algeria, the *colons* hastily abandoned their property and left for France. In the four months between the Evian Agreement and independence on July 3, almost the whole *pied noir* population of one million fled for France. By the end of June, only 40,000 French civilians remained in Algeria. The six years of war had cost the French military 17,456 enlisted men and 892 officers killed. Approximately 3,500 European civilians had been killed, that number including those killed by the OAS. In contrast, the Algerians paid a very high price in lives. The French military estimated that it had killed 140,000 Moslems during the course of the war. An estimated 66,000 Moslems had been killed by the FLN. Including those disappeared and killed in factional fighting, a round figure of 300,000 dead seems a fair estimate.[74]

The real killing only began after the end of the war and independence. While the *colons* found new homes in France, the *harkis* and Algerians who had served the French administration were left to their fate. Once the ALN forces training in Tunisia returned to their homeland and the surviving FLN guerrillas came out of hiding, they began a ruthless slaughter of the *harkis*, and often of their whole families. No figures were kept. Estimates of pro-French Algerians murdered by their countrymen in the weeks after independence run from 30,000 to 150,000 dead. Thousands more Algerians died in the post-independence disorder as local factions of the FLN fought each other for local power.[75] Ben Bella established his authority as the first president of Algeria, but he would be overthrown and imprisoned in 1965 by Colonel Boumédienne, the army commander. Although rich in oil, Algeria remained a poor and economically backward and unstable nation. In the 1990s a guerrilla war mounted by Moslem fundamentalists resulted in large-scale massacres and tens of thousands of civilians slaughtered. The FLN's idealistic dream of a free Algeria with basic rights for all citizens guaranteed is further away today than it was when proclaimed in 1954.

Conclusion

Algeria is a classic case of winning the battles and losing the war. The French armed forces performed admirably in the Algerian War. There is no doubt that the French armed forces defeated the FLN in the field. In many respects, especially in their civic action program and creation of Algerian home guards, the French military proved themselves adept at the basics of counterinsurgency. Unfortunately, from 1945 to 1958 the French government consistently failed to craft an adequate political solution to the Algerian crisis to go along with the effective military operations. Only with the advent of De Gaulle to power in 1958 did the French government produce a solid political/economic plan. It would have been the basis for cutting a deal with the Algerians for independence along with the protection of French property and rights. However, the intransigence of the *pied noirs* killed the deal and brought France into chaos—a good example of how a small minority can derail a strategy.

The end of the Algerian War was a boon for the French economy. Without the burden of the war, French economic growth accelerated and France and the economy boomed throughout the 1960s. France also learned some lessons in decolonization from Algeria. France began to prepare its other African colonies for independence on a schedule and in an orderly manner during the next four years. France established amicable relations with its former West African colonies, and French investments and interests were protected. While the economic costs were not too heavy and the military losses relatively low, the war left deep wounds in the French national psyche that are still not healed today. The trust between the professional army and the people was broken, and the war created deep divisions in French politics that still rankle—witness the popularity of the right-wing party of Jean-Marie Le Pen who served as a paratrooper in Algeria. For decades no one would refer to the "Algerian War" but rather to the "Algerian incident" or "troubles." The memory of widespread torture and abuse by the French military in Algeria is still a painful one for the French.

For the Algerians the consequences of the war, and especially of the peace, were disastrous. Even with huge oil reserves the Algerians never found a way to translate the oil revenue into jobs and prosperity for its people. Today Algeria remains a desperately poor land. The Algerian nation was born in factional warfare, and that tradition continues today, with a succession of authoritarian governments in power since 1962. In the 1990s Algeria was plagued by a terrorist campaign mounted by Islamic fundamentalists against their countrymen. Tens of thousands of Algerian civilians, mostly simple workers and peasants, were brutally massacred. While Algeria is relatively quiet today, terrorist incidents are still common as Algeria limps along as a crippled nation.

CHAPTER 2
British Strategy Against the Cyprus Insurgents, 1955–1959

■ ■ ■

> "One of the most baffling problems which I can
> ever remember."
> —British Prime Minister Harold Macmillan

> "Why do they hold Cyprus against us? It was nothing but a quarrel between the
> Greeks and Turks—and we settled it."
> —British Prime Minister Harold Macmillan[1]

Background to the Insurgency

THE COLONY OF CYPRUS PERFECTLY fits the description of one of those places that the British government acquired in "a fit of absentmindedness." The British first occupied the large island in the eastern Mediterranean in 1878, with the consent of the Ottoman Turks, during the Balkans crisis of 1878. Indeed, the British acknowledged formal Ottoman sovereignty until the 1920s and paid a yearly rent to the Ottoman government in Constantinople—a rent coming from the taxes paid by a resentful local population that was overwhelmingly Greek.

For seventy years Cyprus remained something of a colonial backwater. The British government did not consider Cyprus to be strategically important. The island was a relatively poor colony and possessed no major resources or industries. Although the British established naval and air bases on the island, the bases were small and played no major role in the two World Wars.

79

The island had about five hundred thousand residents in 1955, of whom 80 percent were ethnically Greek, 18 percent ethnically Turkish, and 2 percent other (mostly British and Armenian). Ever since the island had been acquired by Britain, the overwhelming majority of Cypriots had been absolutely clear about their political desires: they wanted "enosis," or union, with mainland Greece. Since no one in the British government or military saw Cyprus as strategically important territory during the first sixty-five years of Britain's colonial regime, the British government twice considered giving the island to Greece. During World War I, Cyprus was formally offered to Greece as one of several inducements to convince Greece to join the Allies. Again during World War II, the British government considered ceding the island to the Greek government in exile.

When the insurgency broke out in 1955, the relationship of the British and the Cypriots had been strained for a generation. Prior to 1931 the Cypriots had enjoyed limited self-government, with a constitution and an elected legislature. However, largely because the issue had been raised during World War I, the 1920s saw a dramatic increase in political agitation for enosis. Leaders of the Greek Orthodox Church on Cyprus, the most important institution for the Greek community, joined in the pressure for Britain to evacuate the island and cede it to Greece. In 1931 the enosis agitation, which had generated a series of protests and demonstrations, turned ugly when a demonstration turned into a full-fledged riot. The clash escalated, and a Greek mob burned down both the colonial government house and the barracks of the local army garrison. Reinforcements from the British army and Royal Navy were rushed in, the island was placed under emergency regulations, and the government proceeded to arrest the Greek Cypriot ringleaders. One of those arrested was the Bishop of Citium, a staunch advocate of enosis. He and several other clerics were forcibly exiled from the island. After the nationalist outburst was quelled, the British suspended the constitution and made Cyprus a direct rule colony. This meant that the full power of the government now resided with the governor general and that the Cypriot legislature was disbanded. After 1931 the only elected government for the Greek Cypriots were town and city councils, and these had very limited authority. The only popular representation to the government consisted of an appointed advisory council of prominent Greeks and Turks, who could merely advise the governor. As a rule the governor only appointed very compliant, pro-British Cypriots to the council.

With the world crises of the 1930s and the beginning of World War, the issue of Cypriot enosis—even of re-establishing a form of limited self-government—became a low priority issue with the British government. Through World War II and into the early 1950s, it was virtually a forgotten colony. Of the 38 colonies administered by the UK in 1947, Cyprus was rated as a class two colony for purposes of establishing pay and rank for colonial administrators. Cyprus was in the middle of the Colonial Office's pecking order, ranked behind the class one colonies such as Jamaica, Hong Kong, and the Gold Coast, but above the Leeward Islands.[2]

The Greek Cypriot goal of enosis remained constant from 1931 onwards. The Greek Cypriot before 1955 would have accepted from the British some form of a constitution and self-government if it had been offered, but only on the condition that it would lead to full independence and enosis. Although Greek Cypriots were driven by a simple nationalism, the Cypriot patriots were not infected by any hatred of the British, nor did they see the British as especially oppressive. Before the insurgency, when hard lines were drawn by both sides, there was plenty of room for reasonable discussion and compromise. As we shall see, the one vital strategic issue for the British—maintaining large military bases on Cyprus—was never a problem for either the Greek government or the Greek Cypriots. When the time for negotiations came, the matter of guaranteeing sovereign base areas was quickly settled.

Indeed, the lack of personal rancor on the part of the Greek Cypriots towards British rule before the insurgency explains why the British government did not take the Greek community's repeated demands for self-government and enosis seriously. Even after the Greek Cypriots had begun a terrorist and guerrilla campaign, it was difficult for the British to accept the idea that the majority of Cypriots opposed any continuance of British rule. Before the insurgency—one could say even today—the Greek Cypriots liked the British. However, the Greek Cypriots simply did not want British domination—a fact that successive British governments found exceptionally difficult to grasp.

Before 1947 Cyprus would have been high on any list of colonies to be granted independence—if decolonization had been part of the British strategy.

Cyprus had no major resources, did not generate any significant revenue to the Empire, and was not considered strategically important. This would change dramatically with the major realignment in British strategy after World War II, and the changes in British postwar military strategy would form the basis for the conflict over Cyprus.

Strategic Realities Versus Imperial Sentiments in Postwar Britain

With the end of World War II, a major realignment of the British Empire became necessary. At this point the British government's assessment of Cyprus' strategic value changed dramatically. Ironically, just as Britain was forced to grant independence to its most important colonies and speed up the independence timetable of others, the British came to the conclusion that this one colony that had seemed very dispensable a few years earlier had now become strategically indispensable.

In terms of strategic position, Britain after World War II could no longer maintain its status as a major world power. For one thing, Britain was bankrupt, deeply in debt and reliant on American financial aid. Britain managed to muddle through only with an American loan of $4.34 billion in 1945, an enormous sum for the era.[3] Clement Attlee, the Labour Party prime minister who replaced Winston Churchill in the 1945 elections, faced a Britain in crisis. Britons had struggled under strict rationing of coal, food, and clothing since 1939. Taxes were high and Britain's massive debt and foreign exchange balance required strict controls of imports and exports. Simple things that prewar Britons had taken for granted, such as oranges, bananas, and chocolate, were unobtainable luxuries for the average person. And conditions would not get better for a long time, as the UK would maintain the strict rationing and controls regime until the early 1950s. Older Britons still recall the hardship of the winter of 1946–1947, which featured exceptionally cold temperatures at a time that the coal shortage was acute. On top of all these crises, more than 2.4 million British workers were unemployed in 1947.

To compound the economic crisis at home was the cost of maintaining huge military garrisons for the empire. The military cost of British home defense and imperial commitments in this postwar world were enormous. In 1946–1947 the British armed forces budget was £1.091 billion and took up 15 percent of Britain's gross national product (GNP). At this level of spending, there was no hope to improve the condition of the average Briton. In short, cutting the military budget was essential to maintaining the health of the British economy. In 1946 the chancellor called for drastic cuts in military spending with a goal of spending no more than £750 million in 1947–1948.[4]

Postwar Britain also faced additional new defense obligations and priorities. The first priority was defending Britain and Europe from the Soviet Union. This would require large forces to occupy Germany while maintaining a reserve force in the UK for the defense of Western Europe. Britain had other immediate priorities. Britain had to bring order to colonies, such as Malaya, that had been occupied by enemy forces during the war. Further imperial emergencies arose. In 1945–1946 Britain had to commit thousands of troops to reoccupy the Dutch East Indies, then in a state of civil war, until the Netherlands government could raise and send troops to control their colony. Britain also had a large force supporting the Greek government, which was engaged in a desperate civil war with Soviet-backed insurgents. The old colonial system was under enormous stress as violent nationalist movements swept through Asia, the Middle East, and the Mediterranean. Within a few years, nationalist and anti-colonialist sentiments would rise up in Africa with a vehemence that astonished the British colonists and government.

The cost of maintaining large imperial garrisons was well beyond Britain's means. Therefore, in early 1946 the government made the painful but necessary decision to grant independence to India, Ceylon, and Burma no later than 1948. Other commitments were reduced or eliminated altogether. In early 1947, citing a lack of resources, the British government asked the Americans to take over the mission of supporting the Greek government in its war against Soviet-backed guerrillas. The American government responded with the Truman doctrine, a policy to provide aid, assistance, and training to any nation directly threatened by the Soviet Union, or threatened by insurgencies fomented and supported by the Soviets. Greece was the first major test of the Truman Doctrine as American aid and advisors helped the Greek government defeat the communists by the end of 1949.

Britain's postwar plight required a thorough review of British strategic and imperial interests, as the imperial military infrastructure was considerably more than the nation could afford. In 1946 Prime Minister Attlee initiated a discussion concerning Britain's strategic realities. In a memo to the cabinet and military chiefs, he questioned whether Britain needed to commit large resources to defending the Middle East in light of new postwar realities. Britain had traditionally maintained a strong military presence in the Middle East and Mediterranean in order to safeguard communications with Britain's Asian empire. But with India, Ceylon, and Burma slated for independence in the immediate future, and the subject of future independence of Malaya already broached, the traditional grounds for maintaining strong garrisons in the Middle East were gone. Concerned with the urgent need to cut defense spending and reorder the British defense system, Attlee argued that the threat posed by the Soviet Union was Britain's primary strategic consideration. Attlee insisted that developing the defensive and offensive capabilities of the Royal Air Force (RAF), as well as developing a British nuclear deterrent, should be Britain's top priorities and that imperial commitments ought to take a much lower priority.[5]

Attlee's sensible and realistic attempt to prod the political and military leadership into taking a fresh look at imperial commitments met with strong resistance from the military chiefs. While phrases such as "maintaining imperial influence" were abstract concepts for the average Briton, they were very real things to the senior military leaders, who had all served in the colonies when Britain was still a leading world power. Unfortunately, though confronted with the urgent necessity of realigning British strategy to meet its postwar economic and political limitations, the men at the top of the British military failed to act like the hard-headed strategists they had been during the World War. At this juncture, Britain's senior military leaders were driven more by emotion and sentiment than by logic. All of Britain's service chiefs had a deep personal link to the Empire. Field Marshal Bernard Montgomery, chief of the imperial general staff from 1946 to 1948, had served in India and Palestine. The chief of the postwar Royal Air Force, Air Chief Marshal Arthur Tedder, had been a squadron commander in the Middle East in the 1920s and Air Officer Commanding Far East from 1936 to 1938. His successor,

Air Chief Marshal John Slessor, chief of the air staff from 1950 to 1953, had been a unit commander in India in 1921–1923 and had served on India's North West Frontier in 1936–1937. Montgomery, Tedder, and Slessor were all proven military leaders and strategists, and they understood the need to craft a strategy to contain the Soviet Union and to deter Soviet aggression. However, they were also products of the Empire who had spent much of their careers defending imperial possessions. Furthermore, the British Empire that these men had served had been a true world power until then. Adapting to Britain's new role as a second rank power and junior partner to the Americans—all while dissolving the imperial institutions that they had fought for—was apparently "an adjustment too far" for the senior military men.[6]

The senior military men came close to what can only be described as mutiny as they resisted defense reductions. Field Marshal Montgomery was the most intransigent in opposing any realignment of Britain's imperial commitments and treated the Labour government with thinly veiled contempt, describing the reduction of British forces in the empire as "defeatist." Nigel Hamilton, Montgomery's biographer and an admirer of Montgomery's wartime leadership, describes Montgomery's tenure as army chief of staff as the low point in an otherwise impressive career.[7] Attlee failed to get his own cabinet to support his call for a new strategy. Indeed, his own foreign minister, Ernest Bevin, also took up the call of the military chiefs to retain the empire. The military chiefs advised Attlee that the Middle East was "the hub of defence planning and one of the three pillars in the British defence system—the others being the defence of the UK itself and maintaining sea lines of communication. If any of these pillars failed, the whole British defence system would likely fail."[8] Much of this was strategic and military nonsense. Given the enormous size of the U.S. Navy and the minimal threat posed by the Soviet Navy at the time, any reasonable observer could see that maintaining Britain's sea lines of communication would not be a major concern in the near future. One could also have questioned the degree of threat the Soviet Union posed to the Middle East, versus the much closer and more urgent threat to Western Europe. Strategy is largely about setting priorities, and in the postwar British defense staff priorities were skewed by old imperial sentiments and an inability to adjust to new conditions.

The hold of empire was almost as strong among the British politicians as it was among career soldiers, and a sense of unreality pervades the British strategic documents of the era. In 1946 a cabinet committee on manpower described the huge burden of large military forces on the UK economy, but the committee still gave priority to "the maintenance of British prestige abroad" and to living up to "our responsibilities as one of the three leading powers in the world."[9] There were other pressures that should have pushed a realignment of defense spending and basing requirements. In early 1946 the Attlee government committed itself to the development and production of nuclear weapons. Given the nature of the growing Soviet threat, it was a sensible move. Developing a nuclear capability would be an expensive proposition, however, as would developing new, long-range jet bombers to carry the nuclear weapons. On top of those projected expenses was the cost of constructing a large and sophisticated basing and support infrastructure for the air force. By opting for a nuclear strategy, Britain would inevitably have to reduce its imperial military commitments.[10] Finally, Britain was no longer in a position to make independent strategic policy. Responding militarily to any crisis required significant American aid, which, in 1952–1953 amounted to 244 million pounds (at $2.80 to the pound) to the UK—an enormous sum for the era.[11]

The Middle Eastern Obsession

The importance of Cyprus in the minds of the British military and civilian leadership can only be understood in the context of the perceived British role as the great power in the Middle East. From the mid-nineteenth century through World War I, Britain had dominated the Middle East, holding nominally-independent Egypt as a protectorate, controlling Iran's oil industry, and holding Aden on the Arabian Peninsula as a naval base. In the aftermath of World War I, Britain enhanced its position as the dominant Middle Eastern power by acquiring Palestine and Jordan as colonies and taking over Iraq as a protectorate until granting independence in 1932. However, Britain still held military bases in Iraq after its independence. After World War II, even as the British withdrew from Asia and America took over as the dominant power in Western Europe, the Middle East remained the last major region of the world under Britain's imperial domination. Despite the economic crisis of postwar

Britain, British leaders were reluctant to relinquish their last great imperial mandate. The imperial presence in the Middle East was now justified in terms of containing the Soviet Union. With strategic airpower now viewed as the primary means of military deterrence, British defense chiefs argued that the Middle East was a prime location for RAF bomber bases, where a new strategic bomber force, soon to be armed with nuclear weapons, could be staged to strike the Soviet Union. Moreover, a network of British air and naval bases served as a visible sign of Britain's military power in the region.[12]

Maintaining bases in the Middle East and Mediterranean made considerable strategic sense. It was also a strategy calculated to win over American support for a British imperial policy, since large RAF bases could also be used by the U.S. Air Force for strikes against the Soviet Union. Chief of the imperial general staff, Field-Marshal Lord Alanbrooke, first made this argument to the defense committee in April 1946, and the Royal Air Force seconded this strategy.[13]

Considerably overestimating the Soviet Union's ability to project its power and influence far from its southern borders, British military leaders argued passionately that any reduction in British influence in the Middle East would inevitably lead to the fall of the region to communism. In a 1949 assessment, RAF chief of staff Sir Arthur Tedder described the importance of the British role in the Middle East: "The UK armed forces were the only stabilizing influence in areas of immense economic consequence to the Western World." Tedder also predicted that British withdrawal from the region "could hardly fail to lead to the disintegration of the Commonwealth and the eventual fall of Africa to communism."[14]

Britain's ambitious designs for maintaining its imperial role ran counter to the wave of nationalism that spread through Asia, the Middle East and North Africa in the aftermath of World War II. British strategic planning had long seen Egypt as the strategic hub of its Middle Eastern empire and the ideal location for major British bases. However, the British grossly underestimated the depth of anti-British feeling in Egypt and the Middle East at the end of World War II. To the consternation of Britain's military leaders, the Egyptians made it clear that they would not extend the agreement that allowed British bases on their territory. With the imminent loss of Britain's primary bases in the Middle East, the service chiefs considered developing Palestine as Britain's major new base in the region.[15] But this plan collapsed when Palestine blew up into full revolt, and the British government was forced to accept an end to its mandate in 1948. In the meantime the Suez Canal Zone became the primary British base in the Middle East, but the constant friction with the Egyptians—which included strikes by Egyptian workers and terrorist attacks on British forces—made the Canal Zone an increasingly untenable location for British bases.[16] With virtually all other options gone, the British service chiefs finally decided that Cyprus was the best location for the bases that would maintain Britain's military and political influence in the Middle East.

A New Government Reevaluates Strategy

In 1951 the Conservative Party led by Winston Churchill came to power. A Conservative government was even less inclined than a Labour government to question Britain's imperial assumptions. Indeed, the Conservatives perceived the Empire as having significant economic and strategic value. *The Chiefs of Staff Global Strategy Paper* of October 1952 argued for the benefits of empire: "Our standard of living stems in large measure from our status as a great power, and this depends to no small extent on the visible indication of our greatness which our forces, particularly overseas, provide."[17] This was political and economic nonsense of the first order, but it demonstrates the extent of emotional appeal the Empire held for government and military leaders in the early 1950s. At the same moment, Britain faced a series of new defense burdens: the Korean War, the buildup of NATO, and the development of a new force of long-range jet bombers. These forced an increase in defense spending from 8 percent of the GNP in 1950, to 14 percent in 1952.[18] Defense spending placed a huge strain on the economy as inflation rose and economic growth slowed. In addition, Britain was still deeply in debt and still relied upon American loans for economic survival. As for the military leaders' argument that the Empire enhanced the UK standard of living, one could note that Germany, which had been a vast ruin in 1945, would surpass the UK living standards by the end of the decade. However, the emotional attachment to empire still precluded the government from reassessing the value of the Middle East in British military strategy.

Winston Churchill had a passionate and sentimental attachment to the Empire, and was not inclined to favor independence for any of Britain's colonies as long as he was in office. However, he would not be the man to determine Cyprus' ultimate fate. When Churchill again became prime minister in 1951 he was seventy-six years of age, and he was not expected to serve a full five-year term as head of government. The Conservative Party leadership already had identified Churchill's successor. Anthony Eden, the dynamic and well-regarded foreign secretary, was the logical choice for prime minister whenever Churchill decided to retire. Under Churchill's tenure, Eden, as the strongest man in the cabinet, was granted considerable leeway to steer government policy in departments other than his own.

It was a principle of British imperial policy not to allow foreign governments a say in the internal governance of any colony. Earlier governments would not have acknowledged, much less encouraged, any foreign government to become involved in such matters as drafting a constitution for a colony. That was the Colonial Office's view of any Greek or Turkish attempt to become involved in Cyprus policy. On the other hand, Eden believed that Cyprus was an exception to the rule. As agitation over the island's status increased, Eden took over the role of setting policy for Cyprus.

Eden, born 1897, came into office with an impressive resume. He had served as an officer in World War I, and then studied Oriental languages (Arabic and Persian) at Oxford in preparation for a career in Britain's Foreign Service. However, as a student he became involved in Tory politics, and he shelved his idea of joining the diplomatic corps for a chance to stand for Parliament. He was elected as a Conservative member of parliament in 1923. From the start of his political career he was seen as one of the Conservative Party's strongest experts on foreign affairs. He became foreign minister in 1935. In 1938 he won considerable fame for resigning from the cabinet in protest over Chamberlain's policy of appeasement towards Hitler and Mussolini. Brought back as foreign minister during World War II, he became one of Churchill's closest confidants.[19]

Serving again as foreign secretary, with the experience of wartime strategy-making at the top level, Eden was confident in his mastery of foreign affairs. Because of his extensive travels, broad experience, and mastery of Middle

Eastern languages, Eden also took pride in his understanding of the Middle East. As one would expect of a political leader with such a resume, Eden approached the Cyprus question with a set of strong prejudices. Because of his perceived expertise, he was loath to accept any advice on the matter from anyone else, and certainly not from the Colonial Office.

Eden shared the military chiefs' view that the Middle East was of central importance to British strategy. As Churchill's foreign secretary, Eden summarized Britain's strategic priorities. First came the defense of Western Europe and support of NATO. Second came the responsibilities arising from Britain's imperial role, including the need to defend Middle Eastern interests. Last came commitments necessary to great power status, including a major contribution to the Cold War effort and effective membership in the United Nations.[20] Eden resisted the idea of abandoning any of Britain's major commitments, strongly endorsing the position that Britain had to maintain a powerful military presence in the Middle East. However, Britain had retreated from Palestine, and in 1954 the British concluded an agreement with Egypt to evacuate British forces from the Suez Canal Zone. Cyprus was now seen as an indispensable base from which Britain could maintain its military position in the Middle East. Yet Eden's understanding of Middle Eastern politics went beyond the military chiefs' views of the region as a base of operations against the Soviet Union. Eden was also obsessed with Abdul Nasser, a former army colonel who had seized power and become Egypt's president in 1952. Nasser was a dynamic figure who preached a new ideology of Arab nationalism and unity combined with anticolonialism and socialism. He was soon acknowledged as the leading political figure in the Middle East. His ideology of socialism and anticolonialism, as well as his willingness to accept aid from the Soviet Union, was seen as a direct threat to British and Western interests in the Middle East.

Eden, and members of the cabinet that included Harold Macmillan, saw Nasser as another Hitler—a ruthless dictator to be opposed and defeated, rather than a leader one could negotiate with. From Eden's diaries and papers it often seems that he was striving to relive the most dramatic and defining moment of his career—when he resigned from the cabinet in 1938 and led a group of idealistic Tories, including Harold Macmillan, to repudiate Chamberlain's weak policies towards Hitler.[21] As a real threat, Nasser was certainly overblown.

Egypt was certainly no Nazi Germany, and certainly no serious military threat to Western interests. There was also considerable difference between Hitler's demands for the Sudetenland, Poland, and Czechoslovakia and Nasser's demand for control of the Suez Canal. The Canal's occupation by British troops was rightly seen by the Egyptians as an affront to their national sovereignty. Eden believed that Britain had to be ready to conduct military operations against Nasser, and Cyprus was certainly the best base of operations for that mission. Thus, with the threat of Nasser looming, there could be no discussion of Cyprus independence or enosis. In fact, Cyprus would be Britain's main base for the strike against Nasser and invasion of the Suez Canal Zone in 1956.

Eden's policies and actions on the Cyprus issue were also affected by an obvious bias in favor of Turkey, coupled with a strong prejudice against the Greeks. This attitude, which was shared by Eden's successor as prime minister Harold Macmillan, ensured that Turkey's considerations and interests in Cyprus, though considerably less than Greece's, would nonetheless be central to any negotiated solution for the island. Eden was convinced that the Middle East was a top priority for British strategy, and he believed that Turkey held the key to the Middle East. Any policy that offended Turkey or interfered with British/Turkish relations was off the table. While admiring the Turks, Eden felt that General Alexander Papagos, the prime minister of Greece, was untrustworthy. In a Foreign Office memorandum on Cyprus in February 1955, Eden noted that Greece was "an unstable country," and that its support for Cypriot enosis "was doing no good internationally: pressure (on Greece) must be maintained to make life as uncomfortable as possible."[22]

Eden's disdain for the Greeks and their position on Cyprus did much to drive the British policies that led to the insurgency. Greek Prime Minister Papagos discussed the Cyprus issue with Eden in September 1953, assuring him that if the British allowed the island's union with Greece, UK military bases on the island would be guaranteed by the Greeks. Eden replied that New York had a large Greek population, so why didn't Papagos claim New York as Greek territory?[23] Eden's undiplomatic rebuff of the Greeks probably had a lot to do with the Greek government's attitude towards the Cypriot (EOKA) insurgency. Although the Greek government wanted to maintain good relations with Britain, Papagos and members of his cabinet refrained

91

from shutting down EOKA's fundraising and clandestine training operations in Greece, although they were well aware of these operations.

Conflict Within the British Government

One of the greatest handicaps the British faced in crafting a policy for Cyprus, both before and during the insurgency, was the rivalry between the Colonial Office and the Foreign Office. One of the principles of British colonial rule was that issues affecting the governance of a colony were an internal matter of the British government, not open to negotiation with outside states. This sound rule was often used to deflect international criticism of Britain's imperial policies. In practice it also meant that the foreign ministry would not have purview over established colonies. However, as a dynamic foreign minister and presumptive next head of the government, Eden was convinced that he was the right man to deal with the Cyprus issue. From 1951 on, therefore, Eden and his ministry took the lead in all Cyprus matters, and the Colonial Office was simply brushed aside.

In a memo in early 1955, Anthony Nutting, parliamentary secretary for the Foreign Office, expressed his department's viewpoint that the Colonial Office was too conciliatory in dealing with Cypriot dissent. Nutting noted that "the colonial office seem reluctant to take stern enough measures to maintain law and order if things get really tough." The Foreign Office recommended harsh measures to suppress the pro-enosis views of the Greek Cypriots, while offering the promise of self-government at a later date.[24] Another February 8, 1955, Foreign Office memo on Cyprus policy followed Eden's pro-Turkish and anti-Greek inclinations. It asserted that the British objectives in Cyprus were: "To keep effective control in Cyprus, to expose the hollowness of the Greek government's pretence to support the principle of self-determination for Cyprus," and "to keep the support and cooperation of Turkey."[25] The Foreign Office also spoke of strengthening the police and persuading moderate Greek Cypriots to support the UK policy of continued colonial rule with limited self-government.[26]

Macmillan, who became foreign minister when Eden became prime minister in early 1955, maintained the policy of handling the Cyprus issue through the Foreign Office while sidelining the Colonial Office. When the insurgency broke out in April, Macmillan expressed his irritation with the other ministry, referring to the "almost Byzantine incompetence of the Colonial Office . . . the Governor (Armitage) . . . seems ineffective . . . and without any faith in the sacredness of his mission."[27] Macmillan believed that a simple solution could be found for Cyprus, and he adopted the common British opinion that a loyal Greek Cypriot party would emerge to support continued British rule over the island. "It should be possible to organize a pro-British party among the Greeks. After all, Xerxes had no difficulty."[28] Yet the classically educated Eden and Macmillan were soon to find out that Greek political consciousness had changed a bit since the fourth century BC.

Cypriots Prepare an Insurgency

The British in Cyprus had the bad luck to face two exceptionally competent insurgent leaders: Archbishop Makarios III, head of the Cypriot Orthodox Church, and Colonel George Grivas, a retired colonel of the Greek army. Makarios, born Michael Mouskos and taking the name of Makarios III upon his election as Archbishop, was a brilliant young cleric who had been marked by the Cypriot Church leaders for rapid advancement. He studied theology in Greece and was ordained shortly before World War II. Stranded in Athens at the outbreak of the war, he lived in Greece under the German occupation. As an up-and-coming young churchman, he had a quick entrée into Greek society. Thus, while in exile from his homeland, he made numerous contacts with prominent Greeks who would later hold top positions in the postwar Greek government. He also came to know some Cypriots such as Colonel George Grivas, who led a resistance group in Athens from 1941 to 1944. After the war Makarios was sent to America for advanced theological study at Boston University. In 1948, while at Boston University, he was elected by the clergy to be Bishop of Citium—an impressive accomplishment for a thirty-five-year-old priest. Having a reputation for learning, a dynamic manner, and many influential Greek political contacts, he was recognized as a leading member of the church hierarchy. He was known for his powerful sermons, his staunch support for enosis, and his concern with the religious formation and education of Greek Cypriot youth. In October 1950, upon the death of Archbishop Leontios, who had been a rallying point for Greek nationalism,

Makarios was elected the Archbishop and head of the Orthodox Church in Cyprus at age thirty-eight. Makarios was an ideal political leader for the Greek Cypriots. He was a firm nationalist, committed to enosis, but no fanatic. His life in Greece and America had given him a degree of political sophistication not found in a typical monk, and he had a coolly self-controlled manner.

As Archbishop, Makarios became the de facto political leader of the Greek Cypriots. This was a direct result of the British decision to abolish Cypriot self-government in 1931. For decades Cypriots had been denied participation in the normal political process, or even the right to elect representatives. So the evolution of Cypriot political organization and development was stymied. The lack of a political process was especially hard on the Cypriots, as this was a well-educated population by colonial standards with virtually 100 percent of the Greek Cypriots literate. Under the government the British established in Cyprus, the Greek Cypriots were not allowed to develop a cadre of civilian political leaders. By default, the job of representing the Greek Cypriots fell to the Orthodox Church—the one institution that could fairly claim to represent the whole Greek community. It might have been difficult for the British Colonial Office to deal with elected Cypriot politicians, but it also would have been easier to operate a political strategy that exploited the natural divisions between groups and parties that would have emerged in a normal political process. If politicians crossed the line and advocated violence, it would have been relatively easy to detain them or ban their party. By pushing normal political activity and aspirations to the religious sphere, however, it became impossible for the British to maintain any control over the political process. In terms of world and local opinion, it is a much harder task to arrest a bishop than a politician. It is also much easier to ban a political rally than to forbid an ostensibly religious meeting.

George Grivas, born in 1898 to a prosperous and very pro-British grain merchant in the district of Famagusta, left Cyprus at age eighteen after attending the colony's top high school in Nicosia and went to study at the Greek military academy. This was not unusual for the time. As Cyprus had no university, Greek Cypriots desiring advanced education commonly went to Greece. Like Grivas, other Cypriots opted to emigrate and serve in the Greek army, where they were accepted as fellow Greeks. Grivas was commissioned a lieutenant in 1919 and first served in combat in the war against Turkey, in which he was wounded and decorated. In the 1920s his military career prospered, and he was selected to attend the French staff college. At the outbreak of war with Italy he was a colonel on the staff in Athens. After the Germans invaded and occupied Greece in 1941 he went underground. In Athens he formed a decidedly right-wing resistance movement named *Khi* and prepared his group to fight the much larger communist resistance movement when the Germans were driven out.

Grivas had the sharp mind of a properly trained staff officer. His military career had developed his talents as a tactician, planner, and organizer. Living as an underground leader from 1941 to 1944 was the best possible training to fight a guerrilla war against the British. For three years Grivas managed to evade the Gestapo and Greek collaborators while he organized, armed, and trained guerrilla forces, even developing an underground propaganda and intelligence system. When the Greek civil war broke out in 1944, he fought alongside the British as they drove the communists out of Athens and set up a provisional Greek government. Retired after the civil war, Grivas turned his energies to his lifelong ambition of uniting Cyprus with Greece. He began quietly organizing other like-minded Cypriots to prepare for a guerrilla war against Britain if the British government refused Cypriot demands. Unfortunately for the British, Grivas had the ideal background and training to make him one of the most formidable nationalist opponents they would have to face during the long retreat from empire.[29]

After World War II the Cypriot agitation for enosis heated up. The Cypriot Church sent a delegation headed by Archbishop Leontios to Britain in 1947 in the hope that the Labour Party government would grant them a hearing. They were dismissed out of hand. However, the next year the British offered a constitution to the Cypriots that would have allowed for a mostly elected assembly. While the Greeks would have been allowed to have a majority in the assembly (lower house), all bills dealing with external affairs and minority rights, including Turkish issues and the constitution, would require the governor's approval to become law. The executive council provided by the constitution sabotaged any genuinely democratic rule by ensuring that the Turkish representatives and the governor's appointees would outnumber the elected Greek representatives. After denying the Cypriots self-government for seventeen years, the British government expected the Cypriots would accept these proposals. However, in a move that would not have surprised anyone who knew the Cypriots, the Greek majority overwhelmingly rejected the British scheme, which would have ended any chance for enosis or independence. In any case, the veto powers reserved to the governor essentially nullified the majority voice on issues that mattered.[30] As far as the British were concerned, Cyprus would remain British; period.

Makarios was a staunch Greek nationalist, but also a Christian churchman who hoped to achieve the goal of enosis by political means rather than by violence. Upon assuming the Ethnarchy of the Cypriot Church in 1950, he encouraged political agitation geared to embarrass Britain and convince the British government of the islanders' determination to end colonial status. One of Makarios' first acts as archbishop was to create Pancyprian National Organization of Youth (PEON). PEON would be led by hand-picked Greek teachers and would play a central role in organizing political protests. PEON served as an effective means of propagandizing and mobilizing young Cypriots against the British. The British soon banned PEON, but the group went underground. PEON functioned throughout the insurgency in support of EOKA's insurgent fighters by carrying messages, collecting intelligence, and organizing protests.

When quiet diplomacy with Britain failed to resolve the issue of Cyprus' status, the Greek government took up the Cypriot call for enosis and brought the issue to the United Nations. The British government's response was a policy statement before Parliament by Harry Hopkinson, minister at the Colonial Office, on July 28, 1954, that declared that "no change in sovereignty was contemplated."[31] The British declaration clearly meant that while other colonies would be considered for independence and self-determination, no change in the status quo would be allowed for Cyprus. Now that the British government ruled out any chance for change by peaceful means, Makarios and the Greek Cypriots moved ahead with plans to force a change in British policy through violence. Through 1954 and early 1955, Makarios organized a series of mass protests and marches to demonstrate Cypriot will to end British domination, while a small group of Greek Cypriots stepped up preparations for armed resistance. Although Makarios and the Cypriots had hoped for a peaceful means to achieve their goals, they also understood that violent action might also be necessary to induce the British to leave. In 1952 Makarios had authorized his old acquaintance, Colonel Grivas, to organize an underground military resistance movement to be ready to fight the British if necessary. The Greek Cypriot military force was named *Ethniki Organosis Kyprion Agoniston*, "National Organization of Cypriot Fighters" (EOKA). The group initially operated from Greece, where it raised money, developed its organization, and put its recruits through a course in guerrilla warfare that included the use of weapons, small unit tactics, and the use of bombs and booby traps. From Greece, EOKA smuggled weapons, explosives, and trained fighters into Cyprus. Although the Greek government was allied to Britain through NATO and hoped for a peaceful solution for Cyprus, it also tacitly allowed EOKA to operate from Greek soil as long as it remained discreet. Although members of the Greek cabinet knew of Grivas and EOKA, they refrained from arresting its members or shutting down its clandestine training.

In 1952 Grivas traveled to Cyprus under his own name and spent four months recruiting leaders for EOKA while conferring with Makarios and Greek Cypriot leaders. Grivas also carried out a thorough military reconnaissance of the island to determine how he would organize and deploy bands in the countryside to target British installations and infrastructure. He built the foundation for what would be a small, but very capable, guerrilla organization. PEON, the Greek youth organization, acted as a supporting group and served to recruit guerrilla fighters from Cyprus' most idealistic youth. Grivas also developed a cadre of secret EOKA supporters among the ranks of the police, civil servants, and employees of the British military. When the insurgency came, his underground supporters would smuggle weapons and explosives into Cyprus and provided a steady stream of intelligence on British plans and operations. Through his network of agents working for the British military, Grivas was able to smuggle bombs into British bases, and on several occasions blew up aircraft and vital military infrastructure.

From the start, the Cypriots were well organized and prepared for an insurgency. The Orthodox Church enjoined its priests to oppose Britain and urge enosis (union with Greece) from the pulpits. Not only did Markarios and the church justify violent rebellion against British rule, they were willing to decree excommunication for Greek Cypriots who supported the British. The small band of trained rebels who led a terrorist campaign against British rule could rely on overwhelming support from the population as well as the complete support of the Church—including hiding of arms in Orthodox monasteries.

Two years before the insurgency began Grivas wrote a strategic plan to push the British out. His "General Plan for Insurrectionary Action" was a well-thought-out plan to conduct a prolonged guerilla war against the British government and military forces on Cyprus. With a small force of 250 guerillas, organized into small teams spread throughout the island, Grivas did not expect to win a military victory against British power. Grivas noted that "it should not be supposed that by these means we should expect to impose a total defeat on the British forces in Cyprus. Our purpose is to win a moral victory through a process of attrition, by harassing, confusing and finally exasperating the enemy forces."[32] His military campaign consisted of a program of terrorism and small attacks meant to damage and harass the British and to win the attention of the international media. "Activity will be aimed at causing so much confusion and damage in the ranks of the British forces as to make it manifest abroad that they are no longer in complete control of the situation." Constant small attacks, coupled with large scale passive resistance by the population, were aimed to pressure Britain to accept international mediation based on the principle that the Cypriots would be allowed to freely choose their fate. "The British must be continuously harried until they are obligated by international diplomacy exercised through the United Nations to examine the Cyprus problem and settle it in accordance with the desires of the Cypriot people and the whole Greek nation."[33]

During his clandestine trip to Cyprus, Colonel Grivas quietly sought out sympathizers among the Greek Cypriot policemen. With morale and conditions in the police force low, and desire for enosis high among the Greek population, Grivas had no trouble recruiting selected policemen who could provide the insurgents with detailed intelligence. From 1954 to 1958, as many as twenty members of the Cyprus Police worked as active agents for the insurgents. During some of the large British sweep operations, some police officers actually hid wanted EOKA terrorists, on the sound assumption that the last place the British would search would be the home of a police officer.[34]

EOKA took advantage of British complacency. Grivas and his lieutenants were discreet while smuggling weapons to Cyprus and setting up guerrilla cells in late 1954 and early 1955. Still, there were enough indicators of impending trouble to put any reasonably competent colonial government and police force on high alert. EOKA successfully got two boatloads of weapons and explosives to Cyprus in late 1954, but in January 1955 a boat full of weapons was stopped off the Cyprus coast by a Royal Navy patrol. Aside from a brief tightening of local security, the colonial government largely ignored the obvious signs of insurrection.

A Host of Wrong Assumptions— The British View of the Cypriots

Long after the insurgency had started, conservative members of Parliament and top officials in the government and military persisted in the belief that the trouble in Cyprus was fomented by a small group of Greek nationalist extremists and troublemakers. If this radical group could be neutralized—arrested and deported or, if necessary, killed—then it was assumed that Cypriots would see the reasonableness of good British colonial government and accept a proposed scheme for limited self-determination. The British might concede some elections and a small degree of home rule, but no independence and certainly no enosis. Dick Brooman-White, a conservative member of Parliament, told one of his colleagues in October 1954 that "it seems inconceivable that the Cypriots should become vicious like the Egyptians."[35] The fact that the Greek Cypriots were a literate European people, not especially prone to crime or violence, and that many had loyally served in the British forces during the World War was enough to convince British officials to ignore the many signals that an insurgency was imminent. In this attitude British military and political elites were prisoners of their traditional understanding of colonial peoples.

Although Britain faced several major colonial insurgencies between 1945 and 1955, these conflicts were against "native peoples." From the British viewpoint one could understand that Chinese peasants living in the Malayan jungles might be enticed by communists to rebel, or that tribal Africans in Kenya might be whipped into violence by the weird Mau Mau cult. But Greek

Cypriots were Christians, anticommunist, and most spoke fluent English. As Brooman-White noted, for the average Briton, including those who had some acquaintance of the island, it was inconceivable that the average Cypriot would oppose British policy with violence. If violence did occur, it was bound to come from some small extremist group and certainly not supported by the majority of the islanders.

Part of the problem lay in the fact that the island had quieted down in 1931 after the deportation of several orthodox clerics and a bishop. With trouble brewing in Cyprus again in 1950, the first instinct of the British regime was to again clamp down hard on Cypriot dissent—no matter that the dissent was expressed in a peaceful manner. In January 1950 the Greek Orthodox Church sponsored a plebiscite on enosis in which virtually the whole Greek community voted. The result: 95 percent of the Greeks expressed open support for enosis. The response by the island's governor, Sir Andrew White, was a request to the Colonial Office for special emergency powers to stamp out the enosis movement. The requested powers included the authority to shut down the press, broad powers to prosecute sedition, and the authority to deport troublemakers. As a colonial official on Cyprus twenty years before, he had authored similar emergency regulations to suppress the 1931 disorders.[36] But Sir Andrew's heavy-handed approach had barely been acceptable in an earlier age, an age that celebrated empire and where there was no United Nations to provide a forum for nationalist and anticolonial views. After 1945 such an approach to maintaining colonial order was clearly excessive, and many Colonial Office officials were sensitive to the new wave of nationalism that was sweeping the postwar world. Sir Andrew's request for repressive measures was not only rejected, but London officials sharply challenged the governor's understanding of the situation.[37]

In a memo J. S. Bennett, an official in the Colonial Office's Mediterranean Department, questioned Sir Andrew's argument that the Cypriots' enosis demands were the product of a "few irresponsible men." Bennett did not think it was possible "to embark on a policy of repression in Cyprus in the hope that no one will notice." Such a policy had not worked in Palestine or Egypt or other places where Britain's colonial rule had been challenged. Bennett went on to comment, "It is, of course, conceivable that Cyprus is the exception that proves the rule, but it seems more probable that Cyprus has lagged behind . . . . It is too small either to rebel effectively or to become a major international issue. Its very isolation and uniqueness make it doubtful whether this will continue to be true in the 1950s."[38] As a mid-ranking official, Bennett likely went too far in his frank criticism of a senior official, and he was soon transferred to the less prestigious West Africa desk.

Although some in the Colonial Office supported the governor's position, the Labour government was reluctant to carry out a preemptive coercion policy to repress Cyprus first, and then offer some limited self-government. The British government's response to the enosis plebiscite was a traditional bureaucratic one: to wait and delay any decision. In the meantime, the Colonial and Foreign Offices sent a request to the Joint Chiefs to determine whether they still believed that Cyprus remained vital to British defense strategy, as asserted in their 1947 report.

In typical bureaucratic fashion, the Foreign and Colonial Offices blamed each other for the outbreak of enosis sentiment on Cyprus. The Colonial Office argued that the enosis agitation originated from the Greek government, so the Foreign Office was to blame for not keeping Greece in line. In turn, the Foreign Office argued that the situation on Cyprus was the result of bungling by a second-rate colonial bureaucracy. Part of the British government's difficulty in handling Cyprus was the different culture of the two ministries, and the lack of clarity as to which ministry was responsible for determining Cyprus' political future. The Foreign Ministry was involved because Cyprus' status involved Greece and Turkey, and was therefore an international issue. However, some top Foreign Ministry officials challenged the prevailing view that the status quo could be maintained, or even that Cyprus was important to British strategy. Anthony Rumbold of the Foreign Office's Southern Department pointed out that the Greek government would almost certainly grant the British any guarantees for basing rights and base sovereignty that the British Defense chiefs would require, insisting that "the early cession of Cyprus to Greece would be not only the most just but also the most expedient solution."[39] Head of the Foreign Office, Sir William Strang, also believed that Britain's position in Cyprus was untenable in the long run. However, as he was close to retirement, he was unwilling to push for a reevaluation of Cyprus policy.

As far as the British government was concerned, debate on the status of Cyprus was closed once the chiefs of staff reported in June 1950 that the "unfettered" ownership of Cyprus was a strategic necessity for British defense. With the imprimatur of national defense cited, the Colonial and Foreign Ministries were loath to challenge the military chiefs. From 1950 through the Suez Crisis of 1956, the British Joint Chiefs remained steadfast in their position that British bases on Cyprus were essential to Britain's grand strategy for the Middle East. Furthermore, after the unsuccessful negotiations for basing rights in Egypt, the military leaders believed that the only condition that would ensure the security of British bases on Cyprus was to continue the island's status as a colony.

The British government took a more conciliatory tack when it appointed Sir Robert Armitage as governor in 1954. In contrast to his rather authoritarian predecessor, Armitage believed that Cypriot passions could be quieted through friendly discussions with Greek Cypriot leaders. Upon his arrival Armitage embarked on a series of receptions and cocktail parties to which prominent Greeks were invited. The Greeks who came to these events, however, were from the miniscule group of Greeks on the island who were connected to the British administration and known for their loyalty. Armitage steadfastly refused to acknowledge or speak with the one Greek Cypriot who really mattered: Archbishop Makarios.[40]

The governor was one of the few people on Cyprus who was not aware that the island was about to explode. Doros Alastos, a Greek journalist based in London, conducted extensive interviews throughout Cyprus after the conflict and noted that in late 1954 the impending uprising "was known to everyone, including the Police."[41] Yet Armitage was not completely to blame for his self-deception about the situation on Cyprus. None of the senior British leaders understood the enormous gulf that had opened between the British and the Greek Cypriots, or the depth of Greek feeling on enosis. When Armitage was appointed governor, the Colonial Office did not think it necessary to give him clear instructions on dealing with the Cypriots. Up to April 1955 the British believed that the enosis movement, though highly vocal, did not constitute a serious threat, and that there was "no seething discontent, chronically threatening internal order" on the island. Eden described the insurgency not as a mass movement, but as "terrorism led by a few."[42]

The Insurgency Begins

On the evening of March 31–1 April 1955, eighteen bombs went off at police stations, government buildings, and military installations across Cyprus. The insurgents' greatest success was in knocking out the Cyprus broadcast station transmitter. Over the next few days, small teams of guerrillas raided police stations, mainly to capture weapons. The day after the bombing campaign began, posters and pamphlets appeared all over the island announcing EOKA's campaign to end British rule and achieve enosis for the Cypriot people. The posters and pamphlets were signed "Dighenis," the name of a Byzantine-era hero that Grivas had chosen for his nom de guerre. Although the damage was not extensive, the large number of incidents, their obvious coordination, and the attacks spread across the island put the British government on notice that it was facing a well-organized insurgency.

During the next weeks, insurgent actions continued. Governor Armitage moved to combat the violence with the forces he had on hand: a small British garrison of a couple of army battalions and the Cyprus Police. The first problem was the lack of intelligence about the insurgents. Police forces in other British colonies were usually efficient about keeping tabs on suspected subversives and anti-British nationalist groups. If violence broke out, or was simply threatened, the police usually had a good idea of whom to round up and detain. This was not the case in Cyprus, which had a small, poorly led, poorly trained police force. In any case, EOKA supporters within the police force kept the insurgents well informed of the government's counterterror campaign.

This lack of basic intelligence would hamper the British throughout the insurgency. At the start, since the British had virtually no intelligence on EOKA, they likewise had little idea of the likely suspects to arrest. What is most striking is that EOKA had been organizing and building its strength on Cyprus for three years before the fighting began. This says a lot about Grivas' ability to identify and neutralize possible informers, as well as the lack of basic competence within the police. It was a year into the insurgency that the British finally suspected that "Dighenis" was Colonel Grivas—even though plenty of Cypriots had long known of his identity.

The colonial government at first denied that the violence was more than the work of just a small band of malcontents within the Greek community, and Armitage hoped that his continued program of outreach to the Greek community would soon quiet things. Yet the war escalated and became bloodier through the spring and summer of 1955. Grivas' carefully trained teams targeted the police and Cypriots working for the British administration. The insurgents aimed to cripple the police by assassinating selected police personnel, including two of the three Greek Cypriot policemen assigned to the Special Branch (police intelligence staff). In June 1955 EOKA dramatically gunned down a Greek police sergeant who had just been assigned to the Special Branch. The message to the police was loud and clear: EOKA had full inside knowledge of police operations and could target key personnel at will.[43] If a Cypriot policeman wanted to live, his best option would be to do as little as possible against the insurgents. Thus, in the first three months of the insurgency, the regular police were effectively crippled and the military had to take over many basic police duties on the island. With the police out of action, the colonial government lost its best means of collecting intelligence. Thus it became even more difficult to find insurgents hidden within the population.

Throughout the insurgency the police would remain the government's weak link in forging an effective response. The Colonial Office's chief police advisor described the Cyprus Police as "a Cinderella service in a Cinderella colony."[44] British government policies made sure that the Cyprus Police were barely able to function as a civil police force, much less a force capable of tackling an insurgency. Postwar Britain had little money to spend on policing the colonies, so each colony was responsible for funding and supporting its own security forces. Since Cyprus was a relatively poor colony, this fiscal policy meant that as the unrest in the island increased after 1948 there were few funds available to pay, train, or equip the police. The Cyprus Police had always been poorly paid, and postwar inflation made things especially bad. In the mid-1950s unskilled laborers earned considerably more than new police constables.[45] Owing to these low pay scales, the government found it hard to attract recruits with even a minimum standard of education.[46] With little financial support available from the Colonial Office, the government of Cyprus went to extremes in the quest for economies. In 1954 colonial officials even denied a police force request for £175 to equip the constables with flashlights.[47] The entire Cyprus Police budget that year amounted to only £600,000—a little more than a pound for every inhabitant. On the eve of the insurgency in 1954, the Cyprus Police had only 1,386 personnel, with a disproportionate number (37 percent) drawn from the Turkish Cypriots. The large number of Turks on the force was due to lower levels of education and higher levels of poverty among the Turkish Cypriots.

Aside from a basic recruit course, there was no program of advanced training for the Cyprus Police, which had a tradition of being more of a gendarmerie than a normal force capable of dealing with criminal investigation. Indeed, the Cyprus Police was so backward that a criminal investigation branch was only created in 1951. Only when the government became aware that Greek nationalists were smuggling weapons to the island did it authorize the police to form a "special branch," a police intelligence unit to monitor radical or subversive activity. Moreover, when the special branch was finally formed in 1954, it consisted of only three officers. Given this lack of training and resources, as well as the mediocre quality of personnel and leadership of the force, it was inevitable that the insurgency would catch the government unprepared.[48]

Exacerbating the problem was the policy of trying to fight an insurgency on the cheap. At the start of the insurgency, many Greek Cypriot policemen resigned from the force in protest of their low pay. Those remaining were compelled to work longer hours and perform extra shifts for no additional pay. It was the last straw for police morale, and still more Greek Cypriot policemen submitted their resignations from the force.[49] To replace the experienced policemen who had left, Governor Armitage raised a new force, the Auxiliary Police. They were recruited from the Turkish community which, in contrast to the Greeks, was seen as loyal to the British regime. From the moment of their formation, the Auxiliary Police would be a weak force with serious discipline problems. Most of the recruits were semiliterate laborers who viewed police work as a job during the slack part of the agricultural year—hardly the makings of an effective counterinsurgency force. Despite virtually no training and little competent leadership, the Auxiliary Police were quickly deployed on security duties.[50] Britain tried to fill the leadership vacuum by deploying four hundred UK policemen on special attachment to Cyprus. But the British police were largely ineffective because they arrived knowing nothing of the language or local conditions and could barely communicate with their subordinates—if at all.[51]

At first, facing a small army garrison and an ineffective police force, the EOKA rebels could strike virtually at will. With the situation clearly beyond the government's ability to control it, the hapless Sir Robert was fired in September 1955. The government then appointed Field Marshal Sir John Harding, scheduled to retire as chief of the Imperial General Staff, as Governor General.[52] Harding immediately called for army reinforcements. By October 1955, two more infantry battalions had been sent, raising the army garrison to over twelve thousand.[53] The military force on the island would continue to grow throughout 1955–1957.

Field Marshal Harding's Campaign— The Military Solution

In the fall of 1955 Field Marshal John Harding was completing his three-year term as chief of the Imperial General Staff. In short, he was Britain's top soldier. Born in 1896, Harding came from a humble background and had risen through the ranks to become a reserve lieutenant on the eve of World War I. Called to service on the Western Front, he earned a reputation as a brilliant and courageous officer, finishing the war as a major. Staying in the regular army after the war, he earned a superb record as a division commander in North Africa, where he commanded the famed 7th Armoured Division. Severely wounded in combat in 1942, he returned to the front in 1943 and ended the war commanding a corps in Italy. After the war he held several of the army's top posts until appointed army chief of staff in 1952. Harding was an outstanding conventional soldier with a sharp mind.[54] But conventional soldiers often do poorly in unconventional wars, and Harding is proof of this theory. In Harding the government believed it had the right man to take tough and decisive actions—in contrast with a less forceful Colonial Office professional like Armitage. As field marshal and governor, he would have almost complete military and civil authority in the island. As one of his first steps, Harding imposed draconic emergency regulations that allowed him to detain civilians without trial and suppress the press. Both Harding and Prime Minister Eden expected the Cyprus problem to be settled with a quick military victory over the insurgents, after which the British might consider discussing a form of limited self-government with the Cypriots.

Harding did not view the insurgency as a prolonged war, but rather as a campaign that could be won with a few sharp blows. He was consistent in believing that insurgencies could be defeated quickly through the application of military force. As army chief of staff in 1953 Harding had publicly announced that the Malayan Emergency "was nearly won." This infuriated General Gerald Templer, the commander in Malaya who had developed a systematic, long-term civil/military strategy to defeat the Malayan insurgents. Questioned about Harding's comments, Templer declared, "I'll shoot the bastard who says this emergency is over."[55] But Harding was confident that with his ample resources a long-term strategy was unnecessary, and in the Governor's New Year's address on January 1, 1956, he boastfully announced that EOKA's days were numbered.[56] It would not be the only time that Harding would announce the imminent demise of the insurgency. Despite the recent example of a highly successful counterinsurgency campaign in Malaya, with its sophisticated civil/military strategy, Harding preferred a heavy-handed approach to bludgeon the population into compliance with British rule. Harding's willingness to employ firepower soon upset some British officials and senior military officers. Immediately upon his arrival in the colony, to interdict clandestine arms shipments from Greece Harding issued orders for the Royal Navy ships on patrol to shoot on sight any Greek vessel near the Cyprus coast. The commander of the Royal Navy's Mediterranean Fleet protested this order, sensibly pointing out that such actions were liable to cause serious problems with Britain's NATO ally.[57]

From late 1955 through 1956, troops poured in until more than twenty thousand soldiers were on the island. The Royal Air Force and Royal Navy also reinforced their contingents. Harding also more than tripled the size of the police and locally recruited security forces. At the height of the insurgency in 1956–1957, Harding had almost forty thousand military and police to oppose an insurgent force that never exceeded 300 combatants. Indeed, Harding's forces amounted to one soldier or policemen for every ten Greek Cypriots in the whole population, one of the most lopsided force ratios in the history of counterinsurgency. Yet the British would learn that sheer force cannot defeat a clever enemy. Lacking effective police support, British intelligence on the rebels was consistently poor. It was a war of the blundering elephant versus the gnat. EOKA's small bands, supported by the Greek Cypriots, easily evaded British forces. Somewhat over half of Grivas' 250 active fighters were spread throughout the rural districts, where they specialized in placing landmines and ambushing British patrols. Cyprus Police and British soldiers, supported by armored vehicles and RAF helicopters, conducted huge sweep operations to encircle and trap the guerrilla bands. Soldiers stormed in and occupied villages for days, searching every home and harassing the inhabitants. When guerrillas placed mines or ambushed a British patrol, Harding relied on the traditional British colonial tactic of collective punishment. Fines of thousands of pounds were placed on Greek towns and villages where outrages had occurred. Such tactics very rarely worked, for the guerrillas were on their home turf and were adept at hiding their arms and explosives. The British tactics succeeded mainly in further alienating the Greek Cypriot population.[58]

The massive British use of manpower also failed to either interdict EOKA's arms smuggling or inhibit offensive actions against the British. Occasional British successes in destroying small EOKA units tended to come more through chance contacts with patrols than through any clear intelligence information. Despite Harding's prediction of a quick, decisive victory, the program of bombings, assassinations of police and British officials, and attacks on military convoys increased throughout 1956. In the cities Grivas employed assassination squads that carefully monitored the habits of British officers and policemen, planned attacks in detail, and then gunned them down in broad daylight. The EOKA hit squads were especially effective in Nicosia. In almost all cases, the killers escaped into the crowd and found refuge in one of EOKA's safe houses. On more than one occasion, the EOKA killer squads were hidden in the homes of pro-EOKA Greek Cypriot policemen.

This kind of campaign, more akin to terrorism than war, took a steady toll upon the British military and police on the island. Casualties came in ones and twos, and there were no real battles to report. The heaviest British casualties in the campaign occurred in June 1956 in the Trodos Mountains and were self-inflicted. A British army unit mortaring a suspected insurgent position set off a forest fire that spread quickly. A British column was caught in the middle of the blaze. Twenty-one soldiers burned to death, sixteen were injured, and numerous vehicles were destroyed.[59]

Harding's greatest failing was his lack of understanding of the Greek Cypriot mentality, a trait he shared with Eden and the British government. Convinced that the Cypriots would become compliant if their leadership were neutralized, he decided to break the insurgency with a bold stroke. On March 9, 1956, Harding ordered Archbishop Makarios arrested and shipped off to exile in the remote British Colony of the Seychelle Islands in the Indian Ocean. Harding's justification was that the Archbishop was inciting violence, an action of which Makarios was obviously guilty. Harding assumed that, with the Archbishop removed, he could find moderate Greeks who would come to a peaceful settlement on British terms. In fact, the Greek Cypriots responded violently to the arrest of their leader. A week-long general strike was immediately declared. Then EOKA stepped up its activity, carrying out 246 attacks in the last three weeks of March.[60]

What the British did not realize was that Makarios was one of the more moderate Greek leaders. Although he reluctantly approved violence, Makarios urged Grivas to restrain his guerrillas in the hope that the British might start negotiating. With Makarios out of the picture EOKA could step up its activity.[61] The action of the British government in deporting the archbishop had been one of the "lose-lose" propositions often faced by a government defending itself against an insurgency. At home Makarios had been a powerful leader, but was not well known to people outside of Cyprus and Greece. His arrest and deportation in 1956 made world news, turning the monk into a world figure. Once outside of Cyprus, Makarios became a living martyr, an international rallying point against Britain. His deportation brought protests from many sectors of British society, including the Archbishop of Canterbury and other leading British churchmen.[62]

Harding's policies also led directly to the increase in communal tension, and eventually outright war between the Greeks and Turks on Cyprus. Before the insurgency Greek and Turkish Cypriots had lived in relative harmony and there had been little trouble. At the start of the insurgency, EOKA was careful to target only British personnel and facilities in order to reassure the Turks that they would be left alone, and their rights and property respected if Cyprus were united with Greece. Harding saw the Turks, who favored the status quo, as allies, and an additional source of manpower to crush EOKA. So he greatly expanded the size of the Auxiliary Police. This action went counter to the advice of experienced colonial officials, who knew that reliance upon a Turkish police force would alarm the Greek Cypriot population and likely lead to open conflict between the island's ethnic communities—a development that the Colonial Office officials desperately wanted to avoid.[63] Brushing such warnings aside, Harding proceeded with his plan to reinforce the security forces with Turkish auxiliaries. In 1956 the Auxiliary Police was expanded to 1,417 personnel, a larger force than the entire regular police of 1954. Harding then employed the Turkish Cypriots as a main force to suppress the insurgency, again disdaining the advice of civilian officials with long experience in Cyprus. In September 1955, a new police force was formed, the Special Mobile Reserve, which was recruited exclusively from the Turkish community.[64]

Harding was in a hurry to win, and he refused to concern himself with the long-term effects of recruiting most of the police from a small sector of the population. He also failed to ensure that the police had adequate training and competent leadership. General Templer, who had been exceptionally successful in countering the insurgency in Malaya, visited Cyprus in 1955 and was alarmed by the state of the Cyprus Police. He recommended major reforms but little positive action was taken.[65] In early 1956 the British government formed the Cyprus Police Commission, composed of several senior British police chiefs, with the mandate to inspect conditions on Cyprus and make recommendations for the local security forces. The commission issued a highly critical report on the Cypriot security forces, deploring their low standard of training and leadership. The UK police chiefs were especially concerned about the poor quality of the newly raised Auxiliary Police, who had received "little, if any, training."[66] Predicting that serious trouble would arise if poorly trained and led government forces were armed and unleashed on a civilian population, the commission recommended that the Auxiliary Police and the special constables be disbanded as soon as possible.[67] Ignoring expert advice as usual, Harding instead expanded the controversial Auxiliary Police and the all-Turkish Police Mobile Special Reserve.[68]

Harding's counterinsurgency strategy proved dramatically counter-productive. Deploying large numbers of untrained, undisciplined, and poorly led Turkish policemen against the Greeks guaranteed a culture of police abuse and an immediate rise in communal tension. The insurgency soon expanded from a straightforward British/Greek Cypriot conflict into an insurgency that also combined communal violence between Greeks and Turks. In the last two years of the insurgency, most of the violence was between the two communities. Turkish mobs first rose against the Greeks when EOKA killed ethnically Turkish policemen. The Turkish community responded to Greek terrorist violence by establishing an underground Turkish terrorist group, Volkan, which many Greeks believed—very plausibly—received arms and funding from Turkey. Volkan began carrying out attacks against Greek civilians and suspected EOKA supporters. The British response to this Turkish violence against the Greeks was biased, to say the least. When the Turks rose against the Greeks, the all-Turkish Special Mobile Reserve and Auxiliary Police routinely stood by as Turkish mobs assaulted Greek civilians and ransacked their property.[69]

Many Greeks had been reluctant to support EOKA's campaign of violence at the start of the insurgency, but the threat of communal violence triggered by Harding's strategy eventually forced the whole Greek community to support EOKA simply to provide some protection from the government forces and the Turks.

Although EOKA was extremely successful at harassing and damaging the British, occasionally it made fatal mistakes. A botched ambush or careless movement would leave the guerrillas exposed to British firepower. A few dozen of Grivas' guerrilla fighters were killed or captured, and some of the mountain bands briefly disabled. Each small success was heralded by Harding as a decisive, crippling blow to EOKA, followed by announcements that the insurgency would soon be broken. Yet there were always plenty of idealistic young Cypriots, usually members of the underground Greek youth organization, willing to replenish the ranks of fallen guerrilla fighters. Despite steady losses in the rural guerrilla groups, EOKA fielded more fighters at the end of the insurgency than at the beginning.

The inability of the British to interdict weapons and supplies to EOKA, or to cripple EOKA's organization, was demonstrated when the peace agreement was signed and the insurgency officially ended. In March 1959, per the peace agreement that would give Cyprus independence, EOKA disarmed and handed in over six hundred guns, thousands of rounds of ammunition, two thousand bombs and over a ton of explosives. EOKA armaments in 1959 included dozens of submachine guns and even a mortar—far more firepower than they had possessed at the start of the conflict. EOKA fighters bragged that they had only turned in the oldest and least effective of their weapons, carefully stashing away the most modern guns against future troubles.[70]

Cyprus in the International Context

One of the greatest blunders by the British government in Cyprus was Anthony Eden's decision to internationalize the conflict at the start of the insurgency. Even before the insurgency the Foreign Office had largely taken over Cyprus policy from the Colonial Office. Eden had just been appointed Prime Minister in April 1955 when Cyprus blew up, but he had already formulated his approach to Cyprus as foreign minister. Secure in his grasp of foreign affairs, and with little consultation with the Colonial Office or members of the cabinet other than his close colleague Harold Macmillan, Eden believed that there was a simple solution for Cyprus. In Eden's view, the Cypriot population could be bypassed, and the status of the island settled through negotiations with the Greek and Turkish governments. Eden believed that Turkey was the key nation to the Middle East, and that whatever Britain did, Turkey was not to be offended. On the other hand, Eden maintained that Greece could be induced to give up its interests in Cyprus and accept continued British rule, with some minimal semblance of self-determination for the overwhelming majority of the Cypriots.

Unfortunately, Eden's simple solution added an extra layer of complication to the crisis. If Eden had followed the advice of some in the Colonial Office, granting Cyprus union with Greece with an iron-clad guarantee for British military bases, the Turks would have objected, but it would have quickly blown over. After all, the overwhelming majority of Cypriots favored such a course, and Britain could legitimately claim Cyprus' status was a British internal issue. However, bringing Greece and Turkey into the process gave these mutually hostile nations veto power over any plans for Cyprus' future, resulting in more than three years of diplomatic stalemate. Once Turkey was invited to play a lead role in Cyprus' status, the issue became one of Turkish national honor. For the Turks the Cyprus issue was more than just protecting the Turkish ethnic minority on Cyprus. It was a means to play out their long-term rivalry with the Greeks.

In August 1955 the Greek and Turkish governments were invited to negotiations in London. It was unavoidable that representatives of the Greek and Turkish Cypriots were also invited to discuss the island's future. The Greeks and Greek Cypriots, who were represented by Makarios, wanted enosis. The British counted on the Turks to support their position of continued British control of Cyprus, with no enosis under any conditions. As before, Britain proposed arrangements to allow for some very limited self-government for the Cypriots, but with final power in the hands of the British governor. Such ideas were rejected out of hand by the Greeks and the Greek Cypriots. When the negotiations broke up in September nothing had been decided and no one was happy. The Greeks were upset that enosis had been ruled out, which made the Turks happy. But the Turks were upset that the British had not completely ruled out the chance for independence for Cyprus, or a self-governance plan that allowed for true majority rule.

The British thought that they could reopen the negotiations process by getting Makarios out of the picture, but the arrest of Makarios and his exile to the Seychelles in March 1956 only enhanced the archbishop's prestige in the eyes of the Cypriots and the world. In order to get the process moving again, Makarios was released from his exile after one year. However, the British would not allow him to return to his home, so Makarios settled in Athens, where he was able to broadcast his sermons and speeches to the Greek Cypriots via Radio Athens.[71] The archbishop encouraged the Cypriots to hold firm for enosis, while urging the mainland Greeks to support their brothers in Cyprus. As much as the British disliked him, Makarios remained the acknowledged leader of the Greek Cypriots, and he would have to be included in any negotiations over Cyprus' future.

Through 1957 and 1958 the Greek government provided considerable help to the Cypriot insurgents by bringing the issue of Cypriot self-determination before the UN. Although the UN refrained from committing itself on the issue, calling only for a peaceful, democratic, and just solution, even this minimal acknowledgement of their cause helped legitimize the Greek Cypriot case in the eyes of the world.[72] With the constant negative coverage in the

113

British and international press, and the dicussion of British policy in the European Union and United Nations, the ongoing insurgency was becoming a serious international embarrassment to Britain. Moreover, the requirement to keep a large military force on the island for counterinsurgency duty detracted from much higher British defense priorities, such as the defense of Western Europe.

The event that made a negotiated settlement of Cyprus possible was the British/French fiasco at Suez in October–November 1956. The Suez Crisis put a quick end to the decade of British illusions about maintaining a great power status in the Middle East, likewise contributing to the resignation of Anthony Eden as prime minister in early 1957. Harold Macmillan, the new prime minister, was more capable than his predecessor at adapting to the new realities of a smaller, more Europe-oriented Britain. With the grand scheme of British influence and bases in the Middle East in tatters, maintaining Cyprus as a center of influence in the region was no longer a priority. Helping to drive a reconsideration of the value of Cyprus was a new defense policy announced in April 1957 that called for major cuts in British defense spending, less emphasis on empire and the Middle East, and a turn to smaller, better-equipped forces focused on European defense.[73] With the British military chiefs no longer claiming that Cyprus was an indispensable base, Macmillan was now free to consider options for Cypriot self-determination, and even independence.

As the Cyprus insurgency entered its third year and communal violence flared, Archbishop Makarios also shifted his position. As enosis now seemed an impossible goal, he accepted the idea that independence, which would at least allow the Greek Cypriots majority rule, might be the best option for getting the British out and bringing peace to the island.[74] With British objections to independence dropped, discussions between the Cyprus factions and the Greek and Turkish governments in London and Zurich progressed, until all the parties were ready for a final conference to settle the conflict in late 1958. In the final discussions the issue of granting the British military bases on Cyprus was conceded very quickly. The most serious sticking point was to assure guarantees for the Turkish minority in a majority Greek country, and the rights of the major powers to intervene to protect their interests.

Cyprus and the International Media

One of the advantages of the Cypriot insurgents—and one that Colonel Grivas played to in crafting his strategic plan for insurgency, was the use of the media to publicize the Greek Cypriot cause to an international audience. Cyprus was one of the first insurgencies that was well covered by the international press. This press coverage highlighted British mistakes, won considerable sympathy for the insurgents both internationally and in Britain, and played a major role in pressuring the government to give up Cyprus.

Even before the insurgency began, Makarios was successful in mobilizing the Greek population. In a series of nonviolent acts of resistance, he provoked the British to openly repressive measures that demonstrated to the world— and to the Greek Cypriots themselves—the strength of their unity against British rule. Makarios had studied the example of Gandhi, who had used demonstrations and protest marches so effectively in demonstrating to the world the strength of the Indian independence movement. Makarios and Grivas employed similar tactics, albeit with a much more violent confronta- tion than Gandhi would have endorsed.

As the insurgency began, Grivas coordinated with Greek youth leaders to put large numbers of high school students out on the streets for a series of anti-British protests. In the 1950s, before television was the primary means of visual news coverage, newsreels were the best means to get dramatic images before the public. The Greek leaders carefully stage-managed protest dem- onstrations to ensure that the British would react with force against Greek civilians—all while being filmed by newsreel cameras. Sometimes the dem- onstrations turned into rock-throwing melees, in which British troops and police wielding batons and rifles charged in and arrested teenage culprits. One of the more notable newsreels of the Cyprus conflict was one from May 1956 that featured high school girls confronting British soldiers. Mass demonstra- tions emphasized the image of the Greek Cypriots as the underdogs con- fronting the might of imperial Britain, an image that evoked sympathy in the international press.

When the insurgency broke out, the British media largely followed the government line and characterized the widespread demonstrations and civic disobedience by the Greeks as coming from a handful of radicals. Sir

Robert Armitage was heartily criticized by the British press for not being hard enough in suppressing the demonstrations.[75] But the constant demonstrations and other nonviolent means of protest soon convinced the press that enosis sentiment was overwhelming among the Greek Cypriots. At night members of the Greek Youth Movement covered the walls and streets of the island's cities with EOKA slogans—which the British had to paint over the next day. The slogans and flags simply reappeared. Since the British forbade flying the Greek national flag, at night high school students would festoon church steeples and public buildings with Greek flags, forcing the British to go through the futile exercise of removing them. Such widespread and constant activities, and the failure of the huge British forces on Cyprus to suppress them, made it clear to any observer that EOKA had mass support among the population. The government's assertion that the demand for enosis was simply the work of a small, radical band seemed increasingly hollow.

Field Marshal Harding began his tenure with a very favorable impression in the British media as a strong and experienced leader who could be expected to quickly restore order to Cyprus. From the start Harding assumed a confident and almost arrogant tone with the media. There was no insincerity in Harding's boast on January 1, 1956, that "EOKA's days are numbered," and that the large forces under his command would quickly crush the rebels. Such talk resonated with the British press and was exactly what the public and government wanted to hear. But Harding was to learn that the press is a fickle friend indeed. In only a few months of his counterinsurgency campaign, the cry from journalists and politicians went from "show the strong hand" against the Cypriot "terrorists" (as they were characterized by the British government), to cries of outrage when the strong hand was actually employed. When communal violence flared up, exacerbated by Harding's policy of employing poorly trained and led Turkish auxiliaries against the Greeks, British press reporting took a decidedly antigovernment tone. Throughout his tenure Harding was incompetent in his media relations. Though he tried to deal with the press as openly as he could and granted constant regular interviews, the content of his statements could not have been better calculated to wreck his and the government's credibility.

The most serious media problem that Harding had to face, and the one he fumbled most dramatically, was the issue of torture and abuse of the Greek

Cypriots by British police and military forces. Numerous British accounts of the Cyprus insurgency acknowledge widespread abuse of the Greeks by the Cyprus Police and British forces.[76] The police and British military intelligence earned a reputation for brutality. Frustrated by their inability to get information on EOKA through normal interrogation, many police and intelligence personnel turned to torture. Indeed, British journalists on the island nicknamed the Cyprus Police and intelligence personnel "HMTs" for "Her Majesty's Torturers."[77] British abuses in Cyprus were considerably less widespread than in Malaya or Kenya, but the fact that at least six Greek Cypriots died under interrogation implies that brutality was not unknown.[78] Even the Tory press, which had initially called for a hard line against Cypriot terrorists, abandoned Harding. When Harding issued a sixteen-page "white paper" describing the allegations of torture as "monstrous and filthy" the usually pro-government *Sunday Dispatch* stated that ill-treatment was now an accepted feature of Cyprus operations.[79]

The abusive behavior of the Cyprus Police was a godsend to the insurgents, who made the actions of the security forces a central theme in their international propaganda campaign. Claims of British police abuse were made by the Greek media and brought to world attention with the support of the Greek government. There was enough evidence of police and military brutality to lend credence to the charges. In 1956 the Greek government brought the issue of security force abuses in Cyprus before the European Commission, forcing an international investigation of British police and military actions.[80] Although some allegations were later refuted, the political damage to the British government was serious. Harding, who did not order brutal methods or officially condone them, repeatedly took the line that such allegations were nothing more than fabrications broadcast by Radio Athens, and that his troops were the victims of an orchestrated and insidious plan by the Greek government to discredit the security forces.[81] This attitude by Harding was too much for the British and international journalists covering Cyprus, who had witnessed British troop actions and the especially bad behavior of the Turkish auxiliary police units that the Colonial Office staff had warned against using.

Accounts of British abuse, even if exaggerated, were a strong blow to British prestige and her claim to legitimacy in Cyprus.[82] Even though Cyprus was governed under a program of strict emergency regulations and many basic rights were curtailed, the British courts and legal system still functioned. This led to more embarrassing revelations about the security forces. British doctors conducted the normal process of a coroner's inquest and documented the deadly injuries received by several Greek Cypriots who died while in custody of the security forces. In 1957 James Callahan, the Labour Party's spokesman on colonial affairs in Parliament, read extracts of statements describing police torture in Cyprus and coroners' reports into the parliamentary record, demanding an independent inquiry into the behavior of the British forces on Cyprus. Harding replied that an independent inquiry would damage the morale of the police and troops—hardly an answer to reassure the public that the situation in Cyprus was well in hand.[83]

The government's credibility worsened as the insurgency evolved into intercommunal rioting in 1957. Incidents in which the Cyprus Police refused to intervene when Turkish mobs ransacked Greek Cypriot shops, assaulted Greeks, and committed murders were witnessed by news correspondents, and promptly reported in the international press. As the insurgency progressed, the Cyprus Police were not just passive about their duty to protect Cypriots from lawbreaking, but became perpetrators themselves. During a series of searches in Famagusta, the Auxiliary Police were accused of looting Greek homes. While Harding dismissed such claims, his own commanders considered stories of police misbehavior credible. The district police commissioner of Famagusta noted that many of his policemen had come from the lowest level of Turkish society and "are known not to have been beyond criminal activities in the past." Concerning the allegations of police looting that Harding denied, the commissioner commented, "I myself have little doubt that there is substance in a fair proportion of them."[84]

The failure of the British government to respond to credible allegations haunted the debate over Cyprus policy. In time, criticism of the Cyprus administration found its way to the House of Lords, as well as the United Nations and the European Civil Rights Commission.[85] In November 1957 the Labour Party openly broke with Macmillan's Conservative government to call for full independence for Cyprus.[86] Field Marshal Harding left Cyprus and retired in November 1957, convinced that his strategy had worked. He was wrong. Harding's strong-arm tactics, plus policy of throwing large numbers of poorly led, poorly trained police at the insurgency, were a spectacular failure. Harding's policies fueled domestic and international pressure for Britain to settle the issue in favor of the Greek Cypriots. After the British conceded independence to Cyprus in 1959, Colonel Grivas declared that the first act of the new government after independence should be to raise a statue to Field Marshal Harding, "since he had done more than anybody else to keep alive the spirit of Hellenic resistance in Cyprus."[87]

Consequences—Independence and the Peace Settlement, Continued Violence

Through 1958 to early 1959 the British, Greek, and Turkish governments, as well as Makarios and the Turkish Cypriot leader Fazil Küçük, negotiated in London to find a solution to the Cyprus mess. The collapse of the British position in the Middle East after the Suez fiasco changed the British assessment of Cyprus as a military base for projecting imperial power. In 1958 the Macmillan government reversed the position of the previous three governments on the issue of Cyprus independence. Enosis, what the overwhelming majority of the Cypriots wanted, was out of the question with the Turks at the table, having veto power over any final agreement. The Turks favored either continued British rule or partition of the island, an idea anathema to the Greek Cypriots.

Finally, the British conceded that Cyprus could be granted full independence under the Treaty of Guarantee, but only with special rights granted to the Turkish minority, including the right to veto legislation. In order to protect the interests of the Greeks and Turks, both nations were allowed to station a small number of military forces on Cyprus: 950 Greek and 650 Turkish soldiers. Great Britain, Turkey, and Greece were all granted the right to militarily intervene in Cyprus if it were necessary to uphold the constitution or to protect ethnic community or national interests. The Cyprus Constitution was agreed upon by the Greek and Turkish Cypriot representatives in Zurich on February 11, 1959. The final agreement, including the Treaty of Guarantee, was signed by the Greek, Turkish, and British governments in London on February 19, 1959. Cyprus would be granted full independence in 1960, with the right to join the British Commonwealth. In the meantime, the EOKA fighters were to be demobilized and granted full amnesties. Makarios would become the first president of Cyprus, with the Turkish Cypriot Fazil Küçük as his vice-president.

The Cyprus Constitution was guaranteed to fail if even slight internal or external pressure were applied. The Constitution was a complex document that divided the electorate into two communities, with the Turks allowed political rights and power far out of proportion to their share of the population. Under the constitution, Greek Cypriots elected the president, the Turkish Cypriots, the vice-president. The Turks were granted disproportionate representation in the legislature and council of ministers. In addition, the vice-president was granted the power to veto laws passed by the legislature.

Unfortunately, the communal violence that had accelerated in 1957 and 1958 had so inflamed the two communities that a political system based on communal cooperation and respect for the rule of law was impossible to achieve. Shortly after independence both communities saw a revival of underground guerrilla organizations, EOKA-B for the Greeks and TMT for the Turks, and both groups quietly obtained new weapons. Although President Makarios tried to serve as a voice of moderation, the tensions between the communities were such that only a small spark was needed to initiate large-scale violence. In late 1963 a dispute over the Cypriot constitution and tax provisions led to demonstrations and communal violence across the island. In response to the chaos on Cyprus, the United Nations deployed a peacekeeping force of 6,500 troops to the island in 1964 to serve as a buffer between the communities. The next decade saw sporadic violence as the Greek and Turkish communities moved further apart, with the Turks concentrating in the eastern half of the island. In 1964 the Greek Cypriots enacted conscription for their community, creating a national guard that was mostly led by officers of the Greek Army and headed by Grivas, now promoted to general. The presence of Greek and Turkish military forces on Cyprus exacerbated the tense situation. On several occasions Greek and Turkish military forces came close to outright war. In the meantime, both Greeks and Turks used the Treaty of Guarantee to quietly arm and support their militia forces.

Under Grivas the revived EOKA, now known as EOKA-B, still agitated for enosis with Greece. EOKA-B became open opponents of Makarios because of the president's determination to uphold to the 1959 agreement on independence. Greek supporters of independence over enosis were attacked, and there was even one attempt by Greek radicals on Makarios' life. After the 1967 military coup in Greece, the Greek government and armed forces became much more overt in supporting the Greek nationalists (enosis supporters) on Cyprus. Grivas died of a heart attack in January 1974, and EOKA-B and the National Guard fell into more radical hands. With the tacit support of the Athens regime, EOKA overthrew President Makarios in a coup on July 15, 1974, and replaced him with an EOKA leader. Five days later, claiming their rights to intervene under the 1959 Treaty, the Turkish army invaded Cyprus and engaged in an all-out conventional war against the Cypriot National Guard. After heavy fighting a ceasefire was put into effect that left the eastern part of Cyprus—slightly over one-third of the island—in the hands of the Turkish army. With UN peacekeepers keeping the two communities apart, Cyprus was basically partitioned between the Greek Cypriots and the Turkish forces. This is the situation as it remains today. In 1983 the Turkish government proclaimed an independent Turkish Republic of Northern Cyprus, but it remains unrecognized by any state save Turkey, and its existence is denounced by the United Nations.

Cyprus remains a divided island and a potential flash point for conflict between Greece and Turkey. A UN peacekeeping force has been in place for over four decades and there is no sign of this mission ending.

The insurgency in Cyprus from 1955 to 1959 is largely forgotten today. In the context of great events such as the Suez Crisis and the Cold War, it is seen as just one of many incidents in Britain's often painful withdrawal from empire. At the same time that Britain was fighting the Cypriots, it was also engaged in large counterinsurgency operations in Malaya and Kenya. So events on Cyprus did not capture a high degree of interest at home. As insurgencies go, it was not an especially bloody affair. Between April 1955 and March 1959 the Cyprus insurgency cost the British military and police on Cyprus 156 dead and 788 wounded while 238 Greeks died. The communal fighting between Greeks and Turks inflicted another 297 casualties.[88]

The insurgency in Cyprus was provoked by a British grand strategy based on an illusory notion of maintaining British power and influence in the postwar world. Between 1945 and 1958, the British political and military leadership's obsession with the Middle East gave Cyprus an importance in British strategy that it frankly did not deserve. A poorly conceived British strategy was reinforced by a series of false assumptions about the goals and attitudes of the Greek Cypriots. Once the insurgency began, British leaders refused to reassess their initial assumptions about the Cypriots in the light of reality on the island. Only the fiasco of the Suez crisis and a change in government could force the British leadership to reassess British policy in Cyprus and begin to make concessions that would end the conflict.

In Cyprus a misconceived grand strategy was combined with an ineffective military counterinsurgency strategy. At the foreign policy level, the move to internationalize the conflict proved counterproductive and blocked the chances for a reasonable political settlement that otherwise might have been achieved early on. The expectation that military force could quickly solve the problem also proved misguided. In Cyprus the British use of strong-arm tactics and overwhelming force dramatically failed against a very small insurgent force that had the advantage of a coherent strategic plan, superior intelligence, and the support of the overwhelming majority of the population. British counterinsurgency policies actually fuelled the insurgency and provoked vicious communal violence—a problem that remains in Cyprus today.

The Cyprus insurgency remains a good case study of poor leadership and poor decision making—an example of when good leaders go wrong. Anthony Eden had shown his mettle as a brilliant strategic leader in the 1930s and 1940s, but in the matter of Cyprus he was so rooted in his own prejudices and convinced of his analysis that he ignored good advice from the Colonial Office while he proceeded with a series of flawed policies. On the military side, Field Marshal Harding had proved his mettle as a senior commander and conventional war soldier but was completely out of his depth in dealing with an insurgency. Like Eden, he worked from his own faulty assumptions and prejudices. He ignored advice from police and military counterinsurgency experts, as well as Colonial Office officials who had some understanding of the Cypriot mentality and conditions. For two years he conducted a military campaign that only worked to make the situation worse, leaving behind the legacy of a Cyprus that is still an unresolved international issue and has required the presence of a UN peacekeeping force for more than four decades.

CHAPTER 3
Vietnam—America's Longest War, 1950–1975

■ ■ ■

"South Vietnam was a society without leadership and without direction—and these essentials the Americans could not provide."
—Troung Nhu Tang, senior member of the National Liberation Front (NLF)[1]

THE UNITED STATES WAS MILITARILY involved in Vietnam for a quarter of a century, the longest engagement in a foreign conflict in American history. From Truman's administration to Gerald Ford's hapless presidency, U.S. presidents, military leaders, and the Congress grappled with the Vietnam issue. The American engagement in Vietnam ended in a most humiliating manner in April 1975, when the U.S. embassy was hastily evacuated amidst the chaos of a collapsing South Vietnamese regime. The North Vietnamese signaled the end of a conflict that began in 1945 when their tanks crashed through the gate of South Vietnam's presidential palace.

From the start the United States became involved in a conflict whose dynamics were never really grasped by the U.S. civilian and military leadership. When the administration of President Lyndon Johnson decided to ratchet up the U.S. military involvement to full-scale conventional war in late 1964, most of the top American civilian and military leaders were confident that America's enormous advantage in military force, technology, wealth, and

123

diplomatic leverage would make short work of a relatively small and poorly equipped force of third world insurgents then receiving limited backing from their North Vietnamese cousins. After all, North Vietnam was yet another third world country with very limited resources, infrastructure, and military capability. Most American strategists expected that large-scale U.S. military intervention would yield quick and decisive results. Instead, the war became a quagmire resulting in the deaths of over fifty-five thousand U.S. soldiers, as well as hundreds of thousands of North Vietnamese and South Vietnamese soldiers, before the U.S. pullout of forces in early 1973.

The story of America's Vietnam involvement is one of a seriously flawed strategy, a failure to understand the mentality and culture of the Vietnamese, a consistent tendency to overestimate the capabilities of American technology and military forces, and a failure of America's civilian and military leaders to grasp the essentials of counterinsurgency.

The Origins of the War and the Start of U.S. Involvement

When the Japanese surrendered in August 1945, the nationalist Viet Minh forces that had organized themselves during the Japanese occupation of Indochina from 1941 to 1945 took advantage of the power vacuum to seize power throughout Vietnam, establish a national government, and proclaim national independence. Though confronted with a *fait accompli*, the provisional French government still insisted upon reestablishing its military presence in Indochina and reasserting its lost colonial status. The U.S. government, wisely appreciating that old-style European colonialism was dead in the aftermath of World War II, refused to support the French endeavor. A bankrupt and war-weary France chose to rely upon British troops and military aid in order to reestablish a limited military presence in Vietnam in late 1945. French intransigence in refusing to end its colonial status and cut a deal with the Vietnamese nationalists forced a breakdown in negotiations. This led to the outbreak of open war between the French and the Viet Minh in late 1946. From 1946 to 1950, the United States refused to grant aid to the French to support their efforts in Indochina, although the French claimed to be fighting the forces of international communism. The argument that the war was about communism was a weak one, and the American government had other priorities. Europe needed rebuilding. The Greeks and Turks, who were under threat by Soviet forces and client states, needed substantial military aid. Creation of a strategic nuclear force was necessary to deter the Soviet Union. Supporting French colonial adventures in Southeast Asia took a rightfully low place on the list of American priorities. However, the fall of China to Mao's communist forces in 1949 and the invasion of South Korea by the Stalin-backed North Korean army in June 1950 again focused U.S. attention on Asia. A major U.S. rearmament program was plainly necessary to confront an openly aggressive communism.

Finally accepting the French argument that they were fighting communists and not nationalists in Vietnam, the U.S. began to pour in aid in 1950. The next four years of the war were mostly financed by the U.S. and fought with U.S. weapons.[2] Between 1950 and 1954, more than a billion dollars of U.S. military aid flowed to build up the French and the pro-French Vietnamese army they created. Bolstered by U.S. aid, including large numbers of surplus U.S. aircraft, tanks, artillery pieces, and heavy and light weapons, the French saw their chance to actually gain a decisive military victory and force the Viet Minh to surrender. This eventually led to the debacle of Dien Bien Phu in May 1954, when the French Army put thirteen thousand of its finest troops in an indefensible position on the Laotian border. The Viet Minh were able to surround them with a large ground force that also brought in anti-aircraft guns to cut off the French army's air supply.[3] The debacle at Dien Bien Phu put an end to France's presence in Indochina and resulted in a negotiated peace in Geneva. Vietnam was divided between the north, where the Viet Minh were strongest, and the south, where the French forces and government—having established a Vietnamese puppet government—were still generally in control. Cambodia and Laos would become independent monarchies.

Creating the Republic of Vietnam

The Geneva Accords ratified by the Vietnamese parties, the French, and the U.S. government in July 1954 required the French to withdraw to the south. They recognized the Democratic Republic of Vietnam established in North Vietnam and mandated future elections to determine the unification of Vietnam. People in all parts of Vietnam were to be allowed to move to the zone of the other party. This engendered a mass exodus to the south of over nine hundred thousand North Vietnamese. They were mostly members of the Catholic minority, who rightly feared persecution at the hands of the communist government of Ho Chi Minh. The Catholics who moved south brought with them high levels of education and middle class skills but would remain a serious problem for the southern government, as they would have to be resettled.

The Viet Minh were generally popular with all the Vietnamese for their success in the nationalist struggle against the French. Ho Chi Minh was looked upon as a patriot for his leadership in that endeavor. However, the greater part of the population was not inclined towards the communist system that Ho Chi Minh and his cadre wanted to impose. Many Vietnamese remembered well that in March 1946, when the nationalists were negotiating with the French over Vietnam's status, Ho Chi Minh had ensured the supremacy of the communist faction of the nationalists by ruthlessly purging the noncommunist nationalist parties. Thousands of Vietnamese, many of them staunch nationalists and patriots, were executed or put into labor camps in the jungle by Ho Chi Minh and his cadres.[4] Even though they had undergone political indoctrination during the war against the French, probably the majority of the Viet Minh were neither communist nor inclined to favor the northern solution of land collectivization. Most of the Viet Minh, and certainly most Vietnamese in the south, had been less motivated by political ideology than by a simple nationalism and desire to free their country from French control. While the communists had become well established in the north, the south was relatively free of ardent communists. With a flood of almost a million refugees from the north in 1954–1955, most of them staunchly anticommunist Catholics, the southern disinclination to follow a radical communist path was reinforced.

Under U.S. pressure the French pulled their last military forces out of South Vietnam in the spring of 1955, and South Vietnam declared itself an independent republic. While the referendum on national unification as envisioned by the Geneva Accords never took place, the South Vietnamese did have a referendum on a choice of government. They could choose between a monarchy under the Emperor Bao Dai (who lived in exile in France and who had loyally served as the head of a powerless Vietnamese government for decades) or a republic under the leadership of Ngo Dinh Diem. In one of the few nonrigged elections in the brief history of South Vietnam, the Vietnamese voted overwhelmingly to establish a republic and to make Diem its first president. South Vietnamese elites and intellectuals initially welcomed Diem. While looking for eventual reunification with their cousins to the north, they disliked the dictatorial northern approach. They looked to build a state that was genuinely Vietnamese and democratic, but with a moderate approach to social issues. Land reform and a moderate form of socialism would have been popular with both peasants and intellectuals, but the collectivization and antireligious policies of the north found little favor among the southerners.

A good picture of the Vietnamese mindset from the period is found in the parallel memoirs of two notable South Vietnamese figures: Troung Nhu Tang, who served as minister of justice in the National Liberation Front shadow government, and Tran Van Don, who became one of the top generals in the South Vietnamese Army.[5] Both men came from similar backgrounds. Both were southerners from the upper classes of Vietnamese society who had earned commissions as officers under the French, but who still burned with an ardent nationalism and the hope of creating a democratic Vietnamese state. As southerners, both favored a more moderate course of national development, and while looking for reform in the southern society, were generally repelled by the ruthless communist system that Ho Chi Minh and his party inflicted upon the north. While hoping for eventual reunification, both favored the creation of a moderate and democratic southern state as the first step. Both welcomed Diem as a worthy leader in 1954. Then, through the 1950s, both of these well-educated and able men became increasingly disenchanted by Diem. Troung Nhu Tang eventually joined the anti-Diem resistance movement, becoming a National Liberation Front civilian leader (although he was not a communist and never joined the party). Tran Van Don remained in the army. He took part in deposing Diem and then became an adherent of General, later President, Nguyen Van Thieu. Both men regarded the civil war in Vietnam as a tragedy and believed that it would have been possible for the southern factions to have formed a coalition government.

Although he served the Thieu regime, Tran Van Don frankly describes the problems of corruption, incompetence, and poor military leadership that plagued the South Vietnamese government from the start. Troung Nhu Tang, for his part, described the arrogance and rigid dictatorial manner of the northerners, who tended to shunt the southerners of the NLF aside during the course of the war and by the late 1960s came to completely dominate what had begun as an indigenous and reformist southern Vietnamese movement. Appointed to a high government position after the takeover of South Vietnam by the North in 1975, Troung Van Tang found the northern communists even more offensive and corrupt than the old South Vietnamese regime. He soon left Vietnam to live in exile. Both men agree that there was a good chance that South Vietnam could have built a stable, unified, and democratic state in the 1950s—but the Diem regime simply blew it.

The most essential factor in understanding the Vietnamese mentality and culture is the power of nationalism. Unlike many third world nations, whose borders and origins were created with little regard to the boundaries of tribes, cultures, or peoples, the Vietnamese nation and people had been forged by seven hundred years of battling the Chinese. From the 1200s to the 1800s the Chinese tried to establish their rule of Vietnam as an imperial outpost. Over centuries of resistance, the Vietnamese had at times driven the Chinese out and had established their own unique monarchy, culture, local government, and traditions. The Vietnamese had their own law and literature and revered national heroes who had led successful campaigns against the Chinese. By the time the French arrived to install their colonial regime in the nineteenth century, the Vietnamese were probably the most consciously nationalistic people in Southeast Asia. Through the nineteenth century to 1945, the French encouraged the development of Vietnamese elite and middle classes, educated in French schools and groomed to serve the French bureaucracy. Yet these Vietnamese elites never forgot their nationalist heritage.

In many respects the French colonial policy left a positive legacy to Vietnam. By the time of the French collapse in the 1940s, Vietnam, while remaining an overwhelmingly peasant society, had the makings of an energetic and capable indigenous middle class and a small corps of well-trained bureaucrats to manage the country. The rising Vietnamese middle classes generally admired French culture and ideals, and a knowledge of the French language brought the Vietnamese into close contact with the broad world of Western ideas. There was much in the system of French law and administration that provided a positive model for the Vietnamese. During the 1946–1954 war against the Viet Minh, the French created and trained an army and small air force that often fought competently against the Viet Minh. Still, the class of Vietnamese who admired France privately remained staunchly nationalist. Even the sons of the Vietnamese middle and upper classes who went to French officer schools and served in the French armed forces during the independence war secretly longed for the day that the French would leave and Vietnam would be truly independent.[6]

By all accounts, Diem began his government with strong popular support from most groups in South Vietnam. The most powerful force in the state, the South Vietnamese Army, trained and established by the French, stood solidly behind Diem. Uncomfortable with Diem at first, the United States decided to give his government aid and strong backing. Indeed, Diem had many of the characteristics of a great national leader. First of all, he was known for his fervent nationalism. In 1932, when as a rising young political leader he had been appointed interior minister in Bao Dai's government, he had quickly proposed numerous government reforms. When the French refused to consider his proposals, Diem resigned in protest. For the next two decades he refused to take office under the French, although he was approached many times. Secondly, Diem was known for his asceticism and honesty. Corruption was rife in the French colonial administration and in their Vietnamese puppet government, but Diem was never any part of that. He was devoutly Catholic, a bachelor known to work eighteen hours a day.[7]

In the 1950s Diem had the opportunity to build a strong, stable, and popular South Vietnamese government that could have served as a counterpoint to the North. If the preferences of South Vietnam's ruling elites had been heeded, the South Vietnamese government would have been friendly with the United States and the West and readily accepted aid, while refraining from joining any formal blocks with East or West. The strong nationalist character of the Vietnamese would have preferred a neutral South Vietnam—a position that the Eisenhower administration would have accepted.

Diem's term as president started well. With the support of the army, he suppressed the powerful crime lords who controlled trade in Saigon. He established a new constitution. He visited villages and listened to the peasant concerns. He agreed to resettle the refugees from the north. Unfortunately, Diem went overboard in asserting control in South Vietnam and in suppressing all forms of opposition.[8] Although the Viet Minh had been relatively weak in the South, there were regions—especially the Central Highlands—where the Viet Minh had had a strong presence. Diem could have easily reached out to the Viet Minh, who were regarded as solid patriots by the average peasant, and brought them into his administration. Instead, between 1955 and 1957 Diem sent his political operatives, police, and army units to conduct massive roundups of former Viet Minh fighters, imprisoning thousands. Some leaders were killed, still others dispossessed. Many escaped the dragnet and went underground to become a solidly anti-Diem force in waiting. In his eagerness to solidify his control of South Vietnam, Diem suppressed other major groups as well. One was the Cao Dai, a religious sect founded in 1921 that was a syncretic mixture of Catholic, Buddhist, and Western Asian thought. Very popular in some of the central provinces of Vietnam, the Cao Dai sect boasted its own churches, pope, and militia. As with the former Viet Minh fighters, the Cao Dai sect had considerable political power and prestige. It was neither hostile to Diem nor unwilling to join in a broad coalition. However, Diem, growing more authoritarian by the day, came to see any large, well-organized group as a potential threat to his government. So, also like the Viet Minh, the Cao Dai sect was ruthlessly suppressed.

The origin of many of Diem's tendencies towards extremism came from his brother, Ngo Dihn Nhu, as well as Nhu's wife, Madame Ngo Dihn Nhu (Tran Le Xuan), who played the part of official presidential hostess. Nhu served as Diem's senior political advisor and was fascinated by totalitarian/fascist political ideology. Nhu built up a political movement that soon became the only authorized political force in the country. His Republican Youth Movement was formed along fascist lines. Nhu constantly advised his brother to employ police-state methods against perceived enemies. Diem's brothers and in-laws fostered an atmosphere of corruption and worked steadily to funnel U.S. aid funds into their own pockets.

As if his family were not enough of a problem, Diem's personal background and prejudices got in the way of building a unified South Vietnam. The devout Catholic Diem openly favored his coreligionists, a major irritant in a country that was overwhelmingly Buddhist. Under the land reform programs supported by U.S. aid money, Diem's Catholic coreligionists from the North received special preferences in land allocations. Catholics played a central role among Diem's top advisors and senior military officers—another action that led the majority of South Vietnamese to complain of his rule. One of Diem's major attempts to extend his power backfired quickly. In 1956 Diem replaced the traditional village council system of local government with governors and district chiefs appointed by him. Again, outsiders and coreligionists from north and central Vietnam were appointed to run southern villages, an action enormously resented by the peasants, who had strongly supported Diem at the start of his rule. The overthrow of the traditional village council system was viewed as a totalitarian move by Diem as even the French had not interfered with this form of local government. By overriding the village council system, Diem wrecked the most traditional and popular local democratic system existing in South Vietnam.

Between 1954 and 1959 Diem and his family did a masterful job of thoroughly alienating most of the major ethnic groups and factions of South Vietnam. By 1959 broad swaths of the South Vietnamese population had simply had enough, and various factions coalesced into a broad resistance movement. Soon an underground government formed and prepared for open warfare against the Diem government. The national resistance movement, which soon evolved into the Viet Cong, was not communist at first, although some members and leaders were inclined to favor a communist model of government. Nor was the anti-Diem movement initially organized and directed by the north. However, the North Vietnamese government, knowing of the broad dissatisfaction of the southerners with their government, soon provided political cadres to the movement and directed the secret supporters of Ho Chi Minh (who had been underground since the suppression of the Viet Minh), to join the national resistance movement.

The South Vietnamese Armed Forces and U.S. Military Support

Beginning in 1954 the United States provided generous economic support and provided advisors and military equipment to build the South Vietnamese armed forces. The number of U.S. advisors and trainers grew from three hundred in 1955 to almost a thousand by 1960. The initial policy of the U.S. military was to build the South Vietnamese army into a 150,000–200,000-man conventional force capable of meeting an invasion by North Vietnam. Given the recent experience of the Korean War, such a strategy made a good deal of sense. However, sticking to the policy of building a highly conventional army did not address the threat of the insurgency when it began in 1959.[9] The main problems that were to plague the South Vietnamese armed forces for the whole of their existence began early and were never adequately addressed by either the Vietnamese or their American advisors. As noted, the French had left Vietnam with a cadre of well-trained and experienced Vietnamese soldiers. The Vietnamese officer and NCO corps had gone through French military training schools and had compiled a solid record in combat against the Viet Minh. The Vietnamese tradition readily accepted conscription and service to the nation, and the average Vietnamese had the qualities that make up a good soldier—the Viet Minh victory over the French certainly proved that. Yet the story of the Vietnamese armed forces is one of a huge waste of potentially excellent soldiers.

The ruination of the South Vietnamese army began with policies put into place by Diem and never corrected. First of all, the officers of the South Vietnamese army were recruited only from the Vietnamese elites, with no opportunity granted to either superior NCOs or junior soldiers to advance to officer rank. Getting an officer commission required a high school diploma, an educational attainment restricted to Vietnam's elite and middle classes. Under Diem the officer corps was politicized to the point that the only thing that mattered was personal loyalty to the president. Advancement came from having the right connections and the right family. Competent officers would serve in the field for years, prove themselves in combat, and then be passed over for promotion by a Saigon staff officer with better connections. In addition to a renunciation of the meritocratic principle, the South Vietnamese leadership tolerated, even encouraged a huge degree of corruption among the officer corps. Diem's downfall did nothing to decrease either the incompetence or the corruption of the officer corps. When General Thieu came to power as South Vietnam's president, the U.S. advisors recommended changing the promotion system to reflect more merit considerations. Thieu refused such advice and insisted that all promotions to lieutenant colonel and higher rank be personally made by himself.[10]

The South Vietnamese Army also failed to adequately train its soldiers or care for them. The problem centered on the social structure of the army, typical of many third world nations both then and today. The officer corps was recruited exclusively from the upper classes, and virtually all the soldiers from the rural peasantry. The middle class could easily buy exemptions for their sons and avoid conscription entirely. Thus, officers scarcely identified with their men, nor was there an ethic of caring for the soldiers. The officers lived well and managed to enhance their salaries through corruption. The average soldier lived on little pay, and little attention was paid to providing for the soldier's family or the soldier's medical care.[11] Although the army began with a solid training program left by the French, the South Vietnamese officers neglected to provide funds or personnel for proper training of their soldiers. One of the common complaints of South Vietnamese soldiers was that they had never been properly trained to use their rifles and weapons in combat. In many cases South Vietnamese units were ambushed and cut to pieces by the Viet Cong simply because the ARVN soldier did not know basic tactics or even how to fire his rifle.[12] Given the generally low standard of leadership in the South Vietnamese forces, the poor conditions for the soldier and the low level of training, it is a wonder that so many units actually fought fairly well.

When open insurgency broke out in 1958–1959, the U.S. government was highly concerned and responded with increased U.S. aid. Despite the characterization of the Eisenhower era military as being overly concerned with nuclear war and conventional war, there were also substantial efforts made to provide military aid and advisors to allied nations threatened by insurgency. From 1957 on, the Eisenhower administration increased its efforts in the counterinsurgency arena. A program managed by the International Cooperation Agency provided training in police administration and counterinsurgency to over six hundred thousand police in twenty-one countries. A 1959 president's task force to recommend military aid reforms endorsed increasing the training and preparation for American military personnel serving as trainers and advisors, and increasing the number of personnel trained as specialists in counterguerrilla and psychological operations. The army developed a new counterinsurgency doctrine manual in 1960, "Military Operations Against Irregular Forces," based on principles well established from the U.S. and British successful postwar experience in defeating communist insurgencies in Greece, the Philippines, and Malaya. The army also laid the groundwork for a new course in counterinsurgency operations to be opened at Ft. Bragg in January 1961.[13]

The Kennedy administration came into office with an enthusiasm to change the Eisenhower era doctrine. From the start; Kennedy emphasized his interest in counterinsurgency warfare and in developing a corps of elite special forces to spearhead American advisory and aid efforts. Given the efforts of the Eisenhower administration from 1957 to 1961, there was a sound doctrine and small cadre of well-trained personnel to build on, and the air force and army quickly responded by raising special warfare units to specialize in counterinsurgency. With the insurgency in South Vietnam growing, the number of U.S. advisors was immediately tripled to three thousand personnel. In addition, U.S. logistics support units were deployed to Vietnam in 1961 to support the increase in military aid and training programs. By 1963 America would have over twenty thousand trainers, advisors, and support troops in Vietnam.

At this point the U.S. doctrine was to employ the special forces units to support the South Vietnamese in a counterinsurgency campaign. On the surface, Diem's counterinsurgency strategy looked similar to the successful counterinsurgency operations in Malaya and the Philippines. For example, a "strategic hamlet" program was established to provide security for the rural population now under constant pressure from the Viet Cong. Peasants would be moved from their small villages to large villages built by the government and garrisoned by regional soldiers and militia. With the population secure, the regular forces would be free to conduct large-scale operations to seek and destroy the enemy. The problem with Diem's strategy, which was supported by U.S. aid money and encouraged by U.S. advisors, was that it never addressed rural discontent, which was about the misadministration of the country by Diem's officials and the often abusive land tenure and rental system of the great landowners—who were usually Diem supporters. In addition, the strategic hamlet program was a poor fit with Vietnamese culture. The Vietnamese were not only emotionally tied to their native villages, as one would expect in a peasant society, but the Confucian and Buddhist traditions of Vietnam placed great emphasis on being close to and maintaining the ancestral grave sites. Veneration of one's ancestors, a cultural/religious trait that even included the Catholics, was a core element of village life. Moving people away from their ancestral villages so that they could no longer maintain their ancestors' graves was highly resented. Indeed, despite early billing as a great success by U.S. advisors, the strategic hamlet program was largely a flop. The Viet Cong had little problem in infiltrating their supporters into the villages, and from 1961 to 1963 proved that they could overrun the small local garrisons almost at will.

Rise of the Insurgency

After their victory in 1954, the North Vietnamese government concentrated on rebuilding and reorganizing their country on a communist model and organizing a capable professional armed forces. The North Vietnamese, supported with some military and economic aid from the Soviet Union, took the largely guerrilla Viet Minh force and developed it into a large, well-trained conventional army. Officer, NCO, and specialist schools were established, and a competent leadership cadre developed.[14] While North Vietnamese officers were expected to be Communist Party members and supporters, and all soldiers were subjected to a considerable amount of political education, under General Vo Nguyen Giap officer selection and promotion were determined by competence and merit and not by politics. It was the essential difference between North Vietnamese and South Vietnamese military leadership. Under Diem, South Vietnam's army became more and more politicized as promotions went to Diem supporters regardless of competence.

In 1956, with the signs of internal dissent already becoming obvious in South Vietnam, the Communist Party leadership of North Vietnam established contact with some anti-Diem resistance members in the South (the Cochin China Party) and urged them to develop their political organization

135

and create self-defense units. Initially, the self-defense units would merely serve to guard the local party and organization—with the understanding that, in the future, they could be turned into active guerrilla units when the opportunity for military action arose.[15]

By late 1958 the South Vietnamese anti-Diem resistance had raised almost two hundred platoon-sized military units, mostly in central South Vietnam where the Viet Minh had been especially strong. By early 1959 both the anti-Diem southerners and the North Vietnamese leadership believed the time had come for open resistance. The North Vietnamese established a military transportation group to funnel weapons, supplies, and advisors from North Vietnam to the Viet Cong cadres in the south.[16]

Once the insurgency had begun, it spread rapidly. By 1961 large swaths of the countryside were effectively in the hands of the insurgents. At the start of the insurgency, the anti-Diem forces created a shadow government, the National Liberation Front, which was not overtly communist at the time— although it readily accepted advice and aid from the North. The NLF shadow government quickly became a pervasive fact of South Vietnamese life. Large landowners and businesses would not be targeted if they paid a regular tax to the NLF. Special teams of guerrilla fighters carefully targeted pro-Diem local leaders for assassination, thereby sending a message to cooperate with the NLF or else. The NLF shadow government and administration were, in most respects, more efficient than the hopelessly corrupt Diem government. "Taxes" collected by the shadow government financed a regular fighting force as well as professional political cadres to carry out propaganda and organization work among the population. The NLF was thus supported by local resources. Equipped with a hodgepodge of weaponry, left over from the war against the French or captured and stolen from the South Vietnamese Army (ARVN), the guerrilla units of the NLF (which contained many experienced former Viet Minh soldiers) were soon able to take on ARVN companies and battalions and defeat them.

The U.S. Strategic Dilemma and the Fall of Diem

In the early 1960s U.S.A.F. General Edward Lansdale, who had been a very successful advisor to the Philippine government in the 1950s, and British counterinsurgency expert Sir Robert Thompson, who had served in Malaya, urged the U.S. military to undertake a concerted counterinsurgency campaign in Vietnam. They argued for a comprehensive civil/military strategy based on the example of the successful campaigns in Malaya and the Philippines. These campaigns had included land reform, government reform, and economic development as well as a military effort geared to secure the population from the insurgents. It was sound advice, but success in suppressing the Huk rebellion in the Philippines and defeating the communist insurgency in Malaya was highly dependent upon the ability of the Philippine and Malayan governments to carry out major reform programs that met the legitimate grievances of the population and allowed the disaffected factions a voice in the government. In the Philippines General Lansdale had worked closely with the defense minister, later president, Ramon Magsaysay, who pushed reforms at every level and readily fired corrupt and incompetent military officers and government officials. In Malaya British high commissioner General Gerald Templer turned a failing counterinsurgency effort around by building an effective police and Malayan military, ruthlessly weeding out corrupt and abusive officers. Another key factor in defusing the Malayan insurgency was the policy of the main Malayan nationalist parties to include the disaffected Chinese population—the center of the insurgency—in the governance of a new Malayan state.[17]

Unfortunately, no U.S.-backed aid and counterinsurgency program built on such successful models could work in South Vietnam as long as the South Vietnamese government refused to enact fundamental political reform or to decrease the rampant corruption and incompetence in the government and military leadership. Better and more open government in the 1950s and early 1960s would have rapidly defused the grievances that fueled the insurgency. For nine years the South Vietnamese were saddled with the incompetent Diem regime. Although thoughtful analysts and observers saw Diem as the problem, the American media and political leadership tended to see the sophisticated, Westernized, and English-speaking South Vietnamese leader as the salvation of his country.[18] In 1959 *Newsweek* magazine called Diem, "One of the ablest free Asian leaders." U.S. Senator Mike Mansfield, an ex-professor of Asian history, praised Diem for "forestalling a total collapse in South Vietnam and in bringing a measure of order and hope out of chaos, intrigue, and widespread corruption."[19]

But there were plenty of other reports from experienced soldiers and observers that the Diem regime and its counterinsurgency campaign was doing badly. In 1963 the crisis that had been building for years finally forced the Kennedy administration to see reality. Having alienated so many of South Vietnam's groups, President Diem now pushed the nation's influential Buddhist leadership into open opposition. Diem, a Catholic who clearly favored his own minority religion, required that Buddhist flags be flown under the national flag on ceremonial occasions. In protest to several of Diem's official actions that slighted the Buddhist majority of Vietnam, several prominent monks publicly immolated themselves in protest, an event widely covered by the international media. Diem's influential sister-in-law, the president's official hostess, gleefully referred to the suicides of the Buddhist leaders as "barbeques." Through 1963 the country dissolved in riots and demonstrations. Finally the Kennedy administration, seeing no alternative, quietly endorsed a coup against Diem in early October 1963. Diem and one of his brothers were murdered by the coup leaders, whereupon General Nguyen Khanh took over power.[20]

This new government was in power for no more than a few months before it, in turn, was toppled by yet another group of generals and colonels. Through 1964 and 1965, South Vietnam turned into a straightforward military dictatorship as factions of officers fought among themselves, and the military situation in the countryside became ever bleaker. Finally, in 1965–1966 General Thieu came to the front as a compromise national leader with the young air force general Nguyen Cao Ky serving as his premier. Although the American government was continually optimistic that successive South Vietnamese governments would enact major reforms, the militarized and factionalized South Vietnamese never found the will to deal with internal problems.

To the Kennedy administration, South Vietnam was seen as a strategically vital bastion against communist encroachment in Asia. The Truman administration had viewed South Korea as a major battlefront against international communism—meaning the Soviet Union and Red China. Likewise, the Kennedy administration saw Vietnam as a major anticommunist battlefront. There was the domestic policy consideration also to take into account. The Truman administration had been accused, however unfairly, of "losing" China to the communists. Since Cuba had recently become a communist state and communism was spreading its influence in Latin America, Thailand, and Laos, a failure to hold the line in Vietnam was seen as a potential major blow to American power and prestige, and any perception of American failure would certainly become a central issue in the next election. Allowing the NLF or a coalition government that included communists to assume power in Vietnam was an inconceivable option for the Kennedy, and later Johnson, administrations.

American Strategic Decision Making From Eisenhower to Johnson

The strategic decision-making process in the Eisenhower administration was rather cautious, yet comprehensive. The U.S. focus in the era was on building up NATO and Europe and on developing an effective nuclear force that would deter the Soviet Union. In dealing with military issues, the Eisenhower administration favored a deliberate planning approach. The Joint Chiefs of Staff employed a large staff of planners to give the president a wide array of options to deal with probable crises. Although the U.S. military was used to intervene in Lebanon in 1958, mindful of the recent experience of the Korean War Eisenhower was reluctant to directly involve U.S. combat forces into any situation counted in the periphery of U.S. national interests.

Rather than use military force, Eisenhower preferred to combat Soviet and communist influence in the developing nations through a mix of covert operations, information campaigns, and U.S. aid and advisors to support allied nations. In Iran in 1953 and in Guatemala, the CIA helped local forces topple regimes that were considered too leftist. In Europe and the third world, Eisenhower strongly supported a broad propaganda program to combat communist and leftist ideology. The U.S. information program, directed largely through the U.S. Information Service, developed films, magazines, and radio programs showing the American and democratic worldview and opposing the communist ideologies that had such a broad appeal to the people and governments in the developing nations.[21]

Eisenhower viewed U.S. economic assistance programs and military aid programs as a sensible alternative to employing U.S. force. In order to arrange the withdrawal of most U.S. forces from Korea after the July 1953 armistice, Eisenhower poured large amounts of military and economic aid into Korea. He placed a high priority on training and equipping the South Korean army, a mission that was highly successful in rapidly improving South Korea's ability to defend itself and deter aggression from the north. In Eisenhower's view, generous support of America's allies through economic aid and military assistance was far less expensive than committing U.S. forces.

The Kennedy administration inherited a fairly stable world, though one with many major trouble spots. The departing Eisenhower administration, highly concerned about the situation in Laos and Vietnam, warned the incoming president about the potential crises. For their part, Kennedy and his senior advisors wanted a bold new approach to challenge the communist threat. Kennedy led campaigns for building up American nuclear, and especially conventional, military capabilities. He believed that the United States needed a greater range of military options to deal with threats less than a nuclear war with the Soviet Union. The new "flexible response" policy also favored a major increase in the special forces units in the military.

President Kennedy came into office with a team of mostly young, fresh foreign policy and defense experts whom David Halberstam aptly labeled "The Best and the Brightest."[22] McGeorge Bundy, brought in from the deanship of Harvard at age 34 and considered brilliant by his contemporaries, served as President Kennedy's national security advisor. Walt Rostow was another academic brought into the inner circle. Rostow was an economist at MIT who specialized in the economics of developing nations. He had also served as an Army Air Forces targeting expert as a young major in World War II. Rostow served as Bundy's deputy until he took over as the president's national security advisor in 1966. Most central to the policy development of the Kennedy administration was Secretary of Defense Robert McNamara, an expert on management and statistics who had recently been appointed as president of Ford Motors. McNamara had served as a staff officer in the Army Air Corps during World War II and had conducted operational data analysis. He took the helm as head of the U.S. military with a firm belief that the principles of scientific management should be applied to developing military forces and strategy. Convinced of his own brilliance, McNamara considered the top generals not as allies or experts, but as dinosaurs who held on to a view of warfare that was fifteen years out of date and who had failed to appreciate the revolutionary changes that technology and management had wrought. The core members of the Kennedy team, filled with confidence and a belief in their abilities, quickly took action to purge the armed forces' leadership of those officers they viewed as obstacles.

Former army chief of staff Maxwell Taylor, a highly vocal opponent of Eisenhower's strategy of reliance on nuclear weapons, was brought into a special post as "military advisor to the president" created specifically for him. It was actually a holding post until the chairman of the joint chiefs, General Lyman Lemnitzer, could be retired and Taylor given his job. The purge at the top of the military leadership and replacement of top officers with men beholden to the Kennedy administration was a step in creating a politicized military leadership who would not object to the theories pushed by the administration.[23] It was, in fact, highly unfair to characterize the top generals as "Eisenhower's men." Senior officers of the era, such as NATO commander General Lauris Norstad, were fundamentally apolitical. Although they had known Eisenhower throughout his military career and had served with him during World War II, they should not have been suspected of having any hostility to a new generation coming into office. Norstad, who was highly respected by the Europeans, earned McNamara's enmity early in the administration during the Berlin Crisis of 1961. Norstad dutifully and correctly warned McNamara that since NATO allies had only a limited commitment to fighting over Berlin, they would be unlikely to approve U.S. plans of stepped up escalation based on employment of tactical nuclear weapons. As the crisis over Berlin grew, and the NATO allies behaved exactly as Norstad had predicted, McNamara blamed Norstad personally for the European failure to accept his positions. The next year Norstad was rudely fired and retired as NATO commander over the objections of America's allies. At the same time, Maxwell Taylor, who was generally distrusted by the army's senior officers precisely because he was seen as too much of a political "operator," was slipped into the chairmanship of the Joint Chiefs of Staff.

141

McNamara's message to the military was clear: They were subservient to him, and challenges to his policies would not be tolerated.

We can see an interesting contrast in the style of strategic leadership between the Eisenhower and Kennedy Administrations. On strategic issues Eisenhower sought out a broad range of views, tolerating quite open debate between branches of government and branches of the military. Eisenhower, who had the final say, allowed a considerable degree of debate among his top military and civilian leaders. Neither the military nor the civilians were cut out of the process. There was plenty of very healthy friction to ensure that a wide variety of policy options were reviewed and considered. In contrast, Kennedy preferred a looser, more ad hoc strategic process. While Eisenhower had employed the methodology of a military staff to develop strategy, Kennedy's national security staff took on what Lawrence Freedman calls "an academic-type model." Bundy acted much like the Harvard dean that he had been. Instead of a strict hierarchical structure, his preference was to study issues through brainstorming and ad hoc groups. This approach made for a poor circulation of information and considerable confusion. In Freedman's words, nobody was "quite clear on whether the president knew all he needed to know or exactly what he had decided." As we shall see, the academic-style decision-making model also meant that the policy process could be overly influenced by enthusiasts and ideologues, and there was no assurance that all policy options were properly studied and criticized.[24]

The Kennedy administration's preference for restricting national military and strategic policy making to a close inner circle around the president was soon shown to be seriously flawed. The first major crisis of the administration was one of its own making. In April 1961 the CIA embarked on a hapless operation to topple Fidel Castro's Cuban dictatorship through a U.S.–sponsored invasion of Cuba at the Bay of Pigs. The operation was a model of bad planning, poor assumptions, and bad intelligence. Virtually the entire Cuban exile force was killed or captured by Castro's army. While publicly accepting the blame for the disaster, Kennedy privately blamed the military for the failure, although the military had been shut out of the planning for the CIA operation. The Cuban fiasco was followed by the Berlin crisis of 1961, which was also handled poorly by the administration. While the Europeans publicly stood alongside the United States to support the existence of West Berlin, privately there was a considerable loss of confidence in the competence of U.S. leadership. At the 1962 conference of the NATO powers at Athens, America's European allies were again offended by McNamara's blunt demand that Europe dramatically increase its conventional defense spending.

Indeed, the Kennedy administration went blundering through military and foreign policy problems until the Cuban missile crisis of October 1962. Kennedy employed his ad hoc style of strategic policy making during the crisis. Largely through pure luck, war was averted and the U.S. emerged with a Soviet pledge to withdraw its nuclear missiles from Cuba—but only at the cost of withdrawing the U.S. nuclear weapons that had been deployed to Greece and Turkey. The Cuban Missile Crisis was a great public relations victory for Kennedy, but in the end it was something of a draw. Moreover, the Soviets had undermined years of U.S.-led efforts to build a European nuclear force.

One of the primary effects of the Cuban Missile Crisis was to reinforce Kennedy and his national security team in their belief in themselves and their brilliance. The military leaders, who had advised a military solution, were privately denigrated by Kennedy's inner circle. The lucky outcome of the crisis was attributed to the policy of overruling military recommendations and following their own, largely intuitive, judgments. From 1961 through 1963, the Kennedy administration's strategic planning for Vietnam focused on counterinsurgency, although the problems of the Diem regime also called for developing strategies for the direct commitment of U.S. forces to Vietnam if it should become necessary. At this time Walt Rostow began developing a plan to coerce North Vietnam into ending the insurgency in the South through the application of American airpower to destroy selected targets in North Vietnam. Rostow theorized that destroying part of North Vietnam's industrial and military infrastructure from the air would force the northerners to the conference table, and to withdraw their support from the southern insurgents. Under Rostow's theory of gradual escalation, bombing North Vietnam would not, in itself, be expected to annihilate the enemy. Rather, bombing certain targets would send a message to the north and threaten them with further bombing and destruction for refusal to cooperate and compromise.

Rostow's theory of coercion through airpower and the threat of escalation was based on two assumptions—both of which were to prove disastrously false. The first assumption was that the center of gravity of the insurgency in the south was not the NLF forces in the south, but rather the North Vietnamese. The reasoning went that, if North Vietnam ended its support for the insurgency in the south, the insurgency would quickly collapse. The second assumption was that the North Vietnamese valued their limited industrial infrastructure so highly, they would quickly abandon their long-term goals for national unification if that infrastructure were threatened. Both assumptions had little basis in fact or in even the most superficial understanding of the Vietnamese people. Before 1965 and the introduction of North Vietnamese Army (NVA) units into the south, aid to the NLF rebels was quite limited. As to the second assumption, in their war against the French the North Vietnamese leadership and people had shown a tremendous strength of will, operational talent, and readiness to accept massive losses in order to defeat a foreign power. In developing Rostow's gradual escalation plans and the later U.S. Air Force bombing campaign plans, apparently no one at the top levels of the U.S. government or military took the time to truly study and understand the North Vietnamese leadership.

For their part, the North Vietnamese were absolutely clear as to their final goals and the price they were willing to pay. The North Vietnamese repeatedly proclaimed their goal of national unification. One of the most eloquent expressions of North Vietnamese policy was made by Chairman Ho Chi Minh in an address to the whole people of North Vietnam in July 1966, several months after the initiation of a major U.S. bombing campaign in the north. "This war may go on for five more years, ten more years, twenty more years, or even more. Hanoi, Haiphong, and a number of our other cities and enterprises may be destroyed, but the people of Vietnam are not afraid. There is nothing more precious than independence and freedom. When victory finally comes, our people will rebuild our nation so that it is even better, even more beautiful, than it was before."[25]

Through 1964 it became evident that the post-Diem South Vietnamese regimes were not going to be able to effectively counter the growing insurgency. The Kennedy team, now working for President Johnson, developed several policy options to directly employ U.S. forces. Just what form the U.S. direct involvement would take was a matter of some intense debate. After four years of wandering through various policy initiatives, listening to various U.S. military and civilian advisors, attempting several military strategies and dealing with a succession of South Vietnamese governments, President Johnson and the team that he had inherited from John Kennedy were no closer to any clear strategy for South Vietnam than they had been at the beginning.

The Gulf of Tonkin Resolution, passed overwhelmingly by Congress after a minor naval skirmish between a U.S. Navy task force and North Vietnamese torpedo boats, gave President Johnson a virtual blank check to employ U.S. forces in South Vietnam. In November the U.S. government was given a further impetus to increase American involvement in the war when the Viet Cong attacked the U.S. air base at Bien Hoa in South Vietnam, damaging some U.S. aircraft and inflicting several dozen American casualties. Johnson's military leaders offered him three options: He could maintain the status quo, he could carry out a large-scale air offensive against North Vietnam—the solution favored by the Joint Chiefs, or he could accept Walt Rostow's graduated response theory of air attack. The memory of the Korean War stalemate was still fresh in the minds of the president's staff, and the strategic problem was finding a means to convince the North Vietnamese to abandon the war while avoiding a level of escalation that could bring China into the conflict. Rostow, strongly backed by McGeorge Bundy, was one of the most ideological personalities in the circle around Johnson, and also one of the most convincing."[26] With respect to the Vietnam War, Rostow has been called the "Most aggressive civilian member of the John F. Kennedy and Lyndon B. Johnson administrations."[27] In November 1964 an interagency working group chaired by Assistant Secretary of State William Bundy proposed to President Johnson that the United States conduct a series of graduated strikes on the North as a means of signaling U.S. determination.

In contrast, the U.S. Air Force under the command of General Curtis LeMay proposed a strategic bombing campaign reminiscent of World War II, in which ninety-four major targets would be heavily bombed over a sixteen-day period. LeMay argued that this would immediately cripple North Vietnam's ability to wage war.[28] In general, Johnson was leery of bombing strategies and, given the choice, the Rostow theory seemed the best compromise among the options given to him.[29]

McNamara and Johnson had already decided upon committing considerable U.S. forces to Vietnam, but wanted the support of—and cover from—the Joint Chiefs of Staff. In July 1965, before meeting with the president, Johnson insisted that the chiefs were not to discuss appropriations or mobilization of U.S. military forces—the two most important and disputed elements of any strategic discussion. During the meeting of the Joint Chiefs and the president, all of the service chiefs except commandant of the Marine Corps General Wallace Greene, expressed misgivings on the expansion of the U.S. role in Vietnam. The senior U.S. military chiefs also provided some prudent advice. If the United States were to commit to fight a major war in Vietnam, the cost would be considerable. Reserve forces would have to be mobilized to ensure that the United States maintained a strategic reserve in case of crisis elsewhere in the world. The new deployments of forces—up to forty-five combat battalions, the equivalent of five divisions, would cost an estimated $12.7 billion. The deployment of the 1st Marine Division to Vietnam would leave the United States with no strategic reserve. In short, the Vietnam War would require considerable resources, and funding a major U.S. buildup would threaten Johnson's first priority—the "Great Society" programs to cure the ills of domestic poverty and underdevelopment.[30]

Johnson rightly feared that a full disclosure of the extent of the U.S. buildup in Vietnam would undermine his domestic legislative agenda, so he decided that he would limit additional funding for the military to the $1 billion increase already in the 1966 appropriations bill. Somehow, the generals would have to figure out how to fight a major war on the cheap. Secretary McNamara provided a cover for the lack of a strategic reserve in the United States by arguing that his systems analysis had decided that the 4th Marine Division, a reserve unit, could be mobilized in two weeks instead of the ninety days that the military planned for in such mobilizations. The change from ninety to fourteen days in the strategic accounting dumbfounded the generals. However, the generals loyally went along with the president, although army chief of staff General Harold Johnson believed that the failure to mobilize the reserves for such a major military commitment would likely be disastrous.[31] Johnson and McNamara soon went before Congress offering a rosy picture of the U.S. buildup in Vietnam, deliberately underestimating the funding for the war by $10 billion. By such means President Johnson had expanded the war and the U.S. strategy in a deceitful manner, fearing that candid disclosure of his plans to increase U.S. forces in Vietnam would incite political opposition.[32]

The Joint Chiefs were nervous about the introduction of U.S. combat units into Vietnam in April 1965. Nevertheless, Johnson's advisors convinced the president that deploying U.S. troops would "break the will of the NVA/VC by depriving them of victory."[33] The general view in the president's circle in 1965 was that the war would be quickly won once the United States had committed its forces. McNamara was slightly less optimistic than Bundy and Rostow, believing that it would take six months, perhaps a year or two, to demonstrate the Viet Cong failure in the south.[34]

U.S. Strategy in Vietnam, 1965–1968

Despite the recent counterinsurgency successes in Greece, Malaya, and the Philippines, coupled with reports and recommendations from knowledgeable experts such as General Edward Lansdale and Sir Robert Thompson, the senior military leaders refused to see the conflict in South Vietnam in 1964 and 1965 as an insurgency. In the 1960s counterinsurgency warfare, in the minds of a senior officer corps that had fought in World War II and Korea, was something on the fringe, and certainly not what they were trained for or mentally equipped to handle. The Army thought in terms of divisional combat, employing tanks and advanced technologies such as helicopters, guided rockets, and tactical nuclear weapons. The Air Force was wedded to the doctrine of strategic bombing as the most effective and decisive means to end a war. One example of the conventional war mindset of the military leadership when confronted with counterinsurgency was Air Force General Frederic Smith's advocating the use of tactical nuclear weapons against Maoist-type guerrillas. In a 1960 article in *Air University Review* and in testimony to Congress in 1962, the four-star general advocated using nuclear weapons for "situation control," that is, exploiting nuclear fires to obviate enemy assembly, movement, and combat operations. His article specifically used Indochina as an example of how extensive use of nuclear weapons could defeat insurgents, closing with the certain belief that, rather than accept slavery under communism, the Asian peasants would accept the irradiation of their homeland.[35]

From 1962 to 1965, the circle of strategists around the president and the senior American military leaders focused on North Vietnam and its armed forces as the center of gravity. By focusing on an enemy state that had a conventional armed forces and an infrastructure and targets that could be attacked through strategic bombing, the U.S. military leadership could plan for the type of war they understood. Despite frequent lip service to conducting counterinsurgency operations, bolstering the South Vietnamese armed forces, and securing the population, the U.S. military leadership was fundamentally uninterested in counterinsurgency warfare. This conventional war strategic focus ignored the obvious realities on the ground. In 1964 when the United States was planning to take military action against North Vietnam to end the insurgency, General Paul Harkins, commander of the U.S. Military Assistance Command in Vietnam (MACV), would blatantly ignore the fact that 80–90 percent of the guerrilla fighters in the south were locally recruited. Indeed, there was little proof that the insurgent National Liberation Front was dependent upon northern supplies.

Counterinsurgency is probably the most political of all wars, and success at the local political level often determines the success or failure of an insurgency. As recent campaigns had proven, successful counterinsurgency was more dependent upon factors such as building government legitimacy and meeting the economic needs of the peasants than it was upon military force. Countering insurgency required a level of imagination and critical thought that was beyond the mindset of the president's cabinet, staff, and senior military officers. For the Kennedy and Johnson circle of strategic advisors, as well as for generals such as William Westmoreland, war in the 1960s was much more of a science than an art. McNamara stressed the application of business methods and statistical analysis in fighting wars. Once on the ground and in command in Vietnam, Westmoreland enthusiastically followed the same approach, pushing his staff to generate vast amounts of data and analysis that would enable Westmoreland and the senior commanders to fine-tune operations to rapidly destroy the Viet Cong and North Vietnamese.

The war in Vietnam was quickly Americanized with the introduction of U.S. combat troops in the spring of 1965. Once U.S. troops were on the ground, the South Vietnamese army was essentially shunted aside. As for combat operations, the U.S. commanders generally preferred to do without the cooperation of the usually poorly trained, led, and equipped ARVN (Army of the Republic of Vietnam). Most Americans considered the ARVN to be useful only in static defensive roles—if even that. Since Westmoreland and the senior U.S. commanders believed that the U.S. troops and bombing campaign would bring a quick conventional victory, it would not really be necessary to take the time and trouble to retrain, re-equip and develop an effective South Vietnamese army. Although the United States continued to support, train, and advise the South Vietnamese military, it was clearly a low priority mission in contrast to the emphasis on U.S. conventional operations.[36]

Westmoreland's conventional war strategy was outlined in two 1965 directives. In September 1965, with over one hundred thousand U.S. troops already in the country, Westmoreland asserted that his strategy was to resume the offensive to destroy the Viet Cong. If Viet Cong forces were located, an "aggressive operation should be mounted using clearly superior forces, firepower, and mobility." The goal was "to defeat the VC decisively."[37]

Westmoreland insisted on a conventional war campaign that relied upon American mobility, provided by helicopters, and massive firepower, provided by the air force and the army artillery, to find, trap, and annihilate the North Vietnamese army units that had infiltrated into the south. On the other side, the North Vietnamese leadership understood that the Americans would be fighting with major advantages in firepower, logistics, and mobility. The senior officers who had fought against the French knew what it was like to fight a technologically superior enemy. Yet when the U.S. way of war was demonstrated in the first major U.S.–North Vietnamese clashes in the Ia Drang Valley in 1965, the skill and effectiveness of the U.S. forces, backed up with air mobility provided by helicopters, still came as a shock to the North Vietnamese. The amount of firepower the United States could bring to the battle was awesome. These factors forced the North Vietnamese to reevaluate their tactics to deal with Westmoreland's "search and destroy" operations.

From 1965 to 1968, the North Vietnamese often preferred to avoid combat with the Americans, except on terrain of their own choosing or when they could carry out a surprise attack or raid. Whenever possible the North Vietnamese would ambush American units and "hug them close," so that the Americans could not employ the awesome firepower of close support aircraft against them without fear of hitting American soldiers as well. The North Vietnamese also made a practice of choosing good defensive terrain and digging in deep to minimize the American firepower advantage. This tactic forced the Americans to take their positions through infantry assaults, which usually resulted in heavy casualties on both sides. Despite the U.S. advantage in mobility and firepower, North Vietnamese units fought a skilled war and were rarely encircled and annihilated. Despite heavy losses, the North Vietnamese were normally able to pull back and rebuild their units. Both sides ended up fighting a war of attrition, with the North Vietnamese paying by far the heavier price.

The assumption of Johnson's strategic advisors, that the North Vietnamese would fold once U.S. troops entered the war, quickly proved false. The North Vietnamese speeded up their deployment of forces to the south, as did the Americans. By mid-1966 the United States had more than 350,000 troops in South Vietnam. By 1967 there were more than 400,000, with plans to deploy another 100,000 men.[38] The North Vietnamese matched the U.S. effort. By the end of 1966 the North Vietnamese had increased its armed forces to 690,000 soldiers and claimed to have 230,000 troops serving in South Vietnam.[39] Despite U.S. bombing, the North Vietnamese were able to dramatically expand their army and military infrastructure—including their heavy weapons, artillery units, and support units. North Vietnam paid a high price: Their official history notes that losses against the Americans were heavy and that some of their commanders became "gun-shy" of American firepower. The morale and effectiveness of North Vietnamese units in heavy combat against the Americans fell noticeably, and providing adequate logistics support became ever more difficult.[40] On the other hand, simple demographics played into North Vietnam's favor in facing an attrition war. North Vietnam's high birth rate ensured that every year 50,000 more young men would reach military age and be available for service. This meant that the North Vietnamese army, combined with the manpower pool of the Viet Cong, could carry on the fight indefinitely, even if U.S. and South Vietnamese soldiers could kill huge numbers of enemy troops.

In his decision not to implement a counterinsurgency strategy to secure the South Vietnamese peasants, Westmoreland failed to consider the very successful program developed by the U.S. Marine Corps. Starting with their deployment in 1965, the marines had set up small detachments called "combined action platoons" in villages throughout the northern region of the Republic of Vietnam. Platoons of fourteen marines lived in the villages with the Vietnamese, organizing and training village home guard platoons to be responsible for the security of the immediate village. These combined action platoons ranked among the most effective counterinsurgency programs ever developed by the U.S. military. The presence of the marines and the home guards in the small villages made it impossible for the Viet Cong to operate in rural areas where they had once held sway. The villagers, for their part, were reassured by the permanent presence of U.S. forces, which were a guarantee that they would not be abandoned to the mercies of the Viet Cong. The presence of small U.S. units in the villages also assured the villagers that their farms would not become free fire zones for excessive U.S. firepower. At the peak of the program in 1970, the U.S. deployed 114 combined action platoons, with 2,200 marine and navy personnel. General Westmoreland, whose attitude was typical of the army's fixation on large conventional operations and success measured by enemy body counts, did not care for the methodical approach of the combined action platoons. This was an approach that provided little in the way of body counts, or data indicating military success. So Westmoreland devoted only one paragraph in his memoirs to argue that he never had enough troops to carry out such a program in the rest of Vietnam. Actually, to have secured two thousand villages and 7 million peasants in the manner of the marines would have required 28,000 U.S. troops—about 5 percent of Westmoreland's total force in Vietnam.[41]

The other part of the American strategy for quick victory was the bombing campaign against the north. The bombing of strategic targets in North Vietnam that began in 1965 would continue for three years. The initial attacks were intended to shock the North Vietnamese and cripple their military by taking out the fuel storage facilities in the north. The North Vietnamese responded to the destruction of their fuel by bringing in fuel from ships in fifty-gallon barrels and stockpiling it in small depots all around the country. The bombing continued with a switch to other targets. Hanoi remained off-limits for political reasons, and North Vietnam's major port of Haiphong remained untouched out of fear of hitting a Soviet ship, or even a ship of one of our allies, and causing an international crisis. Johnson personally managed the air war during his famous Tuesday afternoon lunches with Secretary of State Dean Rusk, McNamara, McGeorge Bundy, and press secretary Bill Moyers. At these lunches Johnson would personally review and approve the list of bombing targets in North Vietnam. This was a case of civilian micromanagement of the war to the highest degree. Only in October 1967 did someone think of bringing a military representative into the discussions about using military force.[42]

The military complained that the bombing campaign was not enough, nor had the right targets been hit. Admiral U.S. Grant Sharpe, commander in chief in the Pacific, argued constantly for an expanded bombing campaign, as did the Joint Chiefs and the air force staff. However, McNamara rarely consulted with his generals on such matters, preferring the advice of his assistant for international security affairs, John McNaughton.[43] Walt Rostow, promoted to presidential national security advisor in 1966, maintained a firm faith in the efficacy of his gradual response theory, and remained a consistent advocate for bombing selected targets in North Vietnam right up to the suspension of the bombing campaign in 1968. Ignoring the advice of professional soldiers and airmen in developing and ordering bombing strategies left the administration open to decades of "if only" memoirs from retired military men, who would argue that a decisive bombing campaign, unlike the gradual response strategy, would have forced the North Vietnamese to concede defeat.[44]

The point is that bombing simply did not work. By April 1967 the U.S. Air Force and Navy had struck almost three hundred targets in North Vietnam—virtually all the targets on the expanded list first proposed by the Joint Chiefs of Staff. One of the largest sustained bombing campaigns in history, with more than six hundred thousand tons of bombs dropped on North Vietnam, had little impact on North Vietnam's ability to wage war. As with the attacks on fuel, the North Vietnamese usually found some simple means to work around the damage.[45] Damage inflicted upon North Vietnam's transportation system from 1966 to 1968 was restored with astonishing rapidity.[46] Considering that 47 percent of American expenditure in Vietnam between 1965 and 1968 went to air operations, the United States got surprisingly little for this massive expense.[47] On the other hand, the United States lost approximately one thousand aircraft over North Vietnam, and hundreds of American aircrew were taken prisoner—men who could be held as hostages during any diplomatic settlement.

Still, by the start of 1968 the American leadership was optimistic and sure that the strategy was working. In the spring of 1967, Westmoreland analyzed his data and concluded that the crossover point had been reached, that the North Vietnamese and Viet Cong had reached their high point and were in decline.[48] There is no reason to doubt Westmoreland's sincerity when he visited the United States in mid-1967 and stated that he would soon be able to start pulling U.S. troops out of Vietnam. Given such good news from the front, it made sense to keep to the strategy embarked upon in 1965. In actuality, there was still little clear evidence that either the bombing campaign or the conventional ground war strategy was really working.

The Tet Offensive and a New U.S. Strategy

During late fall of 1967 the Viet Cong and North Vietnamese prepared for what would be a major blow to the South Vietnamese government, a plan to seize power in key cities and towns in Vietnam. This grand offensive was to be initiated January 30 during the Vietnamese New Year's celebrations known as "Tet." The initial attacks would be followed by a series of further attacks in the spring.[49] The Viet Cong and North Vietnamese, also tired of the war, saw this as an opportunity to break the South Vietnamese. In many respects the Tet Offensive was a strategic mistake for the Viet Cong and NVA. The Viet Cong and North Vietnamese overestimated their support among the South Vietnamese population, believing that the offensive would initiate a mass uprising of the people. The communist forces also underestimated the fighting abilities of some of the South Vietnamese units, who performed much better in combat than the Viet Cong had expected. Finally, the communists underestimated the firepower of the U.S. forces and the Americans' ability to react quickly.

In January 1968 the Viet Cong had seven divisions, numbering approximately 60,000 men, who were ready to assault key towns and provincial capitals. Forces were also ready to penetrate and seize portions of Saigon and the ancient imperial capital at Hue. The Viet Cong were backed by an estimated 400,000 paramilitary supporters. The NVA had an estimated 70,000 troops in Laos and South Vietnam. The Viet Cong had taken heavy losses between 1965 and 1967, so many of the Viet Cong main force battalions contained a high proportion of NVA soldiers.[50] The communist forces faced more than 500,000 U.S. soldiers and marines and a South Vietnamese Army of 343,000. The Australians, Koreans, and Thais had a combined total of more than 48,000 men fighting in Vietnam in January 1968. Add to this the 70,000-man South Vietnamese National Police, 150,000 Regional Forces, 150,000 Popular Forces and a further 42,000 in civilian irregular defense groups. The combined allied forces totaled more than 1.2 million men.[51] On paper, the Viet Cong task looked impossible, but the main blow would be struck against the South Vietnamese Army, a force that the communists believed to be a hollow shell. This assessment was largely correct. Many of the units of the South Vietnamese Army were in a poor state, with a lack of equipment and training.[52]

A large Viet Cong force had infiltrated into the suburbs of Saigon, taking over some approaches to the city. Another team fought its way onto the U.S. Embassy grounds. A large Viet Cong and NVA force fought their way into the old capital city of Hue, and raised the Viet Cong banner on the ancient citadel, one of Vietnam's most famous national landmarks. The Viet Cong and NVA were always aware of the symbolic value of objectives such as the U.S. Embassy and Hue. In other parts of the country the Viet Cong were quickly repulsed by U.S. firepower and suffered massive losses. In other areas the Viet Cong made initial gains, then dug in to force the ARVN to attack them. The performance of the South Vietnamese Army throughout the battle was varied. Some ARVN divisions, such as the 23rd Division in the Central Highlands, performed very well. Some units fell apart. The deciding factor seems to have been leadership. The South Vietnamese 23rd Division had a first rate leader in Colonel Dao Quang An, but he was the exception among the ARVN senior commanders. More typical was the major general commanding the ARVN forces in the Mekong Delta region, who remained in his fortified headquarters for days. Protected by tanks and artillery, he turned over the defense of the Delta—the most populous region of the country—to his American advisors.[53]

After recovering from the initial shock, the American forces quickly responded with a massive and successful counteroffensive. After a month of hard fighting, the Viet Cong and NVA realized that the offensive had failed and called off their attacks. While the U.S. forces took four thousand casualties, including wounded, killed, and missing, and ARVN an estimated eight thousand killed (although the actual figures are likely more than ten thousand), the Viet Cong and NVA had suffered an estimated forty thousand to fifty thousand killed. Many experienced Viet Cong leaders had died in the offensive, a cadre that could not easily be replaced. The South Vietnamese peasants and urban populations had not risen up to join the Viet Cong. In fact, most urban and rural South Vietnamese simply tried to lay low and survive the battle.

In Hue, following a careful plan, Viet Cong political officers and special units arrested thousands of middle-class Vietnamese and executed them. At least six thousand civilians in Hue were murdered to be discovered later in mass graves.[54] This action by the Viet Cong negated their claim to represent the average Vietnamese, helping to turn South Vietnamese public opinion firmly against them. Few of those murdered in Hue had been liquidated because of government ties, nor were they known enemies. They were killed simply because they were educated, or else their small shops qualified them as "capitalists." No territorial gains made by the Viet Cong were held, and the Viet Cong's cadre force had been decimated and would never recover. Thus, in a military sense, Tet was a victory for the South Vietnamese and Americans.

In political terms, however, Tet was an American defeat. The greatest casualty of Tet was America's credibility. After years of putting forth claims of progress and strongly asserting throughout 1967 that the United States and South Vietnamese were winning the war, the communists had been able to mount a massive offensive and take the U.S. and ARVN forces by surprise.

155

No longer was there any light at the end of the tunnel, and the beginning of a U.S. troop withdrawal. There was only the prospect of many more years of fighting against a tough and relentless foe. The poor performance of the South Vietnamese Army was also disheartening.

Westmoreland and the Joint Chiefs realized that the American strategy was in tatters. On February 27, 1968, Westmoreland, backed by Chairman of the Joint Chiefs General Earle Wheeler, requested that President Johnson authorize a further 206,000 troops for Vietnam.[55] After three years of bombing and conventional war, the only answer that top military leaders could provide was more of the same. It was the proverbial straw that pushed Johnson to call for a negotiated end to the war. Additional troops would not be approved for Vietnam. Johnson finally removed Westmoreland in mid-1968, replacing him with his deputy, General Creighton Abrams. Visiting Vietnam as Abram's took command, Secretary of Defense Clark Clifford (McNamara left the post in 1967) complained that the military had no strategy to win the war. In fact, Abrams quickly developed a strategy, and it was a good one.

Post Tet: The Vietnamization Strategy

Taking command in Vietnam in 1968, Abrams operated under far more strategic and operational constraints than Westmoreland had ever faced. With rising discontent at home over the conduct of the war, there would certainly be no increase in troop strength, nor would more bombing be the answer. That strategy was discredited by 1968 when the bombing of all but the southern panhandle of North Vietnam was put off-limits to American warplanes as a gesture to move negotiations along. Upon taking command, Abrams changed the course of operations and tactics 180 degrees: from seeking out and destroying the North Vietnamese Army in major battles and measuring success by body counts, to a policy of deploying troops with the first priority to secure the South Vietnamese countryside.

A major step in addressing the civil/political side of the war came in May 1967 when a senior CIA official with long service in Vietnam, Robert "Blowtorch" Komer, pushed a new organization through the Washington and Saigon bureaucracy. Now, all U.S. aid and development efforts in Vietnam fell under one organization, the Office of Civil Operations and Rural Development

Support (CORDS). As first chief of CORDS, Komer commanded both military and civilian personnel under MACV. The new office ended more than a decade of interservice and interagency rivalry and friction that had evolved through more than a decade of previous U.S. aid efforts. Supported by State Department funding, the core element of CORDS was a force of more than seven thousand aid officials organized into teams to supervise civic action and economic development programs at province, district, and even village level. The State Department CORDS officials were a mix of bright college graduates, experienced aid officers, and some ex-soldiers, such as the famous John Paul Vann.[56]

With General Abram's new priority on security for the South Vietnamese, the CORDS program had ample personnel and support, as well as a $1.7 billion budget, to systematically support projects to improve the lives of the South Vietnamese peasants. When William Colby of the CIA took over as CORDS chief in 1968, he worked in parallel with the military to secure the South Vietnamese countryside. By every measure, the aid and development programs worked well. Though 60 percent of the hamlets had been under guerrilla control in 1967, relatively few hamlets remained as Viet Cong strongholds by 1970–1971.[57] Between 1968 and 1971, the living standards and income/economic standing of the South Vietnamese peasants improved noticeably. If the increased aid effort failed to transform the populace into enthusiastic supporters of the government, it did take away many of the grievances that had propelled a great part of the peasantry to initially oppose the government. CORDS worked effectively partly because the Viet Cong losses at Tet had greatly weakened Viet Cong power and influence, and partly because the new U.S. military emphasis on security of the population was effective. As rural living standards improved, so did the security in the countryside. Roads and waterways that had been "ambush alleys" in 1967 were open to travel—even at night—by 1970–1971. A leadership vacuum in the enemy ranks resulted, weakening the Viet Cong organization.

After Tet, the Vietnamese government started to pay more attention to strengthening local defense forces, with the emphasis on security for the South Vietnamese population. In the 1950s the Saigon government had established two home-guard-type organizations: the Popular Forces and the

Regional Forces. Locally raised, both were employed to protect the strategic hamlets and rural towns. The Popular Forces were organized into platoons, given minimal pay, a few castoff military weapons, and assigned to protect only their home villages. The Regional Forces, organized into companies and battalions, were better paid and equipped for service in their home province, usually no more than twenty miles from their home villages. Through most of the Vietnam War, the role of the home guard organizations was ignored in favor of funding and support for the South Vietnamese regular army. As with most of the Vietnamese military, officer appointments in the Popular Forces and Regional Forces were arranged largely in reward for political loyalty.[58] Yet, in the latter part of the war, despite mediocre officers, low pay, and poor equipment, these local Vietnamese units nevertheless performed surprisingly well. Despite receiving only 4 percent of the South Vietnamese military budget, they accounted for 30 percent of the Viet Cong and North Vietnamese casualties inflicted during the war.[59]

Soon after Richard Nixon became president, his national security advisor, Henry Kissinger, frankly advised that the only realistic option for the United States was to slowly extricate itself from the Vietnam mess. The war was costing vast sums, and public support had evaporated starting in the previous year. In mid-1969 Nixon announced his strategy for the conflict. The U.S. forces in Vietnam, which had reached a peak of more than 550,000 troops in 1968, would be withdrawn in stages and the fight turned over to the South Vietnamese. This followed a course that had been advocated by counterinsurgency experts such as Sir Robert Thompson for years.[60] The United States would ensure the survival of the South Vietnamese by continuing to provide air support and logistics. As U.S. forces left the country, they turned over vast quantities of matériel to their Vietnamese allies. Nixon's Vietnamization strategy proceeded quickly. By 1970 U.S. forces were at less than half the level of 1968. By the start of 1972, the United States had only one combat brigade still remaining in Vietnam, although there were still tens of thousands of U.S. support personnel in the country.

Although the Vietnamese army was much better equipped and supplied after 1969 than it had been before, the fundamental flaws of corruption, poor leadership, and poor training still remained. U.S. advisors worked hard to cajole their ARVN counterparts to provide for their troops and to exercise common sense in conducting operations. Although the Vietnamization program included turning over a vast amount of equipment and supplies to the South Vietnamese, the U.S. support personnel and advisors had no power to change the Vietnamese forces. When U.S. advisors complained of grossly corrupt South Vietnamese commanders, the Thieu regime might at best transfer the officer to a staff job. Needing the support of his officer corps, Thieu never could bring himself to clean up his army.

Another problem lay in the U.S. military culture, which saw the advisory program as an ancillary and not a central mission. American trainers and advisors with ARVN worked hard to support their allies, but never had the authority—whether implicit or explicit—to either call a halt to misconceived operations, or to see that incompetent ARVN commanders were removed. Serving as an advisor or trainer with the South Vietnamese was not considered prestigious, for Westmoreland and the army staff conveyed the attitude that advisory or training duty with ARVN did not further a professional career or chance for promotion in the way that service with U.S. units or staffs did. As a result, professional U.S. officers sought to serve in U.S. combat units simply to protect their careers.

In his excellent study of the U.S. advisory effort in Vietnam, *Abandoning Vietnam*, James Wilbanks argues that the U.S. record in training and advising the South Vietnamese Army was very spotty. After years of U.S. involvement, some South Vietnamese units were very good, and others were consistently poor performers. Since U.S. advisory efforts never received the full support of the U.S. military establishment, they were never able to overcome many of the serious internal flaws of the South Vietnamese Army, such as widespread corruption, poor leadership, and insufficient resources.

Some parts of the Vietnamization program went well. In general, South Vietnamese army performance improved in 1970 and 1971, although success was still largely dependent upon the U.S. forces in the country being available to get ARVN out of trouble if necessary. The South Vietnamese Air Force (VNAF) took up the burden. In the spring of 1972, the VNAF efficiently flew thousands of sorties in a successful air effort to defeat the grand North Vietnamese offensive. The biggest problem the VNAF faced was the weakness of the South Vietnamese military infrastructure, which could not effectively maintain all the equipment the U.S. was finally providing. While the VNAF had plenty of aircraft, operational rates were generally low due to a shortage of trained personnel, mechanics, and parts.[61]

By June 1971, 90 percent of the combat responsibility had been handed over to the South Vietnamese.[62] In March of 1972, the Vietnamization program met its first serious test when the North Vietnamese Army launched a massive offensive spearheaded by hundreds of tanks and supported by hundreds of artillery pieces. The North Vietnamese were also tired of the war and developed a plan to end the conflict with a swift conventional attack. Unlike Tet, the concept of the campaign was to employ heavily armed North Vietnamese troops. Four major ground drives were initiated: two in the north aimed at Hue, one in Central Vietnam designed to cut the country in two and one to threaten Saigon. The spearhead of the offensive was a force of thirty thousand troops equipped with T54 and PT76 tanks, supported by 130mm guns, 152mm guns, and 160mm mortars. Mobile air defense was carried out by antiaircraft units equipped with 23mm and 57mm antiaircraft guns and the new Soviet SA-7 heat-seeking missiles.

The North Vietnamese expected that with American ground troops withdrawn, the South Vietnamese Army would crack under the pressure of a conventional blitzkrieg.[63] ARVN had not faced tank attacks supported by heavy artillery before. Indeed, some South Vietnamese units did fall apart, but other units held together and fought well. The North Vietnamese attack gave the Americans the advantage. The United States still had plenty of airpower available in the theater, as well as advisory teams and a complete communications network that could call in close air support. In contrast to the infantry battles of 1965 to 1968, the North Vietnamese tank columns, artillery battalions, and troops massed in the open for large-scale attacks made perfect targets for American airpower. U.S. advisors with the South Vietnamese were able to call in B-52s for close air strikes on North Vietnamese forces.

In heavy fighting the North Vietnamese took only one provincial capitol in Quang Tri Province. In a counterattack in June, South Vietnamese Marines—always one of the best forces fielded by the South Vietnamese government—retook it. The 1972 Easter offensive was a major defeat for the

North Vietnamese, and under the sternest of possible tests, Vietnamization had not failed.[64] In particular, the South Vietnamese Air Force (VNAF) had played an important role in the battle. Its effective use was, however, largely dependent on the U.S. command and control system still in place, and the work of U.S. advisors on the ground who could call in air support.[65] Serious flaws in the South Vietnamese forces were also exposed. While South Vietnam had managed to mobilize large numbers of men for the war, the training system was still weak. The quality of commanders throughout the armed forces was uneven, with poor commanders probably outnumbering the good ones.

With the North Vietnamese defeated and the situation on the ground essentially stabilized, negotiations in Paris between the Americans and South Vietnamese versus the NLF and North Vietnamese finally bore fruit when a cease-fire was agreed upon in January 1973. U.S. forces would completely withdraw from Vietnam, and North Vietnam agreed not to reinforce its forces in the south and to hold their forces there in place. The South Vietnamese had to be pushed into the agreement, for they quite rightly suspected that the North Vietnamese had no intention of holding to their side of the bargain.[66] Fighting declined in 1973, although the North Vietnamese quietly reinforced their forces and carried out some limited attacks on the southerners. In the meantime President Nixon won reelection in 1972, but faced an increasingly hostile Democratic Congress, many of whose members were pushing for a complete cutoff of U.S. aid to South Vietnam. With the drawdown of the U.S. commitment to Southeast Asia, conscription was ended in 1972 and the U.S. military made the transition to an all-volunteer force. This move undercut and generally ended U.S. anti-war protests, but also signaled a huge reduction in the size of the U.S. military. Although U.S. troops were out of South Vietnam, there was still a large presence of U.S. troops in nearby Thailand, where the U.S. military quietly supported the Thai government in conducting a very successful campaign to suppress a communist insurgency in the north of Thailand.

In case of a crisis in South Vietnam, the South Vietnamese were now largely on their own. Facing political pressure at home due to the Watergate scandal, Richard Nixon had no political capital to spend in getting an increasingly hostile Congress to support South Vietnam. Nixon would be forced to resign from the presidency in 1974, and Vice President Gerald Ford would take office. Through late 1974 and early 1975, the North Vietnamese prepared a major conventional offensive to improve their position for future operations against South Vietnam. In early 1975 the North Vietnamese leadership assumed that this phase of the war—hopefully the final phase—would likely last for a couple of years.

When the North Vietnamese initiated large scale conventional attacks in the northern part of Vietnam in March 1975, the South Vietnamese forces, now bereft of U.S. advisors and air support, collapsed far faster than the North Vietnamese had ever dreamed possible. The limited offensive was expanded into an eighteen-division attack against South Vietnam with the main weight in the central sector of the country. As in 1972, some South Vietnamese units fought remarkably well, holding off larger, better-equipped North Vietnamese forces for weeks. As before, the competence of the South Vietnamese forces on the battlefield was directly related to the quality of unit leadership. Unfortunately, the South Vietnamese military leadership was generally weak. ARVN defeat in the north and center of Vietnam snowballed. By mid-April the North Vietnamese forces, massively supported by tanks and heavy artillery, were poised to take Saigon. It was a frustrating moment for the U.S. military. The North Vietnamese armored forces, supported by long truck columns, would have been perfect targets for American airpower, which could have been employed as in 1972. However, Congress was determined to end American involvement in Vietnam and all funding authorization for U.S. military operations in Vietnam was cut off.

On April 30, 1975, the war was dramatically ended when a North Vietnamese tank crashed through the gates of the presidential palace in Saigon. The South Vietnamese government fled the country, along with hundreds of thousands of refugees who feared for their lives under communist rule. Ironically, South Vietnam did not fall to guerrilla warriors, but to a highly conventional blitzkrieg spearheaded by tanks and artillery. North Vietnam won in the end for the simple and old-fashioned reason that it had better military leadership than its opponents. The North Vietnamese commander, General Giap, made major strategic mistakes in 1968 and 1972. However, his preparation for the final offensive was masterful. He consistently showed great skill in moving supplies, equipment, and men far faster and more efficiently than his enemies thought possible. He had ensured that the North Vietnamese army was well led at all levels, and that the soldiers were properly trained—something that the South Vietnamese had never managed to do. In contrast, most of the South Vietnamese officer corps could not maintain the trust and loyalty of their soldiers. Dependent upon American firepower for more than a decade, the South Vietnamese had failed to adapt to new conditions and to be ready to rely on their own resources.

Intelligence Failure in Vietnam

The U.S. military and CIA employed a vast array of intelligence assets in Vietnam, from the latest high-tech intelligence collection system to monitor North Vietnamese communications to high-tech sensors employed along the Ho Chi Minh Trail to monitor traffic. The U.S. military also employed an army of intelligence personnel on the ground, from CIA specialists who ran agent teams to spy on the Viet Cong, to field intelligence officers who interrogated prisoners and analyzed captured documents. The U.S. headquarters in Saigon was lavishly staffed and equipped, including a bank of the latest computers to help process the flood of data that streamed in from the field. Despite all of that, American strategic and operational intelligence in Vietnam was surprisingly bad and helped drive poor strategic and operational decision making. The fault in the intelligence system was not one of poor equipment or poor staffing, but rather the problem of careerist military officers and senior civilian intelligence specialists who worked hard to see that the intelligence analysis generated reflected the kinds of results that their superiors wanted to hear. Essentially, bad intelligence analysis was driven by senior commanders eager to bring stories of success to the civilian leadership.

The story of bad intelligence analysis in Vietnam began early. In 1963 General Victor Krulak, the joint chief's special assistant for counterinsurgency, issued a remarkably positive report on Diem's strategic hamlet program, even though the regional forces defending some hamlets had defected to the Viet Cong. Moreover, the VC had recently staged some very effective attacks by easily infiltrating the villages.[67] McNamara's papers show a string of positive reports from Vietnam from 1961 to 1963, insisting that the Kennedy administration's efforts in counterinsurgency were bearing fruit. In February

1962 the Defense Department reported that the South Vietnamese government was "beginning to be effective." In July of that year, McNamara reported, "Our military assistance to Vietnam is paying off." In October 1962 McNamara said, "We are delighted at the progress that was reported to us . . . . Progress is quite apparent." General Harkin, Commander of the U.S. Military Assistance Group in Vietnam, and his staff reported that the South Vietnamese army was pushing back the Viet Cong in the countryside. Indeed, up to December 1963 the intelligence reports on Vietnam were overwhelmingly positive.[68]

The crisis brought on by the fall of Diem and the subsequent failure of the South Vietnamese to form an effective government sobered up the American analysts. It led to the frank assessment that South Vietnam would fall unless American troops intervened. Once General Westmoreland took over the U.S. command in 1964 and American combat troops arriving in South Vietnam began fighting the Viet Cong and North Vietnamese army, the intelligence picture generated by the U.S. headquarters in Saigon again took on a highly positive tone. The false intelligence picture was exacerbated by Westmoreland's attempt to measure effectiveness through the notorious body counts. The body count system soon became an exercise in optimistically estimating enemy casualties, because the Viet Cong and North Vietnamese forces carried away their wounded and dead. This again ensured that bad information made it up the chain of command. Officers who had high body counts would be advanced. Officers who were successful in securing an area, but failed to report a large body count, were considered failures.

Out in the provinces, U.S. advisory teams and commanders employed the Hamlet Evaluation Reports, a statistical tool used to evaluate Viet Cong influence and control in each village and district. The reports contained various shades of measurement, from "completely in VC control" to "completely in government control." The problem was that the reports became a means of self-grading by U.S. officers. One did not have to lie to turn in a highly inaccurate report. By giving the best interpretation to every question, one could come up with an estimate that a given district was 80 percent in government control when in reality the district was effectively controlled by the Viet Cong the moment the sun went down. Under this supposedly sophisticated measurement system, favored by McNamara and Westmoreland, U.S. officers who reported great success in their districts were praised and promoted. Officers who reported serious problems were asked, "The other districts are doing great and you're reporting that your district is 89 percent Viet Cong. Why are you failing?" In short, the U.S. military devised a method to encourage dishonesty and careerism and punish honest reporting.[69]

The push from the top for favorable intelligence analysis led to major disputes between the military and the intelligence community. Westmoreland got into the act of adjusting intelligence in 1966 and 1967, when he disputed the count of Viet Cong military forces that included the village militias. Given the estimate of 420,000 total Viet Cong fighters by the intelligence agencies, Westmoreland directed that the intelligence officers "study further." He then removed the Viet Cong self-defense forces and militias from the intelligence estimates to get a lower figure.[70] When Westmoreland's headquarters did produce accurate intelligence about enemy strength, it got into trouble with the Pentagon. In early 1967 Westmoreland reported to the Joint Chiefs of Staff that enemy battalion-sized attacks had increased. General Wheeler, then Chairman of the Joint Chiefs, told Westmoreland to keep that information quiet, since the official published figure was 45 battalion-level attacks. The actual figure was 174. In order to get more favorable numbers out of the U.S. forces in Vietnam, the Pentagon sent a special team to review the intelligence analysis of the U.S. forces in Vietnam. Military Assistance Command Vietnam (MACV) subsequently lowered its figure of enemy attacks to match that of the Pentagon.[71] In mid-1967 the CIA again produced an estimate that undercut the administration's position that the war was going well. The CIA estimated that there were five hundred thousand Viet Cong members in all categories, ranging from active soldiers, to part-time home guards, to villagers who provided rice to local cadres. Having been rebuked for publishing pessimistic intelligence in the past, MACV now insisted that the numbers for the Viet Cong were far too high and ordered their adjustment downward to a figure of three hundred thousand. Later, senior military officers admitted that they had arbitrarily reduced the estimates of enemy strength under pressure from top administration officials.[72]

In short, during the height of the Vietnam War the administration, the Pentagon, and the U.S. commander in Vietnam all worked assiduously to undermine the intelligence professionals, in a grand operation to deceive not only the American people and Congress but also themselves. Westmoreland and the Pentagon apparently began to believe in their optimistically reworked intelligence; for the time being, it worked. Although there were numerous intelligence indications in early 1968 that the Viet Cong and NVA were about to mount a major offensive, MACV headquarters remained surprisingly complacent.

The preparations necessary to carry out a major offensive could not be easily hidden, even for a force as adept at hiding as the Viet Cong. For weeks before the Tet offensive, the Viet Cong and North Vietnamese army had conducted extensive planning and coordination, moved a large number of personnel and units and stockpiled supplies for thousands of troops. Some American officers saw indicators that a major enemy operation was in the offing, but partly dismissed it as a last ditch effort by an enemy that was desperate and losing. Thanks to the military's program of self-deception—complete with inflated body counts and scientific statistical analysis that proved the enemy was on his last legs—Westmoreland and all but a few competent commanders, who had placed their forces on alert, were taken by surprise the morning of January 30, 1968, when the Viet Cong and North Vietnamese army began the Tet offensive.

It took the grand intelligence failure at Tet to force American commanders and political leaders to change their attitude toward intelligence analysis and accept the less-optimistic figures and reports generated by the intelligence specialists. By 1969, with Westmoreland gone and the body count mania ended, one sees a more realistic tone to the intelligence reports in Vietnam and a better attitude from the top political and military leaders in accepting bad news. A great many American lives had been lost to learn that simple lesson.

Public Support for the War in Vietnam and the United States

The Gulf of Tonkin Resolution that authorized the American use of force in Vietnam was passed with overwhelming congressional support. The resolution was broadly written, however, and emphasized protecting American forces, nor did it specifically authorize a full-scale war against North Vietnam.

However, once the Gulf of Tonkin Resolution was passed, Lyndon Johnson never returned to Congress to ensure a specific endorsement of his war policies. This, argued Colonel Harry Summers, was the prime political mistake of the war. Failure to maintain congressional support ensured that eventually the criticism of the war and of the executive branch of government would become intense.[73] At the beginning, the American leadership had assumed that U.S. airpower and ground troops would settle the war quickly. When U.S. military forces entered direct combat, only a quarter of the American public expressed opposition to the commitment of U.S. troops.

The gradualist approach of Johnson and McNamara for the U.S. military buildup in Vietnam got Johnson full support for his program in the U.S. Congress, with few exceptions. However, the opposition eventually came. It was yet more strident years later, when the public finally understood that the president, his secretary of defense, and the Joint Chiefs had willfully deceived the U.S. Congress in the summer of 1965 concerning the U.S. strategy in Vietnam.

From the start the U.S. military leadership was concerned that support for war could not be maintained if the war looked like another Korea-like stalemate. Admiral U.S. Grant Sharp, U.S. Commander in the Pacific with responsibility for Vietnam, addressed his concerns in a 1966 memo: "The American people can become aroused either for or against this war. At the moment, with no end in sight, they are more apt to become aroused against it."[74] In a 1967 memo General Wheeler, chairman of the Joint Chiefs of Staff, also expressed his concerns with the loss of support for the war. He noted "deep concern here in Washington because of eroding support for our war effort with particular distress over allegations of stalemate."[75]

Westmoreland understood these concerns, so in 1966 and 1967 he enlarged and revamped the MACV Information Office. He brought in top public relations officers to lead the effort to develop good press relations. To put out the MACV view that the war was succeeding, the press was fed a steady diet of reports describing battlefield success and improvements in the South Vietnamese forces. Under Westmoreland's direction, the headquarters for the U.S. forces in Vietnam exuded optimism to the press and to Washington. Before Secretary McNamara's visit in July 1967, Westmoreland instructed his subordinates to emphasize that the enemy was tough, but could be beaten.[76] Westmoreland understood the importance of keeping up congressional and public support, visiting the United States twice in 1967. During one visit he addressed a joint session of Congress. In a speech before the National Press Club, Westmoreland argued for the progress that had been made, suggesting that it might be possible to start withdrawing U.S. troops from Vietnam within a couple of years.[77]

The efforts by Westmoreland and the Johnson administration worked effectively to maintain strong public support for the war through 1966–1967. Even for a time after Tet, press and public support for the Vietnam War stayed fairly strong. However, the cumulative effect of years of optimistic administration and military statements on the success of American operations in Vietnam finally worked to undermine the credibility of the president and the military.[78] The Tet offensive of January-February 1968 came as a shock to the American commanders and the American public coming on the heels of optimistic statements by the Johnson administration. Although the Tet offensive destroyed the Viet Cong as an effective military force, it was portrayed in much of the international and American media as a U.S. military disaster. Thus, as an unintended consequence, the Tet offensive ended up as a North Vietnamese victory because it made clear to the American Congress and people that the war would simply drag on and on. It was not what the Johnson administration had led the American people to expect. Johnson had failed to go back to Congress after getting the initial support in the form of the Gulf of Tonkin Resolution in 1964, which gave the president the authority to "protect American troops," not to wage all-out war in Vietnam. Now he was stuck with the charge that he had lied to the American people about the war.

President Johnson's call for a negotiated solution in the aftermath of Tet also recalled to the public's mind the two years of protracted, frustrating negotiations with the communists in Korea that had finally resulted in an inconclusive end to that war. Public support for that war had also eroded quickly, not because the American people did not support the troops or disagreed with the importance of fighting communists, but because the negotiations process was dragging so badly. By accepting a negotiated solution, something that was politically necessary, Johnson also ensured that the war would quickly lose public support.[79]

When Richard Nixon became president in January 1969, he had little political choice but to start moving U.S. forces out and establish a program of "Vietnamizing" the war. However, Nixon's policy of gradual withdrawal was not fast enough for a public that had lost confidence in its government and military leaders. In 1970 roughly half of the public surveyed in a Gallup Poll wanted the U.S. to be out of Vietnam within a year. That same year 56 percent of the U.S. public believed that the decision to commit U.S. troops to Vietnam had been a mistake. As revelations about the origins and poor decisions that had led the U.S. into the war surfaced, and lucid accounts such as David Halberstam's *The Best and the Brightest* (1972) were published, the American will to support an endless war in Vietnam simply collapsed. By 1973, the year the United States reached a truce agreement with North Vietnam, fully 61 percent of the public believed that the Vietnam War had been a mistake.[80]

One of the constant dilemmas for any South Vietnamese who had served with the French, then later served alongside the Americans, was being tarred with the epithet of being the "puppet" of a foreign power. The term has a strong connotation in Vietnam, a "puppet" not necessarily being under overt control of the foreigner but rather a person who had somehow sold out his Vietnamese identity to stand with a foreign culture. Throughout the war the North Vietnamese State and the National Liberation Front constantly characterized their opponents as "puppets" of the Americans. The northerners also wisely played down any mention of communist ideology, but instead always emphasized nationalist themes. From the beginning the communists showed great skill in playing the nationalist card, which was the one theme that could be expected to resonate with every Vietnamese.

The northerners understood that, to have any credibility, even the basic communist models and theories had to be adapted to Vietnamese culture and conditions. Under the North Vietnamese regime standard communist terms were given a unique Vietnamese terminology. For example, Mao's concept of using guerrilla forces was adapted to Vietnamese use by Troung Chinh, a leading Vietnamese communist theoretician. Indeed, the Vietnamese evolved their own strategy of guerrilla war, which was termed a "war of interlocking," in which both guerrilla and regular insurgent forces would conduct simultaneous operations against the French and later American forces.[81] From the beginning of the Viet Minh through the development of the North Vietnamese government, the communists worked assiduously to remold any foreign intellectual import into something that looked and sounded convincingly Vietnamese. In the internal battle for the hearts and minds of the Vietnamese people, the northerners consistently outmaneuvered the southerners in the essential battle to be the authentic banner carrier of Vietnamese nationalism.

The North Vietnamese and the Viet Cong also proved themselves particularly adept at playing the international media to their advantage—portraying their fight as simply a nationalist one against foreign powers—very much a David and Goliath image. As America increased its involvement in Vietnam, the Viet Cong and North Vietnamese developed the *dich van* program ("action among the enemy"). *Dich van* was a sophisticated psychological warfare program directed against both the civilians of South Vietnam and America, and towards the international media. *Dich van* presented an idealized version of North Vietnam and the Viet Cong to the world, while undermining the international perception of the legitimacy of the South Vietnamese government.[82]

One of the most important themes presented to the international media concerned the U.S. bombing campaign against the north from 1965 to 1968. Through the years of escalation, U.S. bombing was carefully limited to only a few areas, and the major urban areas of Hanoi and Haiphong were off-limits to U.S. warplanes. The U.S. administration set careful rules to minimize civilian casualties. Still, the North Vietnamese turned the bombing into a propaganda coup, overstating the damage and grossly inflating civilian casualties in presentations to a largely credulous and anti-American international press corps. In reality, for all the bombs dropped on North Vietnam, the collateral damage to civilian targets and civilian casualties was very low. The North Vietnamese civilians, most of whom were scarcely affected by the air war, were portrayed in the international press as a heroic people under relentless bombardment by a large, aggressor nation.[83] The leftist European media, many of whom possessed a strong strain of anti-Americanism, readily accepted this message. By 1968 opposition to U.S. involvement in Vietnam by the European and American elites, partly driven by the bombing campaign, grew loud indeed.

In contrast, the U.S. government and the South Vietnamese essentially ceded the international media war to the enemy. There was little coherent effort to counter the constant drumbeat of North Vietnamese propaganda in international forums. The Viet Cong mass murders carried out during the Tet Offensive of 1968 were among some of the most grisly and brutal episodes of the entire war. They were part of a careful strategy to terrorize and coerce the South Vietnamese population. Yet the carnage received little play in either the international or American media, in comparison with the coverage of the U.S. bombing campaign in the north. From the beginning of the war the legitimacy of the South Vietnamese government was questioned and publicly derided by most of the international media. Unable to defend its own policies effectively, the United States also failed to finance and support a coherent South Vietnamese government effort to bring its view of the conflict—likewise, the views of the majority of South Vietnamese, who had no great love for the Viet Cong or North Vietnamese—before the international media.[84]

International Aspects of the War

For the Americans the core problem of the Vietnam War was how to coerce North Vietnam into giving up their dreams for national unification within the framework of a very limited war that would not provoke China into entering the conflict. America's major allies cautioned the Kennedy and Johnson administrations against sending U.S. combat troops and bombing North Vietnam. France warned the United States not to send troops into Indochina but was ignored. Great Britain steadfastly refused to get involved or to cut trade relations with North Vietnam. The British did, however, send a team of counterinsurgency experts led by Sir Robert Thompson to make an assessment of the Vietnam situation. Their advice to fight the war as a counterinsurgency campaign found few supporters among an American political and military leadership determined to fight a conventional war in Vietnam. Canada, one of America's staunchest allies, maintained diplomatic and trade relations with North Vietnam. In 1964 and 1965 Canada offered its services to help mediate an agreement between the United States and North Vietnam but was rudely rebuffed by the Johnson administration. Indeed, neither the Kennedy nor Johnson administration had much success in garnering international support for the U.S. policy in Vietnam.

However, America's Asian allies, as well as Australia and New Zealand, came forward to support the U.S.–led effort in South Vietnam. The Australians committed a reinforced army brigade, support troops, and a training team to support ARVN—a total of more than ten thousand troops by 1968. The Australians had operational control in one province. New Zealand provided a battalion-sized task force to work alongside the Australians. South Korea was America's most committed ally, sending more than forty thousand crack combat troops to South Vietnam. Thailand sent a force of fifteen thousand men and provided the Americans with major air bases for the air campaign against North Vietnam. The Philippines sent a one-thousand-man engineer group to Vietnam.

North Vietnam, which had received considerable military and economic aid from China and the Soviet Union in the 1950s, saw such aid dramatically increase as the war grew in intensity. The Soviet Union and China both saw Vietnam as a proxy war in which they could help a small nation bog down the Americans while paying a relatively small price by providing surplus military equipment as well as vehicles, fuel, and machinery. The air war over North Vietnam gave the Soviets the chance to test some of their latest antiaircraft technology. Aware of the Soviet-Chinese split; the North Vietnamese very cleverly played both nations against each other to obtain the best possible aid packages.

When the Americans carried out their first air attacks against North Vietnam in 1964, in retaliation for the Gulf of Tonkin incident, Ho Chi Minh's government accepted the presence of Chinese forces in North Vietnam. This was partly to help in the country's air defense and partly to help the North Vietnamese keep the transportation infrastructure viable in case the Americans increased the air attacks. The Chinese commitment included two antiaircraft divisions to counter American airpower and eighty thousand engineering troops to repair and expand the North Vietnamese rail system. The Chinese troop commitment gave the North Vietnamese two added advantages. The one hundred thousand Chinese troops in the north freed up a large number of

North Vietnamese forces to go and fight in the south. The presence of a large Chinese contingent in the north also served to deter the Americans from mounting an invasion of North Vietnam, for that action would bring the U.S. into direct military confrontation with China—something that the American leadership desperately wanted to avoid.[85] Allowing the Chinese into their country—a nation the North Vietnamese feared more than the Americans— was a hard decision for the North Vietnamese Politburo to accept. As soon as the American bombing campaign ended in 1968 the North Vietnamese asked the Chinese to leave.

The fact that North Vietnam maintained diplomatic and trade relations with America's allies throughout the war meant that North Vietnam's major port of Haiphong remained off-limits to American air attack. A stray bomb hitting a Russian ship, or even a ship belonging to one of America's allies, would cause casualties and provoke an international crisis—a further problem the Johnson administration did not need.

A major part of the American air effort against North Vietnam was the campaign to interdict NVA logistics over the Ho Chi Minh Trail through Laos. Still, the position of Cambodia as a neutral nation during the Vietnam conflict allowed the North Vietnamese an alternative supply route. Even if the Ho Chi Minh Trail had been closed, the NVA still had the option, which they regularly employed, of bringing supplies through the very porous border of Cambodia. The Cambodians maintained a neutral stance during the war, but their neutrality worked very much to the advantage of the North Vietnamese and Viet Cong. Through the war, eastern Cambodia remained in the effective hands of the NVA and Viet Cong. Soviet Block and Red Chinese ships could dock and unload supplies at the port of Sihanoukville in Cambodia and easily move them to the South Vietnamese border. Small boats and bicycle transport could do the rest.

Learning Lessons

The Vietnam experience showed that the U.S. military was a superb tactical force that failed to learn lessons or adapt to new operational and strategic conditions. An August 1972 Rand Study authored by Robert Komer, founder of the CORDS program, argued that the U.S. approach to the war had been overmilitarized. Right from the start, according to the report, we had "Americanized" the war, in many ways weakening the South Vietnamese ability to defend themselves.[86] Certainly the later pacification strategy and its general success stand in contrast to the conventional war military strategy pursued from 1964 to 1968. By largely ignoring the counterinsurgency aspect of the conflict and concentrating on the big battles against the North Vietnamese Army, the U.S. Army was usually successful on the battlefield, but such success did not support the legitimacy of the South Vietnamese state or provide effective security to the peasant villagers of South Vietnam.

Certainly South Vietnam was not doomed from the beginning. In 1955, when Diem took over a newly independent South Vietnam, he had strong public support, and the national infrastructure was in far better shape than that of many third world nations today. The strong sense of Vietnamese nationalism could have been harnessed by Diem. The elements to form an authentically Vietnamese and nationalist government were in place—if the Diem regime had been willing to build a national coalition. Instead, the Diem regime failed to build a truly national government, turning early in the process to the Americans as their major pillar of economic and military support. From that point on, the Southern government was labeled a "puppet" regime by the North Vietnamese and the National Liberation Front. In short, the foundation for the failure of South Vietnam was not in military tactics or strategy, but in the failure to find a domestic political solution.

After the fall of Diem, the South Vietnamese generals who dominated the government never found the will to initiate the basic reforms desired by the population. Instead of addressing their problems, the South Vietnamese came to rely upon American military power, all the while resenting the American presence in their country and the American manner of shunting the South Vietnamese aside. However, no nation can expect another to fight its wars indefinitely. In the end, it was a war for the South Vietnamese to win or lose for themselves.

Between 1968 and 1972, the Vietnamization programs and the efforts to pacify the countryside and improve the peasants' lives were fairly successful both in concept and execution. One wonders what might have been if that had been the U.S. strategy in 1965, instead of the Johnson administration's strategy of conventional war. One of the major lessons of the war is the danger of a flawed strategic decision-making process. The U.S. leadership was too ready to reject the advice of counterinsurgency experts, who based their advice upon recent successful experience, turning instead to the flawed theories of escalation and graduated response put forward by Walt Rostow, McGeorge Bundy, and Robert McNamara.

The strategy of the latter part of the war that directly addressed the insurgency was quite sound. However, none of the U.S. strategies ever addressed the most critical weakness of the South Vietnamese government: the poor leadership and training of the South Vietnamese Army. American advisors and trainers made an admirable effort, but their work was limited both by the Vietnamese and the U.S. military institutional culture.

Unfortunately, the reaction of the American military was not to learn from mistakes made in Vietnam, but rather to bury the issue. Some important studies and critiques, notably Komer's Rand study, were published during the war. Never widely circulated, they were soon forgotten by the U.S. military establishment and civilian leaders. One of the main problems in discussing Vietnam, even today, is the emotional response of the U.S. military to the Vietnam War. Conrad Crane detailed how the failure to study the Vietnam experience resulted in the failure to learn practical lessons. Although the U.S. Army did many things right in Vietnam, the positive lessons of effective counterinsurgency were not passed on to a new generation of U.S. officers.[87]

The failure in Vietnam left a wound on the American military psyche that has never healed. The U.S. military wrongly defined the war in Vietnam as a counterinsurgency campaign, although for the vast majority of soldiers, marines, and airmen it was actually a conventional war. The false lesson learned was that counterinsurgency strategies did not work. In the 1970s and 1980s the U.S. military services cut the study of counterinsurgency and related operations out of the service school curricula and focused their effort on the big conventional war that could parley America's vast technological superiority into victory. The service leadership, and the army in particular, responded to the experience of Vietnam in an emotional, rather than a rational manner. They simply pledged that they would not fight an unconventional war again. Nevertheless, Vietnam was by no means an "unwinnable war." Americans, in partnership with the South Vietnamese, might have won if a comprehensive counterinsurgency strategy had been practiced in much of the country, and the American combat role been limited to protecting South Vietnam against the North Vietnamese main forces.

Starting in the mid-1970s, the U.S. military essentially became a one-trick circus pony: a force that could do one thing really well, but little else. And the one thing that the U.S. military could do well was the big, high-tech conventional war. This concentration of intellectual effort paid off in the Gulf War of 1991, when the U.S. military quickly defeated the Iraqi army in short order with less than two hundred combat fatalities, but it would leave the U.S. military intellectually disarmed when it had to counter irregular enemies in Afghanistan and Iraq in the first decade of the twenty-first century.

Consequences of Failure

The highest price for the failure of U.S. strategy was paid by the people of South Vietnam and Cambodia. Over a million South Vietnamese fled their country, some of them officers and officials of the South Vietnamese regime, but most of them simple people who feared the rule of the North Vietnamese dictatorship. They were, of course, correct in fearing the northern victory. Hundreds of thousands of South Vietnamese—mostly people who had held low positions in the government or military—were sent to concentration camps for years to be "re-educated." In Cambodia the full consequences of a communist victory were realized when the Khmer Rouge took over the country, turning the whole nation into a killing field. Anyone who was suspected of being middle class, or even of holding middle class sympathies, was brutally murdered. Indeed, the policy of systematically "cleansing the nation" was so brutal that the Vietnamese invaded Cambodia in 1979 and quickly ended the Khmer Rouge regime—but not before it had exterminated more than a quarter of the population.

The loss of the Vietnam War was a serious blow to American power and prestige abroad. In the aftermath of American failure, the majority of Congress (which included many who had been elected based on their opposition to the war) favored an almost isolationist course, in which the tool of military power would be carefully limited even in cases where U.S. national security was involved. Foreign and military aid to allied nations was reduced even as the Soviet Union took a more aggressive posture, massively increasing its forces in Eastern Europe and invading Afghanistan in 1979. That year the United States pulled out its support for the Iranian government, a staunch ally of the United States since 1953. The fairly mild dictatorship of the Shah was replaced with the ruthless dictatorship of the Islamic Ayatollahs, who called America "the Great Satan." They promptly looted the U.S. Embassy, holding the American diplomatic personnel hostage for a year and a half. Power politics is much about perceptions, and for several years after Vietnam, the United States was seen as a power in decline that could no longer shape events but only passively respond.

The consequences of failure in Vietnam for the American military were serious indeed. With the decision to wind down the U.S. involvement in the Vietnam War in 1969, and the strong push to get the troops home to the U.S., the morale of the U.S. forces declined notably. The constant turbulence in the force and the massive post-Vietnam cutbacks forced training to be cut short. The former battle-ready army of 1965 was a war-weary and demoralized force in 1969.[88] The serious problems with drug use, indiscipline, and fragging came not in the years of heavy combat, but in the later years of the Vietnam conflict. As U.S. forces withdrew, unit commanders were instructed to keep casualties down. Thus the war became a constant round of indecisive, small-unit actions, wherein the U.S. forces would strike out briefly, and then let the enemy flow back. For the marines, a service with a strong reputation for fighting ability, the results of the new Vietnam strategy, in the words of Marine Corps historian James Warren, "had terrible effects upon combat performance."[89] Allan Millett noted, "the regular infantry showed signs of slackened enthusiasm and professionalism."[90] Indiscipline, fragging, racial incidents, and atrocities against civilians carried out by the U.S. military in Vietnam rose notably in 1970 and 1971, as the troops were now expected to fight in a war in which victory was not an option.

Vietnam put the U.S. military into a tailspin from which it took more than a decade to recover. The 1970s were a time of cutbacks, low morale, declining budgets, and shortfalls of equipment and personnel. The army had 200,000 fewer men in 1974 than it had in 1964—a drop from 950,000 men to

750,000. Meanwhile, U.S. global commitments had not decreased. The force, which saw the quality of soldiers decline noticeably with the end of the draft in 1972, was highly stressed. Twenty percent of marine recruits in 1972 were mental category IV, the lowest intelligence level. By 1975 almost half of the recruits came into the marines without a high school diploma. Figures for the army were similar. Modernization programs were delayed for all the services, as Vietnam sucked up the defense budgets.[91] When the Iranian crisis came in 1979, the combat readiness of U.S. forces was at a post-World War II low. By the late 1970s all the services were in bad shape. Not until the 1980s, with the Reagan defense buildup and an increase of defense spending to 6 percent of the American GDP, did the military recover. It required a huge effort over a decade to improve pay and quality of life, and to provide new equipment to replace the worn-out equipment of the Vietnam era so that the U.S. military could again be a highly effective warfighting force.

One of the most serious consequences of the Vietnam War was the damage to American civil/military relations. Most of the Ivy League universities took a very public anti-military stance during the Vietnam War, and ROTC programs were kicked off campus. The end of a military presence in elite universities, and the end of the draft in 1973, meant that few members of the American elites had any direct contact with the military, or with military personnel, during their formative years. Since the Vietnam War, the number of Americans with military service elected to office or holding top positions in government has steadily declined. Many members of the American elites who were students in the 1960s and 1970s cut their political teeth on anti-Vietnam protests, and the strong positions of their youth tended to color their attitudes about the military as they moved into positions of influence in academia, politics, and the media. For the first time in American history, most civilian policy advisors at the start of the twenty-first century had never served in, or had even a tenuous connection with, the armed forces. A generation away from Vietnam, the senior members of the military and the civilian elites often seem to be from utterly different worlds. At atmosphere of mistrust between the military and civilian elites remains an important factor in American political life more than three decades after the fall of South Vietnam. The lack of direct contact between the civilian and military elites has several effects on American politics. The liberal elites have a tendency to mistrust the military as right wing, ignorant, and authoritarian—a constant threat to civilian leadership. The conservative elites tend to have a romanticized view of the military and its capabilities. Conservative journals and think tanks tend to enthusiastically favor military solutions, carried out by armed forces full of heroes drawn from the pages of Tom Clancy novels. The military is characterized as a master of high technology that can accomplish almost anything.

The conflicting views, of course, have little basis in reality. The truth about the military lies very much in the middle. The U.S. military is overwhelmingly middle class and reflects fairly conservative American values. They are certainly not the threat to the republic that some liberal elites fear, nor are they the brilliant heroes that conservative elites idealize. But when a false understanding of the U.S. military forces and their capabilities is held by the nation's elites, then the consequences for American strategy are serious indeed. The liberal position can lead to cutting the military out of the strategic process. The conservative position can lead to the armed forces being routinely asked to carry out missions far beyond their capabilities. Both directions have dangerous implications for the U.S. future.

CHAPTER 4
American Counterinsurgency Strategy in Iraq, 2003–2007

■ ■ ■

At last the Dodo said, "Everybody has won, and all must have prizes."
—Lewis Carroll, *Alice's Adventures in Wonderland*

Setting the Endstate

WHEN THE ADMINISTRATION OF PRESIDENT George W. Bush decided to go to war with Saddam Hussein's regime and invade Iraq with a coalition of allied nations in 2003, the first element of strategy—the endstate—was in place. The Bush administration formulated clear goals for the war: the elimination of Saddam Hussein and the whole apparatus of his regime; the transformation of Iraq into a democratic nation; the creation of democratic institutions; the establishment of the rule of law with recognition of individual and group rights; the creation of a free and prosperous economy; and the reintegration of Iraq as a peaceful member of the global community. If it could be done—and it was an enormous "if"—the remaking of Iraq would transform the political dynamics of the Middle East by giving the Arab states a nonauthoritarian model of government, demonstrating the efficacy of democracy. A democratic Iraq would no longer be a potential threat to the United States. Iraq could also serve as a curb to the ambitions of Syria and Iran, improving the political conditions in the Persian Gulf region. A remade Iraq

181

could also serve as an American base in the region, thereby helping the United States with the Global War on Terror. For anyone with the least familiarity with that part of the world, it was a *very* ambitious endstate.

Whether such an endstate was ever feasible will continue to be debated for the foreseeable future. Certainly Iraq had many positive conditions that would help it transform into a democracy, including huge oil reserves and a large and generally well educated population with a large middle class. Because Iraq was one of the most secular Arab countries, the more radical versions of Islam had not taken hold there. It had once been a fairly moderate Arab country—authoritarian, but not excessively so, in the period before Saddam Hussein murdered and intrigued his way to the top. Ethnic relations between Shiite and Sunni Arabs in Iraq were traditionally amicable. Intermarriage between the groups was common, and some tribes even included both Sunni and Shiite clans. Iraq was also one of the most tolerant nations in the Middle East toward its Christian minority, some five percent of the population. The economy of Iraq was fundamentally healthier than that of other oil-rich states in the Middle East. It had a fairly diverse economy, with considerable light and heavy industry. Iraq also had large fertile areas and had exported food from the region before the coming of Saddam Hussein and the militarization of the economy. If any Arab country could be transformed into a democracy, then Iraq was one of the better candidates.

Choosing to Fail

The cause of the internal conflicts now raging in Iraq was not the endstate that the Bush administration proposed for Iraq—although the endstate should have been modified to reflect the many cultural obstacles to establishing a democracy in the Middle East. The real problem was a failure to establish ways and means to reach that endstate. The only part of the ways and means to be realized was the first objective: eliminating the regime of Saddam Hussein through military invasion. Beyond that, the American concept was so vague that it could scarcely be called a strategy.

Because the ways and means to establish a new democratic Iraq were never thought out, the U.S. military forces and civilian administrators in Iraq lost control of the situation the moment American forces occupied Baghdad on April 16, 2003. Without a plan to establish order in Iraq, and with no clear means to transform Iraq into a democratic nation, chaos and violence continued. Any strategies developed by the Bush administration, or the U.S. military thereafter, were little more than reactions to a steadily deteriorating situation. From the beginning of the American occupation of Iraq, American civilian and military leaders were consistently slow to understand the dynamics of the political struggles in that country. The solutions imposed by the United States were poorly conceived and poorly supported. More often than not, American policy made a bad situation worse.

The American civilian and military leadership suffered from a lack of critical thinking at the strategic level. From the first discussions in 2001 that led to the decision to invade Iraq, the methodology of strategic planning and decision making—the ways part of the strategic process—were faulty. The planning—or rather the lack of planning—for the postwar Iraq was driven by a set of monumentally bad assumptions. These assumptions, combined with a failure to understand the Iraqi context, led to chaos. The problems were exacerbated by the failure of the American leadership to quickly identify problems as they arose or to adapt American policy and strategy in the light of new conditions. Lacking a realistic plan, the United States was left with what can be described as a Peter Pan Strategy: "If you wish for it hard enough, it will come true." Unfortunately, what worked in James Barrie's play does not work in the modern Middle East.

American policy and actions in Iraq were limited by a lack of resources, military units, money, and civilian experts—all the essential means to achieve the objective. Inadequate military forces on the ground and the lack of adequate civilian personnel to manage the postwar reconstruction established favorable conditions for an insurgency to become established, and then to grow. The lack of adequate funds and personnel hindered efforts to build Iraqi security forces capable of establishing order and protecting their citizens. This situation forced the U.S. military to take on the primary burden of fighting insurgents—a mission it was neither prepared nor organized for.

The decision by the Bush administration to overthrow Saddam Hussein was not driven by necessity, but by choice. Through the 1990s Saddam Hussein was a nuisance, theoretically a future threat, but posed no immediate threat to the United States or to the countries in the region. However, in the aftermath of the massive terrorist attack upon America on September 11, 2001, the Bush administration decided to go to war with Iraq. The initial discussions about toppling Saddam Hussein's regime began in the aftermath of the 9/11 attacks. After the terror-supporting Taliban regime was toppled in Afghanistan in late 2001, the proposed war with Iraq became the top priority of the administration.[1]

Since it was a war of choice, the Bush administration and U.S. military had ample time to plan and prepare. In the year and a half between the Afghanistan campaign and the start of the Iraq invasion, the U.S. government had ample opportunity to assemble the men, equipment, and resources to fight a war and to prepare for the subsequent occupation of Iraq. Given the vast human, economic, and industrial resources of the United States, it would not have been difficult to increase the military force, call up reserves, fully equip the new forces, and prepare a large corps of civilian administrators to help guide Iraq's transition to democracy. There was time to correct deficiencies within the U.S. military and to train a corps of Arabic linguists to at least a reasonable fluency. There were few economic or domestic political constraints to limit the options of the U.S. government.

The Bush administration had little difficulty in obtaining funds and support from Congress between 2001 and 2004. Even before the 9/11 terrorist attacks, the military was stressed by repeated peacekeeping missions, so many in Congress and the military were calling for an increase in the armed forces.[2] In 2001 American military forces and defense spending were at a record sixty-year low, and the defense share of the GDP was only 3 percent—only half the level of defense spending in the 1980s. In the aftermath of 9/11, there was strong support in Congress to increase U.S. military forces. Proposals to increase the State Department's Foreign Service Corps and to increase military and economic aid to American allies in the Global War on Terror would have been readily accepted by a Congress that was very conscious of the need to secure America and combat radical Islamic forces abroad. Yet the Bush administration decided that the traditional answer of expanding the armed forces for war was no longer relevant. When America went to war in Iraq a year and a half after the 9/11 attacks, it had the same peacetime forces deemed insufficient before the Global War on Terror had begun.

In a forum before a group of soldiers in late 2004, Secretary of Defense Donald Rumsfeld responded to criticisms about equipment shortages with the comment, "Well, you go to war with the army you have."[3] But it had mainly been Rumsfeld's adamant refusal either to expand the armed forces or to request funding from Congress for more equipment that was behind the shortages of troops and equipment. The Iraq War is unique in American military history as the first time that America has gone to war with a foreign power and *not* increased the armed forces. On December 7, 1941, when the United States entered World War II the whole army and air force was 1.4 million men. By 1944 that force had expanded to 8 million men. When the Korean War began, the U.S. Army was slightly over 500,000 men. A year later the army had over a million and a half men. During the Vietnam War the size of the Army was increased by 600,000 soldiers. Indeed, when the news arrived that George Armstrong Custer and most of his 7th Cavalry Regiment had been killed on the Little Big Horn River in June 1876, Congress immediately voted to increase the army cavalry force by an additional 1,000 troopers in order to deal with a resistance mounted by a few thousand Sioux and Cheyenne warriors.

The Bush administration decided that the war in Iraq would be fought as cheaply as possible. This was driven less from the necessity to conserve limited resources than from a desire to prove the validity of new theories of warfare being pushed not only by the top leadership of the Defense Department, but also by many in the U.S. military. From the planning of the war to its execution, all the military options in Iraq were constrained by self-imposed limits on troops, funds, and resources. Even after the situation in Iraq had deteriorated into civil war, the Bush administration refused to deviate from this rigid policy. As of this writing (2007), the Iraq insurgency continues in full force, and the chances for a peaceful resolution in the short term are minimal to nonexistent. This chapter will explain the American strategy for dealing with the Iraq conflict and how it failed.

The Neocon Worldview and the Push for War

The ideological background to the Bush administration strategy in Iraq originated with the rise of a group of academics and political activists who argued through the 1990s for a new, more assertive use of American power to pursue an extremely ambitious set of strategic goals. The neoconservatives, or neocons as they came to be called, were usually connected to past Republican administrations. Two of the most prominent, Paul Wolfowitz and Douglas Feith, had served in the Reagan administration. Wolfowitz had served in the State Department, Feith as a lawyer and policy assistant in the Pentagon. In the 1990s, think tanks and advocacy groups, such as the American Enterprise Institute, the Jewish Institute for National Security Affairs, and the Project for a New American Century, provided neocons with forums for their ideas. The neocons were a small but assertive group that went against the mainstream of the academic community, which had tended to be highly suspicious of the military and America's use of force abroad since the Vietnam War. In contrast, neocons embraced the use of American military force in the pursuit of idealistic policy goals. In the 1990s Wolfowitz and Feith were two of the most hawkish neocons. Wolfowitz openly argued for a policy of preemption against threats to the United States. In a 1997 article he also argued for a more aggressive plan to deal with Saddam Hussein, calling for the United States to use military power to overthrow the dictator. [4]

During the Cold War American foreign policy options and the use of military power had been limited by two strategic requirements: to maintain military forces capable of deterring the Soviet Union, and to avoid open confrontation with the Soviet Union and China. Military power could be employed, but only under carefully controlled conditions that minimized the chance for provoking an open crisis with another superpower. With the collapse of the Soviet Union between 1989 and 1991, America was left as the world's only superpower. The Cold War restraints on exercising power were largely removed. The Gulf War of 1991 brought what appeared to be a new consensus between America and the other powers in building an international coalition to end Saddam Hussein's occupation of Kuwait. The neocons saw in these two events a tremendous opportunity for the United States to use its power assertively to spread the growth of democracy. If this could be achieved, it would lay the foundations for greater world stability and continued economic growth. Spreading democracy would be in the direct national interest of the United States, and under post–Cold War conditions, it could be done with minimum risk.

Typical American idealists, neocons wanted the United States to demonstrate strong leadership. They generally rejected the emphasis on alliance politics, as advocated by the more traditional foreign policy specialists, arguing that if America took the lead, European nations and other allies would naturally follow. Neocons preferred peaceful means of spreading democracy, but readily advocated the use of American force—unilaterally if necessary.[5] The idea that democracy can be easily spread with the assistance of American power is, at best, a dubious proposition. Recent experience has shown that, even with U.S. military support, it is very difficult to build a democracy in ethnically-divided nations such as Yugoslavia, or in countries where illiteracy and poverty are endemic, such as Haiti, Somalia, and Kosovo. The neocons brushed off such historical arguments, or any arguments, that disagreed with their world view.

Neocons generally approved of President Bill Clinton's use of military force to support humanitarian efforts and nation-building. Paul Wolfowitz supported President Clinton's 1994 decision to send twenty thousand American troops to Haiti to force out a corrupt dictatorship that had ruined the country. Wolfowitz believed that such operations were a proper use of U.S. force to bring democracy to that troubled country. In 1995 Clinton ordered the U.S. Air Force to lead an air campaign to pressure the Bosnian Serbs to accept a peace agreement with the Croats and Bosnian Moslems. In 1999 Clinton again ordered the U.S. Air Force to lead a NATO air campaign to force the Serbian army out of the province of Kosovo and place that province under an international peacekeeping force. If there were foreign policy disagreements between the neocons and Clinton administration, it was about the tactics and not principles, as neocons generally favored an even more assertive policy than had Clinton.

During the Clinton years the main opposition to an interventionist policy came from the realists, best exemplified by former chairman of the Joint Chiefs of Staff, General Colin Powell. Powell was an exponent of a set of principles, generally called the Weinberger-Powell Doctrine (named for Powell and for Reagan's Secretary of Defense Casper Weinberger), which advocated a cautious use of American military force. Weinberger and Powell had argued that the United States should only use military force as a last resort, when diplomacy had failed. When U.S. military force was applied it should only be in service of clear national interests, with an attainable endstate in view. Once the decision was made for a military solution, the military force applied by the United States ought to be so overwhelming as to guarantee a favorable outcome. Finally, the U.S. government ought not to use military force without broad support from the American people, and well as Congress. Weinberger's personal reference was to the muddled American intervention in Lebanon in 1982, which left almost three hundred Americans killed by suicide bombers in Beirut as Americans wondered what it was all about. Powell's personal reference was the Vietnam War, fought without either Congressional authorization or strong public support. The Weinberger-Powell doctrine was applied in the 1991 Gulf War: the U.S. indeed applied overwhelming military force, had Congressional authorization, and enjoyed strong public support and international backing. Powell had a hand in arranging all these conditions, and the success of the war proved the soundness of the realist principles.

Inherent in the realist view is the understanding that war is never easy. As the German general and philosopher Carl von Clausewitz pointed out; war's defining characteristics are fog and friction. Things that can go wrong will, and every action is liable to have unintended consequences. This is even truer when one intervenes in third world nations rent by internal strife. When the Lebanese welcomed U.S. troops in 1982, no one anticipated that a year later some Lebanese would blow up hundreds of U.S. Marines, with the approval of many of their countrymen. The specter of more Lebanons weighed heavily on Powell, who had seen the faulty decision-making process that sent the U.S. into that country.

One of the most telling differences between the neocons and the realists is their understanding and experience of using military force. The leading realists have more than a passing acquaintance with the military and war. Weinberger had served as an infantry officer in the Pacific theater in World War II. Powell had a military career spanning more than thirty years, had served two tours in Vietnam, and been wounded. In contrast, the neocons tended to have little to no military experience. Neocons such as Paul Wolfowitz, Douglas Feith, and Max Boot all missed the chance to serve. Characteristic of so many lacking any direct knowledge of the military, they tended to have a romanticized view. For them the Gulf War provided the key lesson that technology was now the dominant factor in conflict. Neocons argued that since the United States has a huge lead in technology, this military-technological advantage could and should be put to use to further the promotion of democracy. Douglas Feith, who became number three man in the Pentagon, responsible for planning the global force structure (undersecretary of defense for policy, 2001–2005), commented on the lessons from recent wars: "We are able to bring about very large military effects with smaller forces than anybody thought were capable of those effects in past eras."[6]

The neocons' enormous faith in the U.S. military, and in the military's ability to employ technology, was shared by many who believed the Weinberger-Powell doctrine was too cautious an approach for the post–Cold War world. Reflecting the neocon view of using the American military was Max Boot, a former editor of the *Wall Street Journal* and member of the Council of Foreign Relations. His 2002 book, *The Savage Wars of Peace*, is a popular history of American military intervention overseas.[7] In it, Boot argues that most American interventions to quell rebellions, rebuild failed states, and punish international transgressors have generally been successful. Boot concludes "that small-wars operations are militarily doable" and that a vigorous American policy of military intervention would be of benefit to the United States and the world as long as accompanied by a nation-building effort."[8]

The flaw in Boot's entertaining history is that most of his book was devoted to accounts of U.S. military interventions in the period before World War II. In that era it was generally accepted that a major power could intervene to punish small nations or conduct colonial campaigns to suppress native rebellions. In an era of empires there was little protest from either the public at home or the world at large for such actions. Irregular enemies before World War II tended to be poorly armed and organized and lacked ready access to the world media. In the post–World War II era, however, military interventions have become infinitely more complicated. Insurgents are better armed, and domestic and world opinion is much less tolerant of military intervention. Boot glosses over more recent examples of American military intervention, which would include some notable failures such as Lebanon and Somalia. Continuing to argue for an interventionist policy, Max Boot coined the term "the new American way of war" in an article that described the early operations in Afghanistan in 2001. Those airpower-intensive operations were held up as a model for the new doctrine of high-tech, minimal manpower war. Boot insisted that this way of war leveraged America's overwhelming technological superiority, especially its information superiority, in order to swiftly defeat enemies with a minimum of ground troops. It is a notion of "hit and run, not fight and stay."[9] Boot's argument found an enthusiastic audience not only among the neocons, but also with many in the U.S. military leadership. It fit perfectly with the views of Donald Rumsfeld.

The neocons were welcomed into the Bush administration after the 2000 election. Wolfowitz was already serving as foreign policy advisor to candidate George Bush. When Rumsfeld was selected as Secretary of Defense, he was glad to have prominent neocons Paul Wolfowitz and Douglas Feith on his team and appointed them respectively to the second and third top positions in the Defense Department. Wolfowitz and Feith brought an ideological fervor to their jobs, coupled with overwhelming confidence in the truth of their views. They believed that questioning their views, or those of the defense secretary, was not a legitimate part of the policy process. Senior officials and officers who expressed skepticism of the neocon concepts were either ignored, bypassed, or referred to contemptuously as "dinosaurs." Rumsfeld and his neocon deputies knew exactly how the U.S. military had to be transformed, and discussion was a waste of time.

The U.S. Military and the New Way of War

The U.S. military, and especially the army, went into Iraq unprepared to fight a major insurgency. Counterinsurgency thinking had almost died out in the armed forces after the Vietnam War, and was only taken seriously in the Special Forces, which were outside the mainstream of the military. The military took little notice of the lessons learned from Vietnam, or from ongoing counterinsurgency campaigns in which America was involved, such as in Colombia. The study of insurgency was virtually cut out of the service schools where mid-level officers are prepared for higher command and strategic planning jobs.[10] The focus from 1975 to 2001 was on fighting big, conventional wars.

The 1991 victory in the Gulf, in which airpower and precision weapons had played the starring roles, was so one-sided that many in the U.S. military took the war's results as proof that the U.S. had found the right way of war. A few critics noted that the Gulf War victory had been won under some unique conditions. Saddam Hussein and his Iraqi commanders had demonstrated an impressive level of incompetence. The Iraqi army had been poorly trained, badly led, and poorly motivated. Few Iraqi soldiers were willing to die for Saddam Hussein's ego. Many in the American military knew that they had been lucky: that, if the Iraqis had used better tactics, they could have inflicted a far greater number of casualties on the Coalition forces.[11]

There were a few critics of the new war doctrine, but the enthusiastic voices predominated. A broad consensus arose among American military leaders, political leaders, and civilian defense analysts that superior technology was now the answer for warfare. The argument that had been made by Clausewitz and his followers since the early nineteenth century—that war was dominated by fog, friction, and confusion—was deemed largely obsolete by many in the top military leadership. They believed that new technology would give commanders a nearly perfect picture of the battlefield, and in real time. Through digital technology, information could be passed instantly to subordinate commanders. What now mattered was not having masses of men and equipment on the battlefield, but rather a few highly lethal weapons systems directed by high-tech command and control systems. Airpower would be the primary means of employing firepower on the battlefield of the future.[12]

Richard Cheney, Secretary of Defense during the Gulf War, was one of the leaders most impressed with this vision of high-tech warfare. Shortly after the conflict, Cheney commented, "This war demonstrated dramatically the new possibilities of what has been called the 'military technological revolution in warfare.'"[13] Military literature abounded with articles explaining how the nature of war had dramatically changed, and how technology had virtually eliminated the factors of friction and confusion from warfare.[14] In the 1990s chairman of the Joint Chiefs of Staff, Army General John Shalikashvili, argued that the old form of planned and sequenced operations was gone: "Instead of relying on massed forces and sequential operations, we will achieve massed effects in other ways. Information superiority and advances in technology will enable the United States to achieve desired effects through the tailored application of joint combat power."[15] The policy of the military became "Transformation," which meant that the budget priority was buying high-tech weapons and digitized command and control equipment. Maintaining force structure was a bottom priority.

When Donald Rumsfeld became Secretary of Defense in 2001 he adopted "Transformation" as his slogan. Despite his claim that he would make fundamental changes in the military and overhaul an outdated force structure, Rumsfeld's program actually amounted to little more than adhering to the force structure and modernization policies set by the Clinton administration—right down to the buzzword "Transformation," which had been in general use since the 1990s. Rumsfeld only proposed to accelerate the force structure changes of the Clinton era, and make the ground forces even smaller in favor of increased funding for the air force and space technology.[16] Immediately after 9/11 Rumsfeld and senior civilian appointees saw the chance to put their ideas into practice. It was their opportunity to show that the United States could not only win wars, but could do so quickly, at low cost, and with minimal deployment of troops. It was a lot to hope for.

Civil-Military Relations from Clinton to Bush

Relations between America's elected civilian leaders and military leaders from World War II through the early years of the Cold War were generally healthy. During that period the top military leaders had regular access to the president, and the cabinet. Strategy was developed under an established system that allowed for frank discussions between civilian and military leaders. While military leaders tried to understand the concerns of the civilian leaders, for their part the civilian leaders granted the military a respectful hearing—even if they did not agree. During the Vietnam War, however, the process took a bad turn. Kennedy's and Johnson's inner circles worked—sometimes deceitfully—to cut the Joint Chiefs out of the strategic decision-making process. These actions created an atmosphere of distrust which damaged the American strategic process for a decade.

From World War II to the 1980s, the primary means by which top military leaders communicated with the president was through the Joint Chiefs of Staff, with the military heads of the services serving as a committee. The Joint

Chiefs met with the cabinet, civilian service secretaries, and the defense secretary on a regular basis to present military plans and options for the president's decision. Recommendations for military force structure and funding were also frankly discussed through a committee and formal meeting process. This methodology ensured that the president, as commander in chief of the armed forces, was fully informed of the concerns of the military leadership.

The post-Vietnam era saw a fundamental change in the status of the Joint Chiefs of Staff that worked to the detriment of the strategic process. The Goldwater-Nichols Act of 1986 forced jointness upon the services, which led to a notable improvement in operational efficiency and effectiveness on the battlefield. But the reforms also cut the senior military leaders out of the chain of command. Formerly the service chiefs had held command authority over their services. After 1986, the service chiefs were relegated to the status of force trainers and providers, no longer serving as commanders. In case of conflict, the command chain ran straight from the president, through the secretary of defense and to the theater commanders. The Joint Chiefs still existed, but no longer as a body specifically empowered to review military plans and strategy and take those recommendations to the president as a group. The chairman of the Joint Chiefs, formally a position with command authority, now served as senior military advisor to the president. While the Goldwater-Nichols reforms left the military better organized for joint operations, the military's access to the president and cabinet was now limited to the Chairmen of the Joint Chiefs. Communicating the military's concerns to the president, and ensuring that the military was fully involved in developing national military strategy, was now completely dependent upon the personalities of the president and the chairman. If the president readily sought the advice of the military, and if the chairman was a strong figure who could insist upon access to the president, then the strategic process worked with input from all the major players. However, if the president, defense secretary, or presidential inner circle wished to exclude the military from strategic discussions, it could be done much more easily than in Robert McNamara's day.

These potential problems with the command system were not evident during the Gulf War of 1990–1991, when Chairman of the Joint Chiefs General Colin Powell served as a central member of President Bush's strategic policy team and insisted on his prerogative to give the president and cabinet frank advice on strategic and military issues. At the time, however, Powell's influence was also deeply resented by many Washington defense pundits and by many in the top levels of the Bush administration, because of Powell's cautious insistence on building up overwhelming American military forces in the Gulf before combat began.[17]

When Bill Clinton came into office, he and his inner circle were generally uncomfortable with Colin Powell and the military leadership. Part of the problem was Clinton's record as an anti-Vietnam protester and his indiscreet comments in the 1960s, when he told a decorated army colonel that he "loathed" the military. The core of the friction was not the old issue of Vietnam, but rather the question of American military intervention in the Balkans. Clinton and his inner circle strongly favored employing U.S. troops to settle the ongoing civil war in Bosnia, while General Powell gave Clinton the same advice that he had given the previous administration. Powell regarded the region as a quagmire and questioned the importance of the Balkans to America's national interest. Powell also pointed out the negative aspects of U.S. intervention if the administration failed to get congressional backing for a conflict. Unfunded interventions require the military to cut resources for operations and training, which would lead to a decline in American military capability. As the president's chief military advisor by law, General Powell had the obligation to present such views to the president—however unwelcome.

Powell's stance on military intervention raised the ire of some pro-administration academics, who argued that Powell's behavior was proof that the military was "out of control."[18] In articles in political and academic journals these academics argued that civil-military relations had gone badly wrong— and that the fault was completely the military's. The core of the argument was that the military leadership was undermining the interventionist preferences of the administration by bringing up the negative consequences of proposed intervention in the Balkans. Academic critics of the military argued for a model of civil-military relations in which civilians had total control of the strategic process, with the military put in the position of functionaries carrying out the will of the administration, without discussion. The military tendency to point out problems in policies that were still in the planning stage was labeled "shirking" at best, insubordination at worst.[19] Colin Powell was singled out as a special villain for undermining proper civil-military relations.

Clinton's answer was to cut Powell out of the picture. Powell was highly respected by both parties in Congress and by the military leadership. It would have been a very popular decision to retain Powell as chairman of the Joint Chiefs. Nonetheless, Powell was retired when his term ended and replaced with Army General John Shalikashvili, who had a reputation within the Pentagon as being a "lapdog" towards his civilian and military superiors. Shalikashvili could be expected to be a "tame" chairman who would put no obstacles in the way of the administration's interventionist policies.[20] Still, the service chiefs did not roll over completely. In 1999 and 2000, operating under the strain of the unfunded conflicts and peacekeeping operations, the army staff went to the Clinton administration and made a strong case for a small increase in the army. They were turned down.

Ironically, it was the Bush administration that would create exactly the model of civil-military relations that the academic critics had proposed with the appointment of Donald Rumsfeld. From the first day of his tenure, Rumsfeld insisted that he was in complete charge: "The Constitution calls for civilian control of this department. And I'm a civilian."[21] Rumsfeld quickly acquired a reputation as being another McNamara—purposeful, arrogant, and unwilling to tolerate either debate or discussion. Rumsfeld brought an unprecedented degree of politicization to the top military leadership, dismissing and retiring generals who did not agree with him, promoting officers not for their performance, but for their support of Rumsfeld's ideas. In the words of Barry Watts, a top military analyst, "He [Rumsfeld] also favored military officers who would acquiesce almost completely to civilian control, and his personal style tended to silence divergent military advice, which was not a good idea."[22]

Rumsfeld followed the Clinton administration playbook by selecting exceptionally compliant officers as chairmen of the Joint Chiefs. General Richard Myers, chairman from 2001 to 2005, was certainly no Colin Powell. Unlike Powell, who had taken the lead role in explaining military operations in Washington press conferences during the Gulf War, during the Afghanistan and Iraq campaigns Myers stood behind Secretary Rumsfeld—who dominated all discussion of military operations and tactics. Myers would meekly agree with Rumsfeld if he was asked to speak at all. Myers was regarded as such a nonentity by Rumsfeld that he was cut out of any say in major military decisions, such as the decision to disband the Iraqi Army.[23] Myers earned a notable reputation as a "yes man" under the domineering Rumsfeld. During Congressional hearings on the Iraq War Senator John McCain noted that he was not interested in hearing any testimony from General Myers after Secretary Rumsfeld had testified. "I don't need General Myers' response. I know it will be exactly the same as yours [Rumsfeld's]." McCain then pointedly asked to hear the views of the theater commanders.[24]

Rumsfeld and his top deputies, Wolfowitz and Feith, established their leadership in a heavy-handed way, making it clear that they would brook no dissent or discussion of their ideas within the Defense Department. In February 2003, when the Army Chief of Staff Eric Shinseki testified before Congress and gave his assessment that the occupation of Iraq would require hundreds of thousands of troops, he was refuted the next day by Paul Wolfowitz, who testified that a small force could deal with Iraq and the occupation would be inexpensive and of short duration.[25] Rumsfeld and his deputies saw Shinseki's testimony as a disloyal act. When Shinseki retired, no senior Defense Department officials were present at his retirement ceremony—a classic sign of the secretary's displeasure. After Shinseki retired, the post of army chief of staff remained vacant for several months because no four star general could be found who was willing to work with Rumsfeld. Leaving the army without a chief of staff is unprecedented in wartime, but Rumsfeld's tenure as secretary of defense was filled with unprecedented acts.

In 2005 the compliant General Myers retired and was replaced by Rumsfeld with an equally cooperative chairman, Marine General Peter Pace. The new chairman was described by one marine colonel who worked in the Pentagon as "a man who never met a superior with whom he did not completely agree." As chief military advisor to the president, Pace followed Myers' example and dutifully repeated Rumsfeld's positions and policies. But the act had worn thin. From 2001 to 2006, as the U.S. military fought two wars with the smallest force in sixty years, it was glaringly obvious that the armed forces, especially the U.S. Army and Marine Corps, were too small for the burden of ground combat assigned to them. Congressmen, defense analysts, and retired generals all argued for a larger force.[26] Rumsfeld rebuffed all such criticism, pointing out that the top military commanders had not asked for more troops.

In December 2006, under pressure from all sides demanding that someone be held accountable for the mistakes of the Iraq War, President Bush asked for Rumsfeld's resignation. Within a month of leaving office, the joint staff and military services abruptly changed course and formally requested an increase of ninety-two thousand soldiers for the army and marines.[27] But there had been no noticeable change in the military situation between December 2006, when Rumsfeld left, and January 2007, when the services requested more troops. Either Rumsfeld had not been honest when he said that the generals had not requested forces, or the nation's top military leaders had withheld their strategic requirements from the secretary of defense in wartime—most likely for fear of incurring Rumsfeld's displeasure. Either way, Rumsfeld's tenure signifies an almost total breakdown in honest communication between the top military and civilian leaders.

Rumsfeld and his deputies established an unprecedented level of civilian micromanagement of military operations in wartime, which caused many to wonder if it were a case of the civilians trying to prove that they were better generals than the professionals. After making the strategic decision to go to war with Iraq, Rumsfeld threw out the military's carefully drawn list of unit deployment schedules, and insisted on deciding which units would go where and in what sequence.[28] During the preparation for the Iraq War, the service chiefs were all marginalized in the planning and troop deployment process.[29] Rumsfeld threw out existing operational plans for Iraq, which had evolved over a decade and called for a force of 250,000 troops. Rumsfeld insisted that the whole operation could be done with a minimal force, something on the order of 80,000 men supported by airpower. After a months-long process of developing new plans, Rumsfeld agreed on an increase over his minimal force policy. The final number of troops for the invasion of Iraq was 140,000.

The army's original plan for 250,000 men was not based on the need to defeat the Iraqi army—which was seen as not likely to put up much resistance. With considerable prescience, the army wanted 250,000 men on the ground in Iraq to control the country and establish order after Saddam Hussein's regime fell. Yet, within the Pentagon, the army's position on troop strength for Iraq was ridiculed by Rumsfeld's admirers among the military staff. [30]

The Dysfunctional Process — Strategic Decision Making in the Bush Administration

Since the 1950s the standard means to develop strategic plans and policies was for senior civilian and military staff members from the different agencies and services to meet in committee to develop strategic options for issues that the National Security Council sent to them. Senior officials of the civilian agencies and military services would develop various options which outlined the role each agency would play, what resources could be employed, and what advantages or disadvantages might accrue if the option was implemented. Since getting different U.S. government agencies to agree is like herding the proverbial cats, a representative from the National Security Council (NSC) chaired these meetings, acting as an umpire between the agencies and seeing that the committee produced an appropriate product for review by the higher levels. Since the NSC worked directly for the White House, the NSC representatives had the authority to push committee representatives to cooperate.

Options produced by the policy committees would be passed on to the Deputies Committee, which consists of the appointed undersecretaries and assistant secretaries of the agencies involved in the issue. For example, defense issues would include representatives from the Defense Department, military services, and State and Justice Department representatives. The job of the Deputies Committee, also chaired by a NSC member, would be to review policy options and make recommendations. Finally, the options and recommendations would be sent to the principals committee, which consisted of cabinet members, the Chairman of the Joint Chiefs, the National Security Advisor, and the President. The principals would decide to accept recommended options, or more likely, to send the issue back to the committees with questions and directives to develop the options further. Once policy decisions were made, the senior civilian political appointees were held accountable to ensure their agencies carried out the assigned part of the plan. It could be a cumbrous process, but it was understood. It also had the advantage of forcing agencies to discuss issues and coordinate operations. The interagency process worked slowly because of the bureaucratic culture of Washington and the continuous rivalry between agencies over budget slices.[31]

In the crisis atmosphere engendered by the 9/11 terrorist attack, the Bush administration turned away from the traditional strategic process and developed an ad hoc process that resembled the Kennedy administration's methodology. Believing that the normal process of developing strategic options through committees was too unwieldy, the Bush administration preferred to decide strategic issues by working through a small circle of advisors. This ad hoc method succeeded in late 2001, when a plan to topple the Taliban regime in Afghanistan combined local allies, covert operations, U.S. airpower, and a minimum of U.S. troops and accomplished the objective in a few weeks. Having succeeded in Afghanistan with this process, the Bush administration came to prefer the small group approach.[32]

The policy committees and deputies' committees still met with mandates to develop options and recommendations. But now the NSC representatives only attended the meetings and did not drive the process as in other administrations. One problem was the lack of clear strategic guidance coming from the president's office. President Bush and the National Security Council issued several major strategic documents between 2002 and 2007. There was the *National Security Strategy of the U.S. of America*, one issued in 2002 and another in 2006; the Defense Department published *The National Military Strategy* in 2004, and the National Security Council published *National Strategy for Victory in Iraq* in November 2005. Despite these impressive titles, none of the documents can truly be called a strategy. Each document outlines broad policy goals (endstates). The discussion of the ways and means to achieve the endstates is so vague as to be useless as guidance for cabinet officers or senior military commanders. The 2006 *National Security Strategy* opens with America's strategic goal: "It is the policy of the U.S. to seek and support democratic movements and institutions with every nation and culture, with the ultimate goal of ending tyranny in the world."[33] The means to achieve this goal include statements such as: "Ignite a new era of global economic growth through free markets and free trade."[34] The document stands firm in the Bush administration's commitment to spread democracy, but such sentiments are of little use to the ambassador or theater commander who has to maintain friendly relations with assorted dictatorships in order to fight the Global War on Terror.[35]

The Bush administration's two national security strategies asserted a new principle of America's right to conduct preemptive attacks. In fact, this assertion tended to make America's allies more nervous that her enemies. Beyond outlines of broad goals and principles, such as "promoting effective democracies," the two strategies lack any specific discussion of ways and means to realize the rather grandiose endstate. For example, no priorities were set to guide agency leaders in funding or resource allocation. While the strategies proclaim America's support for allies, the amount and type of aid the United States will commit, and under what conditions, is left unclear.[36] *The National Strategy for Victory in Iraq* devoted most of its text to an apologia of the administration's Iraq policies and argued: "Our policy is working."[37] None of the Bush administration's major strategic documents provide military commanders or senior civilian officials with specific, or even general, guidance for developing planning options. In 2007 I heard several generals express a common complaint: "We have no strategy."

With haphazard guidance from the top, the policy committees still met. But with no one tasked to drive the process, the interagency effort bogs down in the kind of bureaucratic issues common to Washington.[38] Interagency cooperation became a Washington buzzword, and a new organization was established to coordinate State and Defense Department stability operations. However, the level of funding obtained was so small ($3.3 million for fiscal year 2008) that the interagency hub remains incapable of doing much at all. The Washington culture was alive and well in 2007 when a committee of representatives from the State and Defense Departments, and other agencies, met to coordinate the Iraq reconstruction and nation-building activities in other countries. One committee sensibly looked at the CORDS program from the Vietnam War as a good model. However, the discussion broke down because the agencies bickered over who would get the credit for the program.[39]

Although committees developed options and passed them to the Deputies Committee for review, under the Bush administration system the process could be short-circuited by Secretary Rumsfeld, who had the authority to overrule the recommendations of the Deputies Committee and decide his own course of action. A further complication to the decision-making process was the position of Vice President Richard Cheney. Traditionally the vice president had a small staff of military aides and played a small role in security strategy. However Cheney, as a former defense secretary, created a large national security staff of his own and spent as much as half his time on defense issues. Cheney also had the authority to bypass the committee process, and even the cabinet, and could present major policy proposals directly to President Bush without review by the heads of the government departments or the National Security Advisor.[40] This system makes for rapid policy decisions, but with little review outside a tiny, closed group.

This system was bound to break down in dealing with an undertaking as large and complex as the invasion and occupation of Iraq. Early in the planning process for the Iraq War the interagency process broke down. Part of the problem was the unwillingness of the NSC to take the lead and force agencies to cooperate.[41] This problem was compounded by the refusal of Rumsfeld and his deputies to cooperate with other agencies, even when assistance and resources were offered. Once the Defense Department was given the responsibility for conducting the Iraq campaign, other government agencies, notably the State Department, were largely shut out of the process. In early 2002 the State Department set up a group of Middle Eastern experts called the "Future of Iraq Project" with the mission to plan for a post–Saddam Hussein Iraq. In the run-up to the Iraq War, there were several groups developing plans for postwar Iraq. Contrary to the standard image of Washington infighting, they cooperated to create a plan for postwar Iraq before the war began. Late in 2002 the army set up a planning group at the Army War College, and another group was created from faculty of the National Defense University in Washington. The State Department, with a head start in Iraq planning, produced thousands of pages of reports and analysis. Army planners brought the State Department's top Middle East expert, Thomas Warwick, into the Pentagon to coordinate his group's efforts with army planners. When Rumsfeld heard of the planning coordination, he ordered Warwick out of the building, insisting that the Iraq War was a Defense Department show. Discussions between mid-ranking military and State Department personnel continued, but had to be carried out circumspectly so as not to arouse the ire of Rumsfeld or his deputies.[42] In the end, the plans and studies had little effect as Rumsfeld simply ignored them. One key reason for the hostility of Rumsfeld and his deputies was that the planners' assessments consistently went against the belief held by Rumsfeld and his deputies that a war with Iraq would be quick, cheap, and simple. Planning studies of the CIA, State Department, and U.S. Army all came to the same conclusion: helping postwar Iraq would be very complex, would require a large U.S. force, and it would be very expensive.[43]

Much of the planning directly challenged administration assumptions. The Army War College planners went so far as to criticize the Defense Department's policy of handing the leadership of postwar Iraq over to Ahmed Chalabi of the Iraqi National Congress (INC). The army team, which included regional experts who spoke fluent Arabic, pointed out that Chalabi and his group had little influence inside Iraq.[44] Other recommendations that went against Rumsfeld's preferences were to keep the Iraqi Army intact and to use it under Coalition control to rebuild the country. With considerable prescience, the Army War College study argued that if the postwar process was not tightly controlled by the U.S. then Iraq could "become another Lebanon"—a land torn by sectarian violence.[45]

The Defense Department's top leadership summarily rejected the studies and planning of the State Department and U.S. Army planning groups. Although critical staff studies and developing alternative courses of action have been part of the normal strategic planning process for a century, the Defense Department leadership rejected this conventional process. One explanation for this behavior was the neocon approach, which had been fostered through the highly politicized Washington think tanks. The special-interest think tanks that gave the neocons a venue for their ideas emphasized issue advocacy rather than objective analysis. In the hothouse atmosphere of the think tanks, the intellectual method is less about engaging others to reach a solution, but instead focuses on pushing one's own agenda as far as possible. Critics are viewed as enemies, not as partners. When the neocons arrived in positions of power, they took this mentality with them and applied it to U.S. strategic planning. The military planners saw the attitude of Rumsfeld and the top civilian leadership and likened it to watching a train wreck in slow motion. Warnings about the level of effort that would be required in Iraq, as well as warnings of sectarian likely violence, proved accurate indeed.

From War to Insurgency to Civil War

In the aftermath of the Iraqi rout in Kuwait in 1991, the U.S. leadership expected that Saddam Hussein would be toppled from power by the Shiite rebellion in the south. Unfortunately, the U.S. and Coalition forces had only destroyed half of the elite Iraqi Republican Guard forces in the short ground campaign. Saddam Hussein, with the remaining six Republican Guard divisions that provided the main prop to his regime, suppressed the Shiite rebellion in the south. It was a genocidal campaign that lasted for months, and from 1991 to 1993 Saddam Hussein's forces slaughtered an estimated three hundred thousand to four hundred thousand Iraqi men, women, and children. With his internal hold on power secure, Saddam Hussein proceeded to defy the UN and Coalition powers, routinely breaking the sanctions program, and firing upon Coalition aircraft conducting patrols authorized by the ceasefire agreement of March 1991. By the late 1990s, Saddam Hussein tried to restore his waning prestige in the Arab world by expelling the UN weapons inspectors in Iraq, there under the authority of the cease-fire agreement to monitor the destruction of Saddam Hussein's WMD weapons and infrastructure. Despite such acts, Saddam Hussein was safely contained by U.S. forces and posed little threat to regional peace and stability.

The massive terror attack by al Qaeda on the U.S. on September 11, 2001, profoundly changed the international situation and the attitude of the American public. The United States mounted a rapid campaign in Afghanistan, home of Osama bin Laden and al Qaeda terrorist training camps, and toppled the brutal Taliban regime that had provided a safe haven to terrorists. In 2001 the United States and some allies, notably Britain and Australia, supported a coalition of Afghan anti-Taliban factions, and these formed a new government in Kabul. This campaign was hailed as a brilliant victory. However, Osama bin Laden and many al Qaeda and Taliban fighters escaped to fight on as insurgents.

In the first flush of victory in Afghanistan, the inner circle of the Bush administration turned its attention to Iraq. In the post 9/11 world, Saddam Hussein was seen as a serious potential threat.[46] If the UN ended the sanctions regime, as was likely, then Saddam Hussein could again build up his armed forces and equip them with chemical, biological, or even nuclear weapons. As an implacable enemy of the United States, Saddam Hussein could then make Iraq a base for weapons of mass destruction (WMD) attacks against America and its allies. This scenario was not far fetched. Although Saddam Hussein had few dealings with Islamic terror groups before 9/11, he was also a known threat who was capable of genocidal acts. His past record of aggressive war waged against Iran and Kuwait lent credence to the notion that he was a threat that ought to be eliminated.

Top-level discussions in 2001 and early 2002 led to the decision to topple Saddam's regime through a U.S.–led invasion. Through 2002 the U.S. military refined its attack plan and built up a coalition of nations willing to support the invasion of Iraq. Attempts to get the UN to support full-scale military action failed due to opposition from China and Russia, with both nations doing very well out of oil deals with the Iraqi regime. But Saddam Hussein's continual defiance of the UN, and with evidence presented that indicated that Iraq still had WMD stockpiles, the UN approved a vaguely-worded resolution condemning Saddam Hussein's violations of the ceasefire agreement and warned the Iraqis to cooperate fully with UN arms inspectors.

By the summer of 2002 it was clear that the United States was ready to use force to depose Saddam Hussein. Through late 2002 and early 2003, the U.S. increased forces to the region. Saddam Hussein cooperated in his own destruction by continuing to defy the UN and international inspection regime. Convinced by intelligence that Saddam Hussein maintained a stockpile of WMD after the 1991 war and that he had secret programs to develop and produce WMD, the Bush administration went to Congress, which authorized military operations against Iraq. With military preparations underway, the Defense Department finally considered a plan for postwar Iraq. In late 2002 Jay Garner, a retired army lieutenant general who had dealt with the Kurds in the aftermath of the 1991 Gulf War, was named by the Defense Department as the civilian administrator responsible for directing U.S. reconstruction operations in postwar Iraq. The Defense Department created the Organization for Relief and Humanitarian Assistance (ORHA) to administer Iraq until the Iraqis could hold elections and assume their own governance. Garner had only a few weeks and a tiny staff to prepare for the daunting mission.

The U.S.–Coalition campaign to take down the regime of Saddam Hussein was one of the most successful conventional war operations in history. In a high-intensity campaign between March 19 and April 9, three fast-moving

American divisions and one British division, supported by accurate and overwhelming U.S. and UK airpower, wrecked the four-hundred-thousand-man Iraqi military, overran all of Iraq's major cities, and toppled the Saddam Hussein regime. The Coalition forces suffered only a few hundred casualties. Most of the Iraqi army, including the elite Republican Guards, simply melted away. The U.S. offensive culminated with a rapid dash into Baghdad by the 3rd Infantry Division, where they pulled down the great statue of Saddam Hussein to the cheers of the Iraqi people, who were delighted at being freed from the yoke of one of the world's most brutal dictators.

During the advance on Baghdad some of the forces and tactics used by Saddam Hussein worried the American commanders. The conventional war went as expected, and Coalition airpower destroyed Iraqi armored divisions long before they could engage Coalition troops. But Saddam Hussein had prepared a force of forty thousand irregular troops. Called the Fedayeen, these irregulars used guerrilla tactics and made hit and run attacks against American units, firing anti-tank rockets at U.S. armored vehicles at point blank range. There was little that these light, irregular units could do against U.S. heavy forces. But the logistics units, with their fuel and supply trucks that brought up the rear of the American columns, were highly vulnerable to the Fedayeen.

During the advance on Baghdad, CNN interviews with senior American commanders for a documentary, *Inside the War Room*, provided some revealing glimpses of American military thinking. In speaking of the Fedayeen tactics, General David McKiernan, the Coalition Land Forces Commander, expressed his surprise: "This isn't the enemy we expected to fight." In fact, the Coalition intelligence staff across the street from McKiernan's command center had been studying the Fedayeen for months before the war and knew all about the Fedayeen organization and tactics. Moreover, the intelligence staff had briefed General McKiernan several times about the Fedayeen.[47] McKiernan, like most officers trained in the post-Vietnam army, had learned to focus so completely on conventional warfare that he could not grasp the concept of an enemy that used guerrilla tactics. It was a foretaste of what was to come all too often for the next few years—American commanders who understood only conventional war and were surprised by their enemies' unconventional tactics and ability to rapidly adapt.

205

In the run-up to the campaign, theater commander General Tommy Franks and General McKiernan expressed little interest in what would follow after the conventional campaign. Post-conflict operations are known as "Phase IV" in military jargon. While Franks understood the tactical battle, he failed to understand the objective of the operation. He was there not just to destroy the Iraqi forces, but also to secure the country and establish conditions for a transition to democracy. Army Lieutenant Colonel Tony Echevarria commented that the American military had taken warfare out of its political and strategic context, and now only understood the combat phase of a war. He noted that the U.S. military had a "way of battle," but no "way of war."[48] When Baghdad fell and a wave of looting swept the country that destroyed billions of dollars worth of infrastructure, Franks and McKiernan failed to respond quickly. Indeed, the postwar disorder caused far more damage to Iraq than the conventional fighting had. Washington was equally shocked at the events. Deputy Defense Secretary Wolfowitz remarked, with considerable understatement, "Some conditions were worse than we anticipated, particularly in the security area."[49]

There was an answer to the problem, and it came from the Iraqis. During the campaign most of the Iraqi army, which was not willing to die for Saddam Hussein, simply went home and took their guns with them. When Baghdad fell, and with it Saddam Hussein's regime, a group of Iraqi generals and colonels who commanded forty thousand troops came to the Americans with an offer to remobilize their forces and place them under American command. Then the Iraqis would establish order themselves. The American staff officers negotiating with the Iraqis supported the idea.[50] In fact, before the war Army War College planners had recommended just such an approach to deal with the Iraqi army. The army was one of the few arms of the regime that was respected by the average Iraqi as a true national institution, a result of the common suffering of Sunnis and Shiites during the war with Iran in the 1980s. However, Washington vetoed the judgment of the commanders on the spot, and the U.S. military lost its best chance to establish order and reconcile the officers of the old regime with a new Iraqi government.

With no plan to establish order and only 130,000 U.S. troops to control a country of 25 million, weeks of looting and chaos followed. The worst part for the Iraqis was the rise in crime. Saddam Hussein opened the prisons before the regime fell, and with little force to maintain order, criminal gangs had a golden opportunity to begin a wave of kidnappings and robberies that made life hell for the average Iraqi. The overwhelming majority of Iraqis were happy to see Saddam go, but even at this early date, the American occupation was clearly not working. Paul Bremer outlined the consequences of the failure to stop the looting in Baghdad: "We paid a big price for not stopping it [the looting] because it established an atmosphere of lawlessness." He added, "We never had enough troops on the ground."[51]

One lesson from recent conflicts was the need to place a corps of trained civilian experts in place to administer a country in the aftermath of the war. In Bosnia a large team of civilians moved in to manage the country in the wake of the peace settlement in 1995. During the peacekeeping operation in East Timor in 1999, the United Nations and a multinational coalition sent 1,500 civilians to help rebuild a country of 700,000 people. In the wake of the NATO intervention in Kosovo in 1999, a force of 3,000 international civilian administrators was quickly moved in to manage a country of 2 million people. In Iraq, a country of 25 million people, the U.S. brought in only 600 civilians to manage the rebuilding effort and to build an Iraqi administration. It was a ludicrously small figure.

Not only was the number of civilian administrators far too small for the task, ORHA, renamed the Coalition Provisional Authority (CPA) in May 2003, failed to assemble an experienced team for the job of reconstructing Iraq. A few experts came over to the CPA from the State Department and other agencies, but many people hired by the CPA to supervise major projects were young and completely without experience or expertise in the mission to which they were assigned. Hiring for the CPA was carried out by political appointees, who preferred solid Republican credentials and loyalty to President Bush over experience in government.[52] The younger CPA administrators soon earned the nickname "Twinkies"—after the dessert snack made from yellow sponge cake and filled with sweet cream and compressed air. The nickname seemed somehow appropriate. While some CPA members did sterling work, the organization earned a reputation for incompetence. A senior congressional staff member who visited Iraq in 2004 remarked, "In Iraq they needed the first team—and instead they sent in the fourth." Iraqi leaders dealing with the CPA complained of the inability of many CPA administrators to understand Iraqi conditions as they tried to replicate U.S. management systems in Iraq.[53]

Garner was replaced by Paul Bremer in May 2003. Despite the continuing disorder, the vast majority of Iraqis adopted a wait-and-see attitude towards the Americans. The Shiite majority (60 percent of the population) was delighted by the fall of Saddam Hussein; the Kurds (27 percent of the population) were busy establishing a virtually autonomous state in the north. The Sunnis (18 percent of the population) had mixed feelings. Many were just as happy as the Shiites that the oppressive regime was gone. But most were also nervous about losing the position of dominance they had held in Iraq since the founding of the country in 1920. Only Saddam Hussein's top people had any real reason to fear retribution.

Soon after arriving, Bremer published two orders. The first disbanded the Baath Party that had dominated Iraq for five decades and banned the upper ranks of the Baathists from holding management positions in government or industry. The Baath Party was a typical product of a totalitarian state. It was a mass organization with almost two million members, most of whom were required to join the party to work in the government or practice a profession. The upper ranks of the Baath Party contained many of the essential personnel needed to run the infrastructure and economy, and Bremer's order summarily threw them out of work. The next order formally disbanded the Iraqi army. At the stroke of a pen, four hundred thousand armed Iraqi men were thrown out of work and faced a bleak future.

The two orders ignited the insurgency. The ban on employing former Baath party members was a signal that there was no place in a new Iraq for former supporters of Saddam Hussein. The Iraqi army had been a top-heavy force with tens of thousands of officers, another typical product of a totalitarian state. Some were staunch supporters of Saddam Hussein, but most had joined the army and the Baath Party simply to have a career. The army officers, many of whom had been ready to work with the American occupiers, were now completely alienated. Moreover, Iraq was awash in weapons and munitions, and there was a large and angry officer corps who knew how to use them. With the former officers and the now-suppressed Baath Party political network, it was easy work for the now-huge number of discontented Iraqis to organize insurgent groups. Four days after the CPA order that disbanded the Iraqi army and Baath Party was announced, the first insurgent bombs went off in the city of Falluja, a Sunni and Baathist stronghold.[54]

The order disbanding the Iraqi army was one of the greatest strategic mistakes of the Bush administration. The story of who actually made the policy is unclear. Although Bremer issued the order under his name, it was a policy crafted in Washington and made without consultation of the senior military commanders in Iraq, who were still talking with the Iraqi officers about using the army to rebuild Iraq."[55]

The Iraqi insurgency was originally motivated by nationalist and ethnic considerations.[56] The vast majority of insurgents were disaffected Sunnis, who began a campaign of harassment and terrorism against the Coalition Forces. Even more disturbing, the insurgents began assassinating Iraqis who were cooperating with the Coalition forces and trying to form a new, democratic Iraqi government. In 2003 the Iraqi population included many genuine idealists who wanted to build a democratic and tolerant Iraq. They were happy to work with the Coalition Forces towards that end. These people, who would be essential to lead Iraq to a better future, were specially targeted by the insurgents.

As the insurgency began, the Shiites used their new freedom to organize political parties. Under the conditions of continuing crime and disorder the parties naturally formed militias, at first simply to protect their neighborhoods. The U.S. military, with too few soldiers on hand to control Iraq, at first welcomed the militias as a means of having the Iraqis police themselves. But as Sunni violence flared, the Shiite militias took on a military character with uniformed and paid members. It was easy to build a militia. Iraq had been one of the most massively armed countries in the world, and arms depots and police stations were open to looters where there were AK-47s, machine guns, mortars, and rockets for the taking. Some of the larger militias acquired heavier weaponry, including artillery. As violence rose, radical Shiite political leaders came to the fore, among them Moqtada al Sadr, leader of the two million Shiites who lived in the Baghdad district called Sadr City (named after his father, a Shiite leader of some note). Al Sadr, young and very ambitious, wanted power for himself and his people and was not going to wait to acquire power through a political process—although he would also use the election process to build up his political support. Since Sunnis were viewed as the main threat to his people, his militia, called the Mahdi Army, began a systematic program of forcing Sunnis out of ethnically mixed neighborhoods and seizing Sunni property for distribution among his supporters.

When the Sunnis turned to violence, the initial intent was to resist the American occupation and destabilize the Shiite-dominated Iraqi provisional government. Sunni insurgents were soon joined by foreign Islamic radicals from all over the Arab world, who the Coalition Forces nicknamed "Jihadis." The foreign fighters brought a special intensity to the anti-U.S., anti-Iraqi government campaign. Many were ready to die as suicide bombers and had joined radical Islamic groups specifically to achieve martyrdom in Iraq. Suicide bombing, often carried out in crowded areas to ensure maximum casualties, became a feature of the insurgency beginning in early 2004. With few soldiers to cover Iraq's borders, infiltration of Iraq by foreign fighters was easy.

The political parties saw their militias as self-defense forces. The act of ethnic cleansing of Shiites from majority Sunni areas, and Sunnis from majority Shiite areas, was also seen as basic self-defense. The thinly spread U.S. forces could do little to stop such actions that further increased the tensions within Iraqi society. As the intelligence agencies, State Department, and army planners had all predicted, Ahmed Chalabi was not the solution to creating a stable Iraqi government. He had been in exile since he was fifteen, and the Iraqi National Congress, regarded by the Bush administration as the key center of Iraqi politics, actually had little support within Iraq. Indeed, the most influential person in Iraq was Grand Ayatollah al Sistani, spiritual leader of the nation's Shiite majority. As Saddam Hussein suppressed the Shiites there had been no outlet for even a limited political life, so many Shiites had turned. Iraq had been one of the most secular Arab countries, but had become much more religious in the last decade. In the meantime, the influence of religious leaders such as al Sistani had been greatly enhanced. American leaders had not counted on this development or expected the immediate rise of popular leaders who would take control of the Iraqi political process out of the hands of Chalabi's Iraqi National Congress. As usual, there was no plan to deal with such developments.

Al Sistani favored a peaceful solution to Iraq and was grateful that the Americans had deposed Saddam Hussein. But also he demanded immediate elections despite the ongoing disorder. Immediately after elections that would surely grant the Shiites total power, he wanted the Americans to leave. It was, in fact, a recipe for large-scale civil war in Iraq. Within weeks of the fall of Saddam, Americans were facing an Iraqi political system that included some moderate parties, but also some very religious parties, and some that openly advocated violence against the Sunnis. All the ingredients for a civil war were in place in 2003—with the U.S. forces in the middle. Since the differences between the parties were so extreme, Iraqi leaders were forced to build a weak government. Ministries were handed to specific parties, and each party in power made sure that all hiring was done to favor their own supporters. Any regard for professional competence was disregarded. Since the ministries were split along party and ethnic lines, and mistrusted each other, each ministry raised its own security force. The cooperation between the many security forces was poor to nonexistent. In contrast, insurgent groups were often better at working together than the agencies of the new Iraqi government. As early as summer 2003, the Sunnis had produced at least eight groups fighting the Americans and Shiites. Built on local or religious loyalties, insurgent groups shared information and cooperated tactically against the Coalition forces and Iraqi security forces.[57]

The scale and intensity of the insurgency took the Pentagon and U.S. military commanders by surprise. General Myers, chairman of the Joint Chiefs, remarked, "This enemy is not like any enemy we've fought before."[58] He was clearly unaware of the many wars that America had fought against irregular forces, including the recent 1993 conflict in Somalia and the 1983 conflict in Lebanon. Myers was typical of his generation of senior officers. Having been trained in the post-Vietnam era, he understood conventional war. But warfare against militias, insurgents, and terrorists was completely new. The only guidance the military headquarters in Baghdad could give to Coalition units in Iraq was to seek out insurgents and fight them. In absence of direction from above, many unit commanders developed their own solutions and proved they could adapt quickly to the requirements of counterinsurgency. On their own initiative, U.S. Civil Affairs officers developed local programs to restart the Iraqi economy. They found funds from the old regime and created a public works program to clear the irrigation canal system in the south and got the farms producing again. Tens of thousands of Iraqis were put to work clearing the canals that had silted up during the 1990s. Over several months the irrigation system was repaired, farms started producing food, and tens of thousands of Iraqi were provided jobs. Throughout Iraq, local U.S. commanders met the challenge of local issues.

Most of Iraq was relatively peaceful, with the Kurds and their Peshmerga Militia in firm control in the north and the Shiites and their militias in control in the south. However, the insurgency flourished in the central part of Iraq, in the four provinces that included the majority of the Sunni population. From 2003 to 2005, U.S. forces carried out sweep-and-clear operations to drive the insurgents out of towns, but there was no pacification effort to follow the military operations. The Iraqi government was unable to establish a presence after the U.S. troops drove out insurgent bands. So as soon as the U.S. troops cleared an area, the insurgents came right back in.[59] Troops on the ground called this the "whack a mole" strategy after the arcade game in which the moles pop up at random. Many U.S. soldiers learned the politics of counterinsurgency: how to deal with local leaders and sheiks and negotiate local settlements. From 2004 to 2006, U.S. forces made considerable progress in pacifying one of Iraq's most violent provinces, the majority-Sunni al Anbar Province. U.S. commanders learned that working through Iraq's tribal system was the best method for winning cooperation of the Iraqis. It certainly was not the Westernized, parliamentary democracy that the U.S. policy had proposed for Iraq, but it worked.[60]

Accelerating the insurgency was the poor state of the Iraqi economy. The Bush administration's optimistic projections that the cost of rebuilding could be borne by the Iraqis proved 100 percent wrong. Ever since the Iran-Iraq War of 1980–1989, Saddam Hussein had poured the country's oil revenues into the military and his own pocket and paid little attention to maintaining the nation's oil infrastructure. The decade of sanctions and neglect of basic maintenance had left the oil production and distribution system in a shambles, and Iraq could only pump a small fraction of its oil capacity by 2003. The Iraq oil infrastructure needed billions of dollars of investment and a vast rebuilding program to produce large quantities of oil. Even if everything worked perfectly, it would be years before Iraq would see large oil revenues. In the meantime the Iraqi economy could survive only with a vast amount of U.S. and foreign aid.

In 2003 the U.S. Congress voted $18 billion for Iraq reconstruction aid and a large number of construction and infrastructure projects were initiated. But the effort was badly managed. The undermanned and disorganized CPA handed out expensive contracts, but it had only a handful of personnel to provide oversight. Much work was done, but many of the projects were shoddily constructed or never finished. Billions of dollars of funding was lost to simple waste and mismanagement between 2003 and 2007.[61] By 2007 the whole effort had produced only a moderate improvement in Iraq's economy. Although much of the vast destruction caused by the postwar looting had been rebuilt, electricity production still languished and Iraq was pumping only a bit more oil than it had in 2002. High unemployment continued to help fuel the insurgency.

Facing the disorder in Iraq in 2003, U.S. forces initially tolerated the militias that sprang up after Saddam Hussein fell. The sectarian militias at least kept some kind of order—something U.S. forces were unable to do. But the Pentagon failed to see the dangers inherent in the formation of party militias. In 2004 Paul Wolfowitz argued before Congress that the U.S. could accept the militias in Iraq as an aid to dealing with the deteriorating security situation.[62] In encouraging the formation of sectarian militias in 2003, Washington policy makers and senior commanders in Iraq helped create conditions for sectarian civil war. The parties resorted to taxing the local population to create full-time forces and, with unemployed military officers as leaders, many militia units were better led, trained, and organized than Iraqi military and police units. The hastily trained and organized new Iraqi security forces had to accept the authority of the militias in large parts of the country. For example, the police commander for Sadr City, a district of two million people, had only three hundred poorly armed men to keep order in 2004. Moqtada al Sadr had ten thousand heavily armed men in his Mahdi Militia. To merely survive, the police had to accept al Sadr's authority.[63] By early 2004 the Iraqi government had little real authority in the urban areas where the militias held sway. By late 2003 U.S. forces had already skirmished with al Sadr's militia units in an attempt to establish government authority in Baghdad.

Rather than rush more U.S. troops to Iraq to deal with the escalating violence, the U.S. solution was to stand up Iraqi security forces as quickly as possible.[64] Yet the Pentagon established only a small staff under General Paul Eaton, the Coalition Military Assistance and Training Command, for the huge task of building a new Iraqi military from scratch. Without a plan to build a new Iraqi military, the Pentagon insisted that a new armed forces be built quickly, at minimal cost and with minimal use of U.S. troops. The result of this policy could have easily been predicted.[65] The plan was crippled from the start.

Other essential tasks fell through the cracks. The Pentagon ignored the need to train the Iraqi military leadership, and no training program was provided for the Iraqi Defence Ministry civilians who would have to manage, supply, and equip the forces being created. With no program to train the mid-level and senior officers, the new army fell back into the old habits of complacency and corruption that they had learned so well under the Saddam Hussein regime. Promotion in the army and police went by party or faction membership, not by merit. Poorly performing or openly corrupt officers could not be relieved.[66] It was the old South Vietnamese officer corps all over again. The first battalion of the new army trained by American contractors collapsed even before it saw action. As soon as training was completed in late 2003, half of the battalion's soldiers deserted over pay problems and out of fear for the security of their families.[67] The second battalion that was trained collapsed when it was ordered into battle against insurgent strongholds in 2004. Throughout 2004, the police and regular army units experienced high desertion rates before going into action. The remainder tended to run away as soon as battle was joined.[68]

Since the Iraqi police and military forces proved incapable of operations of any kind, the U.S. forces were forced to carry the burden of fighting a clever guerrilla enemy on his own turf.[69] On the occasions when the insurgents stood and fought, as in the campaign to clear Fallujah in 2004, Americans could bring their massive firepower and high-tech weapons to bear. But the insurgents mostly fought the Americans with random sniping attacks and ambushes. The most lethal weapon used against the Coalition forces was the IED (Improvised Explosive Device)—explosives set up along roads and detonated to destroy passing Coalition military vehicles. With vast quantities of munitions stored throughout Iraq, it was easy for insurgents to take old artillery shells and aircraft bombs and turn them into bombs.

It took almost two years of insurgency for Washington and the U.S. military leadership to begin to understand that the hastily-conceived strategy to stand up minimally-trained Iraqi forces was not working. In January 2005 retired General Gary Luck was sent to Iraq to assess the needs of the Iraqi forces. He recommended that the U.S. army triple the number of trainers to eight thousand.[70] But the U.S. military culture worked against establishing an effective training program. Secretary Rumsfeld and the Pentagon leadership showed little interest in the training mission, preferring direct action operations by U.S. forces. U.S. officers picked up that attitude, and thought of the training mission as a "B Team" job. As in Vietnam four decades before, serving as an advisor or trainer with Iraqi troops counted for far less than leading U.S. troops when it comes to one's career resume.[71] A common practice was to assign National Guard or Reserve units to the complex task of training Iraqis, while U.S. combat units focused on finding and engaging the insurgents. Just as often, the National Guardsmen and Reservists were assigned to the training mission without any preparation beforehand. Because the coalition had failed to train a civilian staff for the Iraqi Defense Ministry, the Iraqi military remained almost completely dependent on the U.S. forces for logistics and support. By 2007, four years into the training effort, U.S. commanders in Iraq still rated very few Iraqi military units as capable of combat operations. Iraqi forces continued to suffer from high desertion and AWOL rates, poor leadership, and a lack of equipment.

By 2005 the Iraq War had changed from an insurgency into a sectarian civil war—with Sunnis supported by foreign fighters on one side, and the Shiites supported by Iran on the other. But it was not just a two-sided civil war. In the south of the country, notably in the city of Basra, rival Shiite militias fought among themselves for control of the city. In many locales, the Iraqi National Police became a branch of the most powerful local militia. Al Sadr's Mahdi Army remained one of the largest and most effective armies in Iraq. Other Shiite militias included the Iraqi Hezbullah, the Dawa Party Militia, and the SCIRI (an Iranian-trained militia force).[72] Each militia was aligned with one of Iraq's political parties and, once elections were held and a parliament convened in 2005, the party militias gained political cover from their sponsoring party. A weak Iraqi government could scarcely take action against al Sadr's Mahdi Army when that party controlled thirty of the seats in the Iraqi parliament.

Both Sunni and Shiite groups engaged in a systematic program of cleansing areas of members of the other ethnicity. In a resurgence of Islamic fervor that increased during the conflict, Iraqi Christians, who were not armed and posed no threat to anyone, were ruthlessly expelled from Sunni neighborhoods where they had lived peacefully for generations.[73] All through Iraq there was widespread ethnic cleansing from 2004 to 2007. Sometimes the ethnic cleansing was accomplished by threats. In other cases militia units ran death squads to kill enough of the rival group to force the others to flee. With the practice so widespread, U.S. forces could do little to protect Iraqis from the violence directed against them by their countrymen and even neighbors. By June 2007 the United Nations estimated that there were two million internal refugees in Iraq—almost all of them people who had been forced from their homes in ethnic cleansing campaigns.

An equally disturbing fact is the exodus of middle class and professional people from Iraq. The United Nations estimated that by 2007 more than two million Iraqis had fled the violence of their own land for neighboring countries—almost 10 percent of the population. Of these, the great proportion was the educated middle class and professionals: the teachers, technicians, and businessmen that Iraq desperately needs if the economy is ever to be rebuilt. An estimated 40 percent of all Iraqi professionals left by mid-2007, with many of the rest trying to leave. With the loss of the middle class, Iraq has become increasingly a nation of the semi-literate and warriors led by factional leaders—not a basis to establish a functioning economy, a democracy, or even a minimum level of stability. By voting with their feet, many Iraqis have decided that Iraq has no future.

The central driver of the insurgency, and also the way out, is a political settlement by the different Iraqi factions to share power and resources. There are five major issues dividing Iraqis. The first is the question of sharing the vast potential oil revenue fairly among all the Iraqi ethnic groups and regions. The second is a reform of the 2005 Constitution to grant more power to local regions and, thus, appease the Sunnis. The third issue is a reform of the laws excluding former Baathists from management and government. Most Baath Party members were compelled to join the Party, and punishing them denies the country their managerial talents and continues a sense of alienation. The fourth issue is reform of local elections. Finally, the Iraqi government has promised since 2004 to disband the political party militias and carry out a demobilization program to ensure that political power is not based on military force.

These reforms have been discussed in the Iraqi parliament for more than two years. Most Iraqis understand that the conflict can only end with some form of wealth and power sharing among the Iraqi groups. The problem has been the incredibly fractious nature of Iraqi politics and the weakness of President Nouri al Maliki's government. The Iraqi Parliament contains several major factions and party blocks, and several parties have powerful militias. In their own regions, those parties have almost complete control of civil life, and the Iraqi government is either irrelevant or co-opted by the regional leaders. Political parties have managed to block any legislation and reforms, even as their militias carry out ethnic cleansing operations. These issues have all been on the table since 2004—and have been consistently blocked.

By late 2006 the Bush administration, although maintaining its upbeat message on Iraq, had no clear way out of the impasse. Violence and casualties in Iraq were still increasing, and an estimated twenty-three thousand to twenty-eight thousand Iraqi civilians had died in 2006.[74] The Republican Party took a beating in the 2006 elections because of the public's unhappiness with the administration's handling of Iraq. That year the Republicans lost their majority in both houses of Congress, which meant that the Bush administration policy in Iraq would come under increasing attack from Congress. The Bush administration policy of funding the war with supplemental appropriations had finally caught up, as Congress was in a good position to cut off funding for the war without cutting off funding for the U.S. military. By 2007 President Bush had only one last chance to win some success out of Iraq before even the Republicans turned against him.

In the spring of 2007 the Bush administration latched on a military operations plan developed by Frederick Kagan, an academic from the prominent neocon American Enterprise Institute. To carry out a new strategy,

217

General David Petreaus was appointed commander in Iraq in early 2007. General Petreaus had shown considerable understanding of the requirements of counterinsurgency while he commanded the 101st Airborne Division in Iraq in 2003–2004. As commander of the Combat Arms Command from 2005 to 2006, he oversaw the production of a new counterinsurgency doctrine for the U.S. Army and Marine Corps. Kagan's strategy, approved by the White House, was to flow an additional thirty thousand U.S. troops to Iraq—mostly through the expedient of keeping many of the troops in Iraq for a longer tour and scraping up the last deployable units available in the United States. U.S. troops would "surge" into Baghdad with the mission of bringing greater stability to a city that had seen a major increase in ethnic killings in 2006 and early 2007. The idea was that if Baghdad were secured and ethnic cleansing reduced; the government would be in a better position to establish a general peace agreement between the factions. It was a strategy to buy time for the government and complete the training of more Iraqi military and police units.

There had been other surges during the Iraq War. For example, in early 2005 the force had been increased to provide security for the Iraqi elections. In each case the increase in troops had resulted in short-term success, with a reduced level of violence in some areas. Yet, after every surge the violence levels climbed again. One of the problems with the surges is that the relatively small number of additional troops deployed could only cover a very limited area, and the insurgents and militias always had the option of moving their operations to other areas while waiting for the U.S. forces to be reduced again. This consistent problem has been the weakness of the Iraqi government and its security forces. Pacification could be only temporary, since the Iraqis were incapable of establishing a strong government presence in areas that had been quieted by the U.S. troops.

The surge strategy of 2007 is likely to have little long term effect unless the Iraqi government can use the opportunity to enact necessary reforms and also field effective Iraqi security units capable of controlling areas on a sustained basis. However, as of summer 2007, American generals in Iraq still rated the Iraqi army as poorly trained, poorly equipped, and, in the words of a U.S. general, "not quite up to the job yet."[75] The United States faced the classic dilemma of a country using military means to strive for victory against an insurgency. U.S. forces could wage a perfect counterinsurgency campaign in Iraq. They could kill insurgent leaders, break up insurgent groups, and restore some order to Baghdad. But none of those things could bring success. The strategic center of gravity in Iraq is the Iraqi government. If President Nouri al Malaki and the various Iraqi factions are unable to come together and share power, resources, and reform the constitution, then the insurgency/civil war will continue and perhaps escalate. As of this writing (fall 2007), the situation in Iraq is still in doubt, but by no measure could one call the war a success.

Understanding Iraqis—Intelligence Failures

The Iraq War has been notable for some major American intelligence failures. The first was the CIA's assessment that Saddam Hussein had an active WMD program. In the words of the CIA chief, George Tenet, that assessment was 100 percent reliable: a "slam dunk." To be fair, intelligence collection and analysis is anything but a perfect art. The idea that Saddam Hussein, who had readily used chemical weapons against the Kurds and Iranians and had a large nuclear development program in the 1980s, would revive his programs was very believable. But the embarrassment for the United States was enormous when no active program was discovered—even after months of effort by specialist teams combing Iraq.

Another intelligence failure by the CIA had equally great consequences for U.S. planning and international relations. Bush administration thinking on postwar Iraq was based on the optimistic projection that Iraq's vast oil reserves would cover the cost of rebuilding the country. The administration believed that once Saddam Hussein's regime was gone, the Iraqi economy would thrive, and a prosperous economy would form the basis for a democratic nation. All such optimistic assumptions proved as false as the WMD intelligence.

According to his own account, when Paul Bremer arrived in Iraq in May 2003 he had little to no information on the state of the Iraqi economy: its organization, the condition of the oil infrastructure, its financing, and its management. A rapid assessment of the Iraqi economy produced a report that the economy was in utter disarray. It would take a vast effort to reorganize and rebuild the economy. Getting oil production to even a moderate level would require years of effort and billions in American and foreign investment. All of a sudden, the task of quickly transforming Iraq into a prosperous, democratic country became a mirage. Bremer would have to sort out decades of economic mismanagement in the middle of an insurgency.[76] Yet none of this ought to have been a surprise. The CIA did not have to look far to conduct a survey of the Iraqi economy before the war. Western oil engineers who had worked in the Middle East were well aware of the state of Iraq's oil infrastructure. There had been many high-level defectors from Iraq who could have provided information about the economic organization of Iraq, as well as the condition of major industries. Bremer ought to have arrived in Iraq with an economic analysis of the country in hand. Instead, George Tenet and the CIA had failed to do something as elementary as provide an economic survey of a country we were going to war with. This intelligence failure would have an even greater impact on the U.S. mission in Iraq than the false assessment of WMD.

At an even more basic level of strategic analysis, the U.S. civilian and military leadership failed to understand the nature of Iraqi culture and politics and the motivations that drove many Iraqis to insurgency. Before the war, the policy of viewing Iraq through the lens of the Iraqi National Congress and exile groups led to a poor understanding of contemporary conditions in Iraq. In testimony to the House Armed Services Committee in July 2004, Army General John Keane, who served as the acting army chief of staff in the summer and fall of 2003, admitted that many in the Department of Defense leadership had been "seduced by the Iraqi exiles in terms of what the outcome would be after the war." He also admitted, "There were very few people who actually envisioned, honestly, before the war what we were dealing with now after the regime went down .... We did not see [the insurgency] coming, and we were not properly prepared to deal with it."[77] The Islamic revival in Iraq had been ignored by U.S. intelligence, which meant that American soldiers would have to deal with a far greater degree of religious fervor and militancy than expected. Failure to understand such dynamics led the American leaders to overestimate Ahmed Chalabi's influence and underestimate the role that Grand Ayatollah al Sistani would play in setting a political course for post Saddam Iraq.

A further problem for the American leaders was their failure to understand the tribal nature of Iraqi society. All Iraqis belong to a tribe, and to a clan within the tribe. As in most Arab nations, there exists a traditional tribal leadership headed by sheiks and elders who exert enormous local influence. Under Saddam Hussein the Iraqi tribal system was largely suppressed, but after Saddam's downfall, and in the stress of postwar disorder, Iraqi tribalism quickly returned. With the resurgence of tribalism, Iraq's old ethnic rivalries revived. In the postwar power vacuum, traditional leaders reasserted themselves. This meant that most Iraqis would first turn to local leaders for authority, and not to the national government. Tribalism also worked against government efficiency. Senior government officials appointed to head government departments naturally favored members of their own tribe—with no regard for the competence or honesty of employees. This ensured that a large proportion of Iraqis would see their government as an enemy, or at least rival, force.

One of the greatest mistakes in understanding the dynamics of the civil war in Iraq was the U.S. emphasis on the foreign fighters in Iraq, the Jihadis, as the main enemy. American strategic estimates saw the foreign groups in Iraq, to include al Qaeda and its allied groups, as driving the resistance to the Americans. This interpretation fit the 9/11 frame of reference: to see Iraq not as its own conflict, but part of the global conflict against Islamic radicalism. The *National Security Council's National Strategy for Victory in Iraq*, published in November 2005, listed the main enemy insurgent forces in Iraq as: 1. Rejectionists (mostly Sunnis), 2. Former regime loyalists and, 3. Al Qaeda. This analysis was flawed. The Shiite militias, which possess far larger fighting forces than the insurgents and enjoy broad public support, were only briefly mentioned as a military threat. Yet, unlike the insurgents and al Qaeda, the Shiite militias (some closely connected to Iran) are far more dangerous to the long-term stability of Iraq. Al Qaeda forces can destabilize the country, but have no capability to control more than a few regions. The Shiite militias have the capability to control most of the country. Al Qaeda came into Iraq as an opportunistic move to inflict damage upon the Americans, but that organization does not drive the conflict because they are, like the Americans, foreigners. Al Qaeda and other foreign groups cannot easily hide among the population. Foreigners, even those from Arabic-speaking countries, are easily

221

identified by their dialect and accents. They can only exist in Iraq if they are provided cover among a large part of the local population. As long as the civil war exists and large elements of the population believe that they need the foreign fighters to help them against the other Iraqi groups, then Jihadis will be a major force. But if the Iraqis were to agree upon a national peace settlement that was broadly acceptable to the different ethnic groups, al Qaeda and the foreign fighters in Iraq would be quickly apprehended.

A further broad failure to develop a strategy for success in Iraq was the inability of America's military leaders to understand the requirements of training the Iraqi security forces. The original strategic goal was to see Iraq become a stable country, with security forces capable of defending against internal and external threats. This was a very tall order if one considers the largely dysfunctional nature of Arab armies. To use the term dysfunctional is no exaggeration. A small group of Americans have decades of experience in training Arab military forces, and they have noted some consistent cultural problems. The most thorough study of the culture of Arab armies was written by Kenneth Pollack shortly before the war in Iraq.[78] In a study of the Iraqi, Syrian, Jordanian, Egyptian, Saudi Arabian, and Libyan armies, Pollack noted that the main problem Arab armies face is poor leadership. Arab armies tend to reflect their societies, which are authoritarian and strongly hierarchical. Officers, who are from the higher strata of society, tend to have little regard for their soldiers' well-being. Since knowledge is power, higher ranking officers are reluctant to share information with their peers or lower ranking officers. Authority is carefully circumscribed, and initiative in the officer corps discouraged. In addition to the cultural problems are the technical ones. Arab military forces might have excellent weapons but not use them effectively because of poor logistics and maintenance systems. All of these problems are exacerbated by weak training programs.[79] A 1999 study by Norvell De Atkine, a retired U.S. Army colonel with long experience in training Arab military forces, further outlined the problems of training soldiers in a culture with extreme social stratification, little delegation of authority, and a system of tribal loyalties that undermines any concept of meritocracy.[80]

The U.S. military's experts on the Arab nations agree that building an effective Arab army requires working against a whole series of cultural barriers.

Success is difficult to achieve and would certainly take a long time. Yet none of this experience was taken into account by U.S. leaders who counted on a quick-fix solution to Iraq's security. Little attention was paid to a systematic training program for the Iraqi officer corps. When a new army was created, all the dysfunctional elements of the old regime became part of the new force. Early programs focused on training the privates, and not the officers, although U.S. advisors on the ground with the Iraqi army identified poor Iraqi leadership as the single greatest obstacle in developing the security forces. Nor was any special attention paid to logistics and administration—which are the well-known weak spots in Arab armies. The Pentagon decided to establish a civilian Iraqi defense ministry but did not provide training for the civilian administrators. So, three years after establishing the civilian-led defense ministry, the Iraqis still cannot carry out these basic tasks and are almost completely dependent upon the Americans for logistics support. All of these difficulties were foreseen by experts, but the requirements were ignored by Rumsfeld and the senior military commanders.

Another major obstacle to waging an effective campaign against insurgents in Iraq is the lack of well-trained human intelligence specialists in the U.S. military. The problem was identified early in the Iraq War as a serious weakness in the U.S. military, which has vast amounts of high-tech intelligence systems, but little in the way of fluent Arab interpreters and interrogators. A blunt report in October 2003 by the U.S. Army Center for Lessons Learned, and several other reports, all argued that deficiencies in the military human intelligence organization undercut U.S. efforts to fight insurgents in Iraq.[81] The lack of military linguists, a problem well known before 9/11, was ignored by a Defense Department leadership that went along with Rumsfeld's idea that the requirement for interpreters could be met by contract personnel. It was another money-saving Pentagon idea that never panned out. Many of the people contracted by the military in Iraq could barely speak English, and they lacked security clearances. Indeed, many of the interpreters hired by the U.S. military in Iraq were forced to quit after insurgents threatened their families. Six years after the start of the Global War on Terror, the U.S. military has yet to realistically assess its language requirements. Lack of trained military linguists means that U.S. commanders are limited in their ability to collect basic intelligence and understand the local context—both basic requirements for effective counterinsurgency.

The Media War—Losing Public Support at Home and Abroad

How George Bush lost the support of the American people between September 2001 and 2007 is a remarkable story. After the mass murder attack on the United States in September 2001, President George Bush rallied the nation and took quick action to attack al Qaeda camps and their Taliban supporters in Afghanistan. In 2001 President Bush's approval ratings in national polls were in the nineties—a natural reaction for a country that traditionally rallies around the president in time of war. Bush also had strong public support for his policy to invade Iraq and depose Saddam Hussein when he went to Congress in 2002 and won congressional approval for the action.

In contrast to the Vietnam War, where the American public strongly supported the Johnson administration's strategy from 1964 to 1968, the Bush administration lost the support of the American people in a remarkably short period of time. By June 2004, only eighteen months into the American occupation of Iraq, the majority of Americans doubted the wisdom of having gone to war in Iraq and doubted the policy of keeping American troops there. During the Vietnam War the majority of the American public supported the government policy until August 1968.[82] From 2004 to 2007 President Bush's popularity ratings steadily declined. George Bush now holds the record of the lowest sustained popularity of any American president since polling began in the 1930s. The public's perception of his leadership, and his handling of the Iraq War, were the primary causes for his unpopularity.

In 2004 the Republicans lost Congressional seats because of their support of Bush's Iraq policy. In 2006, their continued support of Bush cost the Republican Party control of both houses of Congress. The Republicans were replaced by a Democratic majority that was firmly united in opposing the U.S. presence in Iraq and determined to force an American troop withdrawal. By 2007 some top Republican congressmen and senators who had loyally supported Bush's policies had declared their lack of confidence in the administration's Iraq policy. In the spring of 2007, the Democratic congressional majority tried to force an American troop pullout by voting supplemental funds for the war on the condition that American troops begin to withdraw. After several weeks of impasse, Congress withdrew its objections. But it warned Bush that if no progress were made, then the war funding issue would again come to the fore.

One of the reasons Bush lost public support for the war was the president's poor ability to communicate. In contrast to his predecessor, Bill Clinton, Bush is undoubtedly honest and almost certainly believes what he says. But George Bush is also a notoriously poor speaker who tends to speak in short bullet comments that more often confuse his listeners rather than inform or inspire them. One of Bush's primary arguments for fighting in Iraq was that by fighting terrorists in Iraq, America does not have to fight them on home soil. Yet this argument fails the logic test. There is no reason why terrorist groups determined to kill Americans cannot send people to both Iraq and to the United States. Although repeatedly asserted by the administration, the connection between counterinsurgency in Iraq and the security of the American people at home was never clearly made, and less than a quarter of Americans polled in 2007 accepted the administration argument.[83]

On several occasions President Bush demonstrated an overconfidence that came across to many as thoughtless arrogance. On May 2, 2003, in the immediate aftermath of the campaign to depose Saddam Hussein, and with Baghdad and Iraq still in grave disorder, George Bush flew out to the aircraft carrier USS *Lincoln*. He landed in a jet wearing a military flight suit and stood in front of a huge banner declaring "Mission Accomplished." He announced to the nation that "major combat operations in Iraq are over." In July 2003, after U.S. soldiers had been under increasing insurgent attack for two months, President Bush insisted at a White House Press conference that things were under control in Iraq. "We've got the force necessary to deal with the security situation." Bush commented on the increasing attacks on U.S. troops in Iraq by saying, "Bring them on."[84] Such comments gave many the impression that George Bush simply did not take the war seriously. Such statements would haunt Bush in his second term as evidence that he did not comprehend the situation in Iraq.

The first great blow to the Bush administration's credibility was the failure to find any stockpiles of WMD in Iraq or any evidence that Saddam

Hussein had any functioning programs to develop chemical, biological, or nuclear weapons. Before the war and in the United Nations debates the Bush administration had made Saddam Hussein's possession of WMD the central reason for invading Iraq. The administration argued that the danger was very real, and after the September 11 terror attacks, the American public was very nervous of the possibility of an even more deadly form of attack. The failure to find any WMD in Iraq led to charges that the Bush administration was so bent on war that it had "lied the public" into a conflict. It became a huge international embarrassment, especially for the countries that were supporting the American effort in Iraq.

A better public relations strategy would have been to emphasize the nature of Saddam Hussein's genocidal actions against his own people. Saddam Hussein's campaign against the Kurds in the 1980s had been brutal, and the repression of the Shiites in the south after the Gulf War had been worse. When the Coalition forces overran southern Iraq they found mass graves containing tens of thousands of partially buried men, women, and children. The floor of the desert near Haiditha in southern Iraq, the scene of some of Saddam's massacres of the 1990s, was littered with scraps of clothing, eyeglasses, and even toys that children had been clutching when they were pushed out of the trucks and thrown into the killing pits. Throughout Iraq killing fields were found, and in some the victims had been buried alive. When U.S. Army officers who have seen the Iraqi mass graves talk about it, their eyes will fill with tears and their voices choke.

In cities and towns throughout Iraq, torture chambers were found in the secret police stations and walls of many cells were covered in blood. Saddam had murdered hundreds of thousands of Iraqis. He had arrested, tortured, and mutilated many more. Yet the Bush administration failed to focus a media effort upon the horrors of an evil regime that America might terminate. Accounts of the suffering of ordinary Iraqis featured only briefly in the U.S. and world press. Few films documenting Saddam Hussein's mass murders appeared. One could contrast the lack of a media campaign in Iraq with the concerted effort made in Germany after World War II to document the Nazi atrocities. If the U.S. had mounted a similar effort in Iraq to systematically document and publicize the crimes of Saddam Hussein's regime—complete with graphic photos and evidence—it would have had a stunning impact in the Arab world. The argument that democracy serves as a defense against genocide and oppression of the level of Saddam Hussein is a strong one. An effective media campaign would have confronted the European critics of the war with the argument that sometimes gross injustice can only be eliminated through military force. A campaign to publish evidence of Saddam Hussein's crimes against humanity would have been much more effective in maintaining U.S. and international support for the war than the Bush administration's media campaign consisting of esoteric technical data and photos of chemicals and equipment that could theoretically be used for making WMD.

At the start of the war there was a naïve confidence among the American military and civilian leadership that the American position on the war would be readily accepted in the United States and around the world, so the Bush administration failed to develop a strategic media plan. The military also failed to understand the dynamics of media operations after the conventional war was over. In 2005 one American general in Iraq argued that there was no need to publicize the U.S. position to the Iraqis and the world because "our deeds will speak for themselves."[85] The failure to have a coherent media plan, coupled with such attitudes, put the United States at a grave disadvantage in dealing with the world media. Arab and world opinion quickly turned against the war. By 2007 the story of Saddam Hussein's atrocities, the most powerful justification for taking down his regime, is largely forgotten.

Like the Johnson administration in Vietnam, the Bush administration exuded confidence in the ultimate success of the Iraq operation. From 2003, every time there came a major step in building the Iraqi government (sovereign government in 2004, elections of 2005, and the national referendum on a constitution) the Bush administration declared that a "turning point" had been reached—only to see the violence escalate further. As under the Johnson administration, U.S. leaders hinted in 2005 and 2006 that conditions would soon improve and the Iraqis would be able to take over their own security. But the public can take only so many "turning points" before losing confidence in their leadership. As with Vietnam, the American public saw the contrast between increasing casualties and growing disorder in Iraq versus the administration's confident message and the insistence to "hold the course." The administration's credibility was undermined from the start when Defense Department leaders predicted a short and cheap war. When the reality of Iraq was so clearly different than the administration's vision, then the public could only conclude that the administration was either incompetent or lying. Indeed, that public support for the Iraq War lasted as long as it did says a great deal about the willingness of the American people to support their government in wartime.

The Bush administration and many in the military have tended to blame the press for the loss of public support. The military command in Iraq provided a daily dose of good news including stories of schools rebuilt, businesses starting, and successful operations against insurgent groups. But the military today controls the message from the front much less than in previous wars. One great change in wartime media has been a soldier's access to computers and e-mails—and many American soldiers in Iraq have set up their own websites and write daily blogs on their experiences. More than in any other war, family, friends, and the public have immediate and daily access to the views and opinions of the soldiers in the war that are uncensored and unfiltered.

Soldiers blogging from Iraq often complain that the good work they have done in Iraq is being ignored by the press and only negative stories about Iraq have appeared in the mainstream media, and the claim of media bias has some validity. Reporters in every war zone have a tendency to exaggerate, sensationalize, and to publish accounts based on unconfirmed information. Indeed, one of the most common Iraq War blogs has been of soldiers writing refutations of press accounts of operations they participated in that bear little resemblance to what was reported by the media. Yet the broad thesis that the media has played the main role in undermining support for the war does not hold up. While some journalists demonstrate a remarkable ignorance of the military and hold an obvious anti-U.S. military bias, and the author has come across some of these, there are many journalists who have extensive experience with the U.S. military and are highly respected by those in uniform for their understanding of the military and their commitment to getting the story right. Some of the most knowledgeable and respected journalists have written devastating critiques of the Bush administration's leadership and the many mistakes made in Iraq.[86] Moreover, it is not only journalists who have leveled the charge of incompetence at the Bush administration. Much of the hardest-hitting criticism has come from retired generals such as General Anthony Zinni, former Centcom commander, and General Bernard Trainor, to name two of the most distinguished senior officers who have criticized the Bush administration's strategy.

The Bush administration's handling of the Iraq War is a story of numerous self-inflicted wounds, which include the failure to properly equip soldiers for combat in Iraq, followed by a failure to take care of the soldiers wounded in the war. The cause of the scandals was, yet again, the cheap war policy insisted upon by Defense Secretary Rumsfeld and the senior military leaders. In 2003 one of the top news stories about the U.S. military was the inability of the U.S. Army to provide all the soldiers in the combat zone with improved body armor, able to stop bullets, not just shrapnel fragments like the Vietnam-era body armor. Not expecting an insurgency or war without front lines, the army actually put a halt on buying new armor for the troops as supply chiefs figured they could get by with providing modern armor only for the front line troops. The army figured that the fifty thousand support troops in Iraq could do with the old, Vietnam-era armor. The savings amounted to $700 per set of armor. It was a miniscule sum by Pentagon standards but part of the army's culture of "do more with less." Under the Pentagon contracting system it took 167 days to start getting armor sets to the soldiers in Iraq. The army general overseeing the procurement system bragged that this amount of time was "historically pretty good."[87] Distrusting their leaders to equip them for war, many deployed soldiers bought their own sets of body armor privately, at $1,400 a set.[88]

In early 2007 the military was rocked by a series of national scandals about inadequate care provided for wounded soldiers. At Walter Reed hospital in Washington DC, the flagship hospital of the army, soldiers wounded in Iraq and Afghanistan were sent to live in substandard buildings with leaky roofs, peeling paint, and poor sanitary conditions. Some senior officers had known of the situation for months and had done little as they followed the Pentagon policy to keep war costs down. Finally, when the story broke in the national news, the secretary of the army was finally forced to resign—one of the few cases in which a senior official has been held accountable for incompetence during the Iraq War.[89] A survey of military health care across the United States showed that Walter Reed was not unusual. Military hospitals were grossly underfunded and understaffed, largely because the cost-conscious Pentagon would not pay enough to hire qualified medical personnel. Not only soldiers suffered from long waits and poor treatment, but their families also. Medical care was so scarce that a soldier or military family member had to wait a week to be treated for a cold or back pain. Military wives had to wait for weeks for gynecology examinations.[90] Such stories should make one wonder about the competence of a military leadership that went to war without planning for casualties. Or one might wonder about an administration that makes "support the troops" its message—and then fails to make support of wounded soldiers a priority.

The United States is losing the media war in world opinion. It is also losing the media war in Iraq. Before the war, the Army War College planning group argued that transitioning postwar Iraq into a democracy would require a well-functioning media system, and developing a media program for the Iraqis was high on its list of priorities as one of the means to help restore order and stability and begin the process of building a democracy.[91] One proposal was to ban antidemocratic sentiments and incitements to violence by any Iraqi media organs in order to inhibit the formation of parties that preferred a violent path to power.[92] Unfortunately, the U.S. military failed to understand the importance of a media program in occupying Iraq. Without a plan to develop a free Iraqi media, Coalition forces allowed insurgents and violent factions to fill the void upon the downfall of Saddam Hussein's regime in April 2003. Neither the military nor the civilian administrators of ORHA planned to distribute broadcast frequencies or license the Iraqi media so, in the post-invasion chaos, Iraqi factions simply seized assets of the old regime and set up their own newspapers, radio, and television stations. It was described as a "free for all—if you have enough armed men."[93] Rather than working as a means to promote stability and democracy, the post-Saddam Iraqi media mostly worked to support the opposite.

Some Iraqi factions used their new media outlets and their newfound freedom to demand the violent suppression of their opponents. Major factions used their seized television and radio stations and newspapers to openly oppose the new Iraqi Governing Council, which was composed of the more moderate and democratic elements in Iraq. Neither the CPA nor the Iraqi

Governing Council was able to suppress the newspapers and radio stations calling for violence.[94] In the crucial period of 2003–2004 when the Iraqi political future was being debated, the Coalition made only a small effort to help the pro-democracy Iraqis to present their side of the story. The Iraqi Media Network was established with a small band of dedicated volunteers who managed to cobble together some old equipment in a studio in Baghdad and begin broadcasting. The lack of adequate equipment was compounded by a shortage of trained Iraqi media professionals willing and able to work for the new Iraqi government. The problem was low pay. Networks of the Arab nations hired many of the best known and most experienced Iraqi media specialists to manage their broadcasting in Iraq. They were offered five times the salary that the resource-strapped CPA was willing to pay. So the most experienced Iraqi news commentators and media personalities went to work for the Arab networks which generally put an anti-American slant on the news. The small, idealistic band of amateurish Iraqis working for ORHA and the Iraqi Governing Council tried their best—but with few resources they could not compete against the media of the Iraqi factions or the Arab networks.[95] By 2005–2006 the Iraqi media had evolved into a highly partisan force that primarily promoted the factional and more radical agendas. There is little voice in the media for moderation in Iraq.

International Context of the War

From 2001 to 2003 the Bush administration worked to build an international consensus to support an American invasion of Iraq. Months of effort in the United Nations from mid-2002 to early 2003 failed to gain support authorization from the international body to invade Iraq. Unlike the widespread foreign support for the 1991 Gulf War, China and Russia and even France were determined to block any authorization from the UN Security Council. The best the United States got was a general warning to Saddam Hussein to stop defying UN inspections and sanctions.

Yet U.S. policy still won considerable foreign support. Colin Powell, as secretary of state, rounded up allies to support the UN resolutions warning Iraq. Thirty nations volunteered to support the effort with soldiers or civilian administrators. But the Coalition military support for the 2003 war was much less than the 1991 war. With the exception of Britain, which committed a division and took over the occupation of the Basra area, most national contingents were relatively small. Italy, Spain, Poland, Japan, and Korea sent forces, and El Salvador contributed an infantry battalion. Most countries contributed noncombat forces such as engineers and civil affairs specialists. Counting the large British force, the international coalition never amounted to more than 40,000 soldiers, civilian administrators, medical workers, and so on. It was a welcome addition to the effort in Iraq—but it was far from meeting the huge needs of postwar Iraq.

In 2004 General Tommy Franks, Centcom commander, remarked that his planning staff had expected 150,000 additional international troops to help with peacekeeping operations after the fall of Saddam Hussein, but they never materialized."[96] How this assumption originated, and why it persisted, is unknown. But optimistic projections were one of the most common traits of the Bush administration's approach to the war. There was some cause for hope in the spring of 2003 when a UN group arrived in Iraq to assist in the rebuilding of the country. The UN team began discussions with Paul Bremer on their role in the reconstruction of Iraq, but in August 2003 insurgents destroyed the UN headquarters with a massive truck bomb which killed the UN's special representative and over twenty other UN employees. It was a brilliant political move on the part of the insurgents. The insurgents had made the security situation too dangerous for operations, so the UN group pulled out of Iraq. Now the United States would have to deal with Iraq with significant support from only a few allies.

A large part of the assisting Coalition forces could not be readily employed in the most urgent task, which was securing the country. Sending token forces to Iraq was an important gesture of solidarity with America, but foreign governments had their domestic opinion to worry about, and public opinion in most allied countries was strongly against the American invasion of Iraq. So America's allies in Iraq generally limited the deployment of their forces to the most secure parts of the country—and even then insisted that their forces would only engage in combat if attacked. This further limited the already insufficient forces needed to conduct the active patrolling and policing necessary for a counterinsurgency campaign. Within a year of the start of the insurgency, the

Iraq operation was extremely unpopular with the public of America's allies. Foreign governments that supported the Iraq operation were punished by their voters in subsequent elections. Spain changed governments in 2004, and the new government promptly withdrew its forces from Iraq. Italy threw out its pro-American government in 2005, and its new government also announced a troop withdrawal. Other nations, under heavy pressure at home from the voters, reduced their efforts in Iraq.

The U.S. invasion of Iraq inflamed sentiment in the Arab and Islamic worlds and offered Middle Eastern radicals an easy opportunity to strike at the Americans. By early 2004 a variety of foreign Islamic radical groups were well established in Iraq. Osama bin Laden appointed one of his senior deputies, Abu Musab al Zarqawi, to lead "al Qaeda in Iraq." He led a bloody campaign against the Coalition forces before being killed in 2006. Since 2003 the foreign fighters in Iraq have played an important role in the insurgency, with many of the bloodiest mass bombings carried out by them. With the borders poorly secured, it was easy for foreign fighters to infiltrate into Iraq. Syria shares a long border with Iraq, and access through Syria is relatively easy. Iran also shares a long border with Iraq, and the Iranians have had little trouble funneling arms and assistance to Shiite factions. The ready access to outside funds is also important as insurgent fighters and militiamen in Iraq are usually well paid—often much better paid than the Iraqi security forces. Insurgencies require constant cash infusions, as well as personnel and weapons. Unfortunately, the presence of hostile regimes on Iraq's major borders means that there is little chance of limiting the cash, weapons, and fighters needed by the insurgents and militias.

The Iranian connection is especially important to Iraq. Iran, like Iraq, is a majority Shiite country, and Iraq is the site of several of the most important pilgrimage sites for Shiite Moslems. Many Shiite Iraqis feel more comfortable with Iranians than with their own Sunni countrymen. By 2006 there was clear evidence that the Iranian Revolutionary Guards was equipping the Shiite militias and terror groups with highly sophisticated explosives and small arms. U.S. forces have detained some Iranians within Iraq who were there to help train the Shiite militias.

In March 2006, with the Iraq effort clearly in trouble, Congress set up a special commission to develop some strategic recommendations. The committee was chaired by James Baker, a former member of the Reagan cabinet, and Lee Hamilton, Democratic congressman with extensive service on the House Foreign Relations committee. The study group contained a mix of old Washington insiders from both sides of the political aisle. Some, like Lawrence Eagleburger and William Perry, were knowledgeable in foreign affairs. Others, like Vernon Jordan and Leon Panetta, were not. The idea was to find an Iraq strategy that could obtain some consensus from both parties. The Iraq Study Group met for eight months, visited Iraq, talked to a large number of officials and experts and released its report in late November 2006.

The Iraq Study Group Report briefly outlined dozens of recommendations to improve the American effort in Iraq. Many of them were simple common sense. For example, the report proposed that the chaotic management of the Iraq reconstruction effort be placed under one office and director. They also recommended that the State Department increase its corps of foreign aid specialists.[97] The most significant part of the report was the recommendation that the Iraq crisis be solved through a regional solution to include a general agreement between the United States, Iraq, Syria, and Iran. The study group reasoned that if Syria and Iran cooperated in cutting off support to insurgents and militias, it would be a major step towards tamping down the violence in Iraq.

Political leaders from both parties hailed the Study Group's suggestions as forming the basis for a new strategy in Iraq that could help end the insurgency and enable American forces to withdraw from what was becoming an ever more costly war. The uncritical acceptance of the Study Group's recommendations illustrates a high degree of unreality that pervaded the leadership of both parties in Washington and how desperate the desire for a solution—any solution— had become. While the Study Group's concept of regional diplomacy sounded good, the actual chance of such proposals working stood at about zero percent. One could not ignore the fact that Syria and Iran both generously support international terrorism, and both are implacable enemies of the United States. Syria and Iran view the United States as their primary threat. Any chance to weaken American power and prestige, especially in the Middle East, would work mightily to their national interest. A strong democratic Iraq would be an implicit threat to the stability of the Iranian and Syrian dictatorships, as both countries have dissident ethnic groups and movements that would be emboldened if a strong democracy took hold next door. From the Iranian and Syrian view, keeping the insurgency in Iraq going is a very good thing.

The question that the Study Group did not try to answer was: What kind of price might the U.S. have to pay Iran and Syria to get their support to help the Iraqi government? Since continuing the insurgency is strongly in the national interest of Syria and Iran, the price would have to be high indeed. Would the U.S. perhaps allow Syria what it has wanted for decades—full power to dominate Lebanon? As a price for cooperation the Iranians are likely to demand that the U.S. end economic sanctions and stop its opposition to the Iranian nuclear program. Would the U.S. be willing to accept a nuclear Iran for a promise of help in Iraq? These are the tough questions that American policymakers face if they follow a policy of bringing Iran into the negotiating process.

One can expect that any deal the Syrians or Iranians might agree to would be one that would seriously undermine America's position in the Middle East. Even if a deal with Iran and Syria were cut, there would be no assurance that either country would hold to it and not continue covert aid to the insurgents and militias in Iraq. Neither country has a trustworthy reputation. One might remember the last time the United States had diplomatic relations with the Revolutionary Islamic Republic of Iran. The Iranians sacked the American Embassy and took fifty-five U.S diplomats hostage and held them in a brutal captivity for 444 days. If the Iranians cannot be expected to comply with the most minimal international norms of diplomacy, why would they honor an agreement that would shut off aid to their allies and co-religionists within Iraq?

Assessing the Surge

In September 2007 General David Petreaus, commander of U.S. forces in Iraq, and Ambassador Ryan Crocker, the State Department's top man in Iraq, were called back to Washington to testify on the progress of the "surge" of additional forces into Iraq. General Petreaus was able to point to several tactical successes in which local security had been improved by greater U.S. troop presence. However, his testimony on the development of the Iraqi military forces was not so optimistic. After four years of effort and the establishment of 160 battalions of the Iraqi Army, only a dozen Iraqi battalions were rated by the U.S. military as being capable of independent operations. Almost all of the Iraqi Army still depends on the U.S. Army for support, logistics, and command and control—not a very strong result from years of effort and the expenditure of billions of dollars. As of late 2007 there is little prospect that the Iraqi Army will be able to operate on its own for years to come.

Where General Petreaus could offer some positive news, Ambassador Crocker, testifying about the political conditions in Iraq, had an overwhelmingly negative report. Iraqi politics remains highly factionalized, and the efforts to pass the benchmark legislation necessary for national reconciliation remains stymied. The Ambassador could offer little hope that the situation would improve over the next six months.

During the Congressional hearings of September 2007 neither the Congress nor the Bush administration wanted to take a close look at the elephant in the closet—the existence of powerful militias that are now the dominant factor in Iraqi politics. As of 2007, the major parties in Iraq, including the main parties in government, all field large private armies. Whether Iraqis want it or not, politics in Iraq is now based on factional military forces. Disarmament of their factional militia would be seen by any of the major Iraqi political groups as tantamount to suicide. Iraqi politics has developed into something resembling Lebanon during that country's civil war of the 1970s with a weak central government with little power to contain or control the factions.

In September 2007 other reports were presented to Congress that showed a much gloomier picture of Iraq. The report of the Independent Commission on the Security Forces of Iraq chaired by retired Marine General James Jones argued that the Iraqi National Police was incompetent and crippled by sectarianism and recommended that it be disbanded.[98] A report by the General Accounting Office on the Iraqi government that same month also noted the general failure of the Iraqi government to meet its goals of political reform and protecting the population. Both reports emphasized the division of Iraq into hostile, armed factions.[99] Even under the best scenarios, by late 2007 the Bush administration was assuming that the Iraq War would require stationing large U.S. forces and carrying the major burden of the war for another five to eight years.

Consequences

The insurgency in Iraq was caused by a combination of factors: A highly dysfunctional strategic decision-making system, a faulty military doctrine, poor relations between the civilian and military leadership, deeply flawed intelligence assessments, and a civilian and military leadership that found it difficult to adapt. There were also the internal factors in Iraq: the ethnic tensions and the economic breakdown that set the right conditions for an insurgency. The foreign factors that helped the insurgency included minimal support for U.S. policy from allies and active Syrian and Iranian support for violent factions in Iraq. Finally, the lack of a plan for postwar Iraq guaranteed a bad outcome. All these factors came together to form a perfect storm in Iraq and set the United States up for failure.

The consequences for the failure of U.S. strategy in Iraq are severe. As of late 2007, the best endstate that the United States can hope for Iraq was the worst case envisioned by the prewar planners of the Army War College—that Iraq will be like Lebanon of the 1970s and 1980s. It will be a country with a weak and ineffectual government, a largely powerless military, dominance of the nation's politics by armed factions, a broken economy, and a state of ongoing civil war. Even if the Iraqi government were to arrange a peace settlement among the warring groups, the party militias and system of ethnic/party domination of the ministries is now so well established that effective governance will not be possible. That's the best case.

There are several other probable scenarios that would be even more detrimental to U.S. interests than the current dilemma. If Kurdistan breaks away to form an independent nation then Turkey would likely invade. A ruthless Shiite victory over the Sunnis could bring Sunni nations such as Saudi Arabia to the side of their co-religionists as Iran sides with the Shiites. A regional war is not at all an unlikely scenario. The worst case for the United States would be to see American military forces and influence pushed completely out of the region and Iran, soon to have nuclear weapons, established as the hegemonic power in the Gulf Region. In short, in any realistic assessment there are no good outcomes likely to come from the Iraq War. The U.S. strategy in the near future, or in the administration after George W. Bush, will have to be oriented to managing the Iraq war so that America's failure in that country is only serious, but not catastrophic.

One of the outcomes of the Iraq War is a U.S. military close to the breaking point. By 2007 the U.S. military was gravely weakened by repeated deployments of units to Iraq. The military forces have been stressed beyond their limits, and American military capability is in rapid decline. Military services have had to drastically drop standards to recruit enough personnel to man the force, always a bad policy for the long-term health of the military. The professional officers and NCOs of America's grossly undermanned military are now in their third tour in Iraq and Afghanistan. National Guard and Reserve units have been sent to second tours. As of 2007 retention rates for mid-ranking officers and NCOs, the core group for effective unit leadership, had fallen. Billions of dollars of equipment has been destroyed, damaged, or simply worn out in Iraq. Units in the U.S. are drastically short of equipment, and funds for the future of the army, such as training and education funds, have all been cut to keep the Iraq deployment going.[100] With half of the army's forty-three brigades deployed overseas, and the other half recovering from combat tours in Iraq or Afghanistan, the United States has no strategic reserve force to deal with crises. The Iraq War has so consumed the U.S. military's resources and personnel that the U.S. Army's new chief of staff, General George Casey, testified to Congress in September 2007 that "the current demand for our forces exceeds the sustainable supply . . . and we are unable to provide ready forces as necessary for other potential contingencies."[101] In short, if a serious crisis were to erupt over the next several years, the United States would be hard-pressed to deal with it. This means that, whatever the outcome of the war in Iraq, the United States has assumed an enormous strategic risk of not being able to respond to major crises or threats because of the heavy commitment to Iraq.

Another serious consequence of the Iraq War is the loss of international support for U.S. efforts. After seeing the quagmire of Iraq, few of America's allies will be willing to participate in any U.S.-led military operation for a long time. Governments of allied nations have taken a beating in domestic elections for supporting the U.S. effort in Iraq. Future military involvement with the U.S. will face increased opposition in the parliaments of America's allies.

Finally, the Iraq War will erode American domestic support for military operations in the future, no matter how necessary or justified they might be. The long-term public reaction to the Iraq War is likely to be a public inclined to isolationism. Just as public opinion in America was skeptical of military operations for years after Vietnam, even aid to allied nations will be increasingly criticized as such aid might lead to "another Iraq." At a time when there are very serious threats in the world, and when the United States might have to use its power to support endangered allies or meet threats from radical regimes such as Iran's, public support for any operation will be weak.

The problems caused by the Iraq War will take years to fix. It took the military a decade to recover from Vietnam, and will likely take longer to recover from Iraq. Rebuilding America's foreign relations will be a major problem for any U.S. administration after President Bush. Unless the United States suffers from another major terrorist attack, public support for military operations abroad will be lacking. In the meantime, the United States will be much more limited in the military and foreign policy options it can employ.

CHAPTER 5
What is Needed

■ ■ ■

"The conduct of small wars is in fact in certain respects an art by itself, diverging widely from what is adapted to the conditions of regular warfare."
—Colonel C. E. Callwell, *Small Wars: Their Principles and Practice*

"The shooting side of this business is only 25 percent of the trouble, and the other 75 percent lies in getting the people of this country behind us."
—General Sir Gerald Templer

BY ITS VERY NATURE, INSURGENCY is a fundamentally different kind of war from a conventional war between states. In terms of strategy, fighting insurgency is a more complex process. Influencing the insurgency center of gravity, the population, is more difficult than influencing an enemy government. The support of the population, necessary for the insurgent and counterinsurgent alike, is fickle. Individuals and groups commonly switch allegiances during the conflict, something rare in conventional war. The resources required to address the causes of insurgency are less military in nature and weighted more towards civilian aid. A nation will employ soldiers in the counterinsurgency role, but an effective counterinsurgency strategy also requires large numbers of policemen, civilian aid workers, engineers, teachers, media specialists, and other nonmilitary personnel who will interact with the civilian population.

While a good strategy for counterinsurgency is a complex endeavor, it is also an absolute necessity for success. As these case studies illustrate—and one could bring in many more examples to make the point—vast resources and

241

military superiority are no guarantee of success in counterinsurgency. Success depends on using those resources in a comprehensive and planned manner and that requires a strategy.

In the four cases examined in this book the defending government possessed vast resources in comparison with the insurgents. Government forces enjoyed overwhelming military might. The governments had other advantages, such as an established infrastructure of governance, media expertise, and a large corps of military and civilian experts. The governments also had the ability to influence foreign governments. Yet, despite impressive advantages, the counterinsurgent governments failed. Their failure was not caused by military defeat; it was rooted in fundamentally bad strategy. Moreover, each of the counterinsurgent governments examined in this work made similar strategic errors. This concluding chapter will summarize the major mistakes of each nation and try to develop insights into the nature of strategy in counterinsurgency. As I noted on the first page of this book, insurgency has been one of the most common forms of conflict and is not going away. It is my hope that the people and governments of great democracies can learn some lessons from this book and consider them when we confront future insurgencies.

The Role of Vision — Defining and Adapting Endstates

Wars, even those that end with complete victory by one side, rarely lead to the exact endstate the leaders envisioned when the war began. World War II was supposed to end with Germany's surrender, and then all the major powers would cooperate in the occupation and administration of Germany. The original plan was to have Germany divided into three occupation zones but kept as a unified nation. Germany would be de-Nazified and brought back into the world community as a peaceful and democratic nation. The endstate envisioned full cooperation between the British, Americans, and Soviets. But during the latter stages of the war it became evident that Josef Stalin would not change his ways and the Soviet Union would use its position to assert control over all of Eastern Europe. Thus, the Soviet occupation zone of Germany became a Soviet satellite.

After victory over Germany, cooperation between the Western Allies and the Soviet Union ended quickly as Soviet ambitions became evident. It was not the kind of peace that the Western powers had planned for. To deal with the unexpected environment, Britain and America quickly changed their plans for postwar Germany. To their credit, the British and Americans adapted well to new conditions. Britain and America cooperated to build a free and strong West Germany. The Marshall Plan formed the foundation of a strengthened Europe. British and American leaders crafted a new grand strategy to contain the Soviet Union. It was a demonstration of strategic leadership and decision making of the highest order.

The lesson is that at the conclusion of a conflict, a nation attains an endstate that is usually less than originally hoped for. This is especially true when the conflict is an insurgency. Insurgencies might be total war for the insurgent, but for the counterinsurgent they are often limited wars and wars of choice. Because fighting insurgents is a matter of choice for a great power, the national leadership has a much harder job maintaining public support. In total war one can militarize the economy and require great sacrifices from the population—especially when the alternative is national defeat and occupation. But in fighting insurgencies the price of failure is not as high. The question arises: Just how much is a nation willing to pay before the cost becomes too high? If a democratic government chooses to fight an insurgency, it must also convince its own public that the fight is in the national interest and that the cost of failure would be substantial. An additional complication is that conditions quickly change during conflicts. Domestic concerns might come to the forefront of the public consciousness; new international problems develop; the nature of the insurgency and the insurgent demands might change. Dealing with change and uncertainty is the responsibility of the national leadership, and the strategic planner must constantly take such factors into account.

A successful strategic process requires the national leadership to adapt to changing conditions. This, in turn, requires a review of the final objective and asking the fundamental questions: Can the original endstate be achieved? Will attaining the objective require substantial additional resources? Will public domestic opinion support the price that will have to be paid to achieve the stated goal? If the answers to the above questions are No/Yes/No, the national leadership will have to review their policy to see where compromises can be made, whether a more modest objective is realizable, and whether the cost can be sustained. Convincing legislatures and the public to accept new and more modest goals can be difficult, and it will require considerable political effort. Adapting the endstate to something less than ideal requires civilian and military leaders to fully understand their nation's capabilities and limits. It also requires a realistic understanding of the national interest.

In the four cases studied in this book, the endstates envisioned by the major power governments at the start of the insurgencies were highly unrealistic. This is not a judgment from hindsight. Many in the national leadership understood the strategic problems at the time. In Algeria the status quo that France fought to maintain was utterly unacceptable to most Algerians, and many French leaders fully knew this. In trying to maintain a colonial empire in the post-World War II world, France was battling its allies and the tide of history. The British were in a similar situation in Cyprus. The government expected that the Cypriots would settle for the status quo and remain docile colonial subjects. It was an unreal view, and it was coupled to an equally unreal understanding of Britain's changed position in the postwar world. Until the Suez fiasco brought a sense of reality back to British leaders, the government consistently maintained the position that Britain could still play the role of a great imperial power in the Middle East. After Eden resigned, a reevaluation of national strategy correctly concluded that Cyprus had no great strategic worth for Britain.

In Vietnam the endstate envisioned by the U.S. and Western powers in 1954—that of an independent noncommunist South Vietnam—was neither impossible nor unrealistic. It took enormous blunders by the Diem regime to push the country into an insurgency. However, once the insurgency got going, the chance for a program of reconciliation between the many factions in the south became more difficult.

In Iraq, the question of endstate is more complex. There were a host of factors that worked both for and against the establishment of a peaceful and democratic Iraq. The Bush administration developed its policy around the vision of re-creating Iraq as a Western-style liberal democracy. But this was a country and region with no tradition of democracy whatsoever. Something like a moderate regime might have been possible after Saddam Hussein, but the idea of a full-fledged democracy was a step too far for the Iraqi culture. In any case, the highly ambitious endstate was not realizable because of the flawed assumption that building a democracy in Iraq would be an easy and cheap process.

Faulty Decision-making Process

One consistent problem that appears throughout these case studies is a flawed strategic decision-making process. Good strategic decision making requires effective coordination of the civilian and the military agencies of government. It is a difficult task, but not impossible. However, successful decision making requires national leaders to build a healthy system that allows for full consideration of strategic options with a high degree of objectivity.

The structure of the French Fourth Republic was so weak, due to the strong divisions between the party blocks, that between 1945 and 1958 it was impossible for any government to advocate the fundamental reforms and economic programs that would have defused the Algerian insurgency. In 1958, the French government itself was dramatically refashioned, and a new constitution gave the president the necessary powers to implement a broad reform program in Algeria. De Gaulle developed an excellent strategy that addressed the fundamental problems of France's interests in Algeria. De Gaulle balanced French interests against the economic needs and political aspirations of the Algerians in a comprehensive solution. Unfortunately, the reforms of 1958 came four years too late to change the final outcome. As the war continued, the passions of the *pied noir* community in Algeria became so inflamed that any negotiated settlement that protected the core interests of both sides became impossible.

Before and during the Cyprus insurgency, Anthony Eden short-circuited the British strategic decision-making system. He cut the Colonial Office, the cabinet department most knowledgeable about Cyprus and legally responsible for the island, out of the decision-making process. Eden put the issue under the Foreign Office and worked to block out discussion of the more moderate, and more realistic, views of the Colonial Office.

During the Kennedy and Johnson administrations, American strategic policy devolved from a fairly open process into a closed system, where a small circle of individuals close to the president controlled the development of policy. Kennedy and Johnson's inner circle worked to stifle criticism from the Joint Chiefs on Vietnam policy. The closed-group approach to policy making allowed a few determined ideologues, notably Walt Rostow, McGeorge Bundy, and Robert McNamara, to drive the strategic process. There was little debate over Rostow's

245

flawed assumption that a bombing campaign targeting the North Vietnamese economy would be enough to end the North's support for the insurgency in the South. From 1963 to 1965, as the Johnson administration developed its strategic options for Vietnam, numerous voices called for a counterinsurgency strategy for South Vietnam. But such a program would have required a considerable amount of U.S. aid and a long process of advising and building up the South Vietnamese state. On the other hand, Walt Rostow's theory of gradual escalation—victory through an air campaign—promised immediate and decisive results. So rather than address the difficult problem of insurgency in the South, which was the main problem, the Johnson administration focused on North Vietnam. Focusing on the North allowed the Johnson administration to choose a conventional war strategy that the U.S. leadership and military felt comfortable with. In a healthy strategic process, plenty of warning flags would have gone up when Rostow proposed his theory of gradual escalation as the solution. Rostow's theory was based on a false picture of Vietnamese culture and history, and there were American regional experts available who could have refuted the theory if they had been brought into the process. Indeed, the huge sacrifices that the Vietnamese had made in the war against the French ought to have been a warning that the Vietnamese were a people who were not easily deterred.

Once the conventional war and bombing strategy was decided upon, the Johnson administration held to the policy for three years. While Johnson had doubts about the bombing campaign, his immediate circle remained fixed on the air strategy. On the ground, Johnson simply poured more troops into South Vietnam where Westmoreland kept promising a decisive military victory. It took the Tet offensive of 1968 to prove that the strategy was not working. Only after Tet did the administration turn to a strategy that might have been successful if employed from the beginning. But assumptions about the capability of U.S. bombing and U.S. conventional forces were not seriously questioned from 1964 to 1968.

The strategic decision making of the Bush administration took the flawed methodology of the Kennedy and Johnson administrations to extremes. To an even greater degree than the Kennedy and Johnson administrations, strategic policy and decisions were driven by a small circle of men around the president. The Bush administration created a closed process that allowed little input from outside the circle. Those within the circle regarded questions, criticism, and even planning as somehow "disloyal." The small-circle approach allowed a few dominant personalities and determined ideologues like Donald Rumsfeld, Paul Wolfowitz, and Douglas Feith to drive the strategic process. If the strategy under Lyndon Johnson was driven by bad assumptions, then the Bush administration strategy was based on incredibly bad assumptions: about Iraqi politics, force requirements for occupation, the cost of the war, and the economic condition of Iraq. Yet these assumptions were never questioned, and the strategies they engendered were not adapted even when the assumptions collapsed. As the situation visibly deteriorated in Iraq, Rumsfeld and the Defense Department remained rigidly on their course of fighting an insurgency with inadequate resources.

In Iraq, the Bush administration failed to carry out the most fundamental requirement of strategy: developing options and plans. American civilian and military leaders not only failed to produce an adequate plan to deal with postwar conditions in Iraq, they also failed to have a "Plan B"—a series of alternative options ready in case something went wrong with the primary plan. Developing alternate plans to deal with a variety of probable scenarios is not an esoteric political science theory—it is an essential part of any sound strategic process. Simply put, the strategy process of the Bush administration was dysfunctional.

The Algeria, Vietnam, and Iraq examples illustrate the problem of rigid formulaic thinking driving the strategic process. In Algeria the French army fixed on the *Guerre Révolutionaire* as the solution to the insurgency. The problem was that this was essentially a tactical approach to counterinsurgency and failed to address the main issues of concern to the Algerians. Good tactics can, and did, achieve great local successes in Algeria, Vietnam, and Iraq. But tactical success does not win the war.

The strategies for the Vietnam and Iraq wars were driven by dubious theories. Although theories are important for the strategist in providing insightful guidelines in planning, uncritical acceptance of theories and treating them as rigid models invites disaster. In insurgency one is dealing with a more complex environment than in state-on-state relations, and there are no simple models for success. Walt Rostow's concept of graduated escalation was an elegant theory, but it was based on wholly wrong assumptions about the Vietnamese interests and character. In contrast, the neocon approach to strategy cannot even be described as a coherent theory. It was more of a broad optimism: "Everything will work out fine." The neocon doctrine was grounded in a naïve belief in the power of democracy, and real problems were wished away.

Applying Appropriate Resources

Effective counterinsurgency requires applying the right resources to deal with the problem. Military and security forces are certainly a high priority, but effective counterinsurgency operations also require a large component of economic aid and civilian administrators. Determining the right type and amount of resources to be applied is a major component of the art of strategy. In all four case studies, the counterinsurgent government had considerable resources at its disposal. And in each case, the government made critical mistakes in applying these resources.

British strategy—from the end of World War II to the Suez Crisis—is a striking case of a nation trying to do too much with too little. In the postwar world, Britain did not have the money or military forces to carry out its objective of maintaining an imperial status in the Middle East.[1] Yet both Eden and Macmillan, as cabinet members and government leaders in the mid-1950s, staunchly supported the position that British power had to be maintained in the Middle East. Both men, as well as the British Joint Chiefs, failed to recognize the limitations of postwar British power as they insisted on maintaining the appearance of empire without the economic substance to back it up.

The strategy built around Cyprus as a grand imperial bastion was an illusion. Early in 1956 Harold Macmillan, then chancellor of the exchequer, took note of Britain's debts and economic troubles and concluded that major defense cuts were necessary in order to restore the economy. Yet, later that year, Macmillan strongly supported the last great attempt to exert an imperial presence at Suez.[2] Even if the Cypriots had happily acquiesced in the status of the island as a permanent colony, Britain never had the necessary resources to fulfill Cyprus' role as an imperial base for Middle East operations. It took the Suez fiasco of 1956 to bring a degree of reality back to British strategy.

The French government had been warned for a decade before the Algerian insurgency began that the Algerian population was in desperate need of a program to alleviate the marginal condition of a great part of the population. The economic conditions did not cause the insurgency, but they fomented a deep dissatisfaction among the Moslem population. The poverty of most Algerians was convincing proof of the justice of the Algerian cause in the eyes of many in France and around the world. Once the insurgency broke out, France applied ample military force to deal with the insurgents. The French military campaign was highly successful, and the French army broke the military power of the FLN. But the effort to improve the infrastructure and living standards of the Algerians lagged until 1958, when De Gaulle put the Constantine Plan into effect. Had France employed such a plan early in the insurgency, it would have alleviated the economic distress that made the FLN so popular.

America followed a course in Vietnam that was similar to the French approach. The United States employed its resources to a conventional war strategy and put a low priority on developing the South Vietnamese economy and securing the rural population. When the U.S. changed its strategy in 1968, putting the CORDS program into action and securing the rural population, the results were impressive. If such a strategy had been applied early in the conflict, the Viet Cong would have had much less appeal.

In Iraq the U.S. national leadership had vast economic and military resources available and simply decided not to use them. Conditions for an insurgency were established when the Defense Department sent a force into Iraq that was far too small to establish stability for the population. It might have been possible to turn the situation around in 2003 if the Pentagon had adjusted its plans and sent in a much larger force. But this was not done. The civilian side of the U.S. occupation in Iraq was also poorly supported. There were considerable funds available for Iraqi reconstruction, but the number of civilian administrators and supervisors sent into Iraq was so small that they were unable to efficiently manage the reconstruction program. The Pentagon's insistence on fighting a cheap war with minimal forces doomed the Iraqi social and economic recovery effort.

Understanding the Context

A key requirement in waging a successful counterinsurgency campaign is to understand the context of the country and population one is dealing with. Insurgencies are about politics, and the political goals of the insurgents are usually easy to understand. Yet in the four insurgencies examined in this book, the government's top military and strategic leadership repeatedly failed to understand the political and social context of the population and the insurgent viewpoint. The national aspirations of the Greek Cypriots and Vietnamese were well known. The grievances of the majority of Algerians were well known, and senior French officers had warned of the conditions for revolution for years before the outbreak of conflict. That various ethnic groups in Iraq were likely to use violence to attain power was recognized by U.S. military planners before the war.

This failure to understand the views and motivations of the population is what an aircraft pilot would call "poor situational awareness." Politicians and senior military leaders need to be alert to potential problems and have a "feel" for the things going on around them. In these four insurgencies there was plenty of warning and ample information available about the politics and sociology of the population. The growth of insurgent movements should not have been a surprise. Yet, in every case the national leadership misinterpreted the signs of an impending insurgency and then misunderstood the seriousness of the situation when the violence began. In each case, the first response of the government was to dismiss the insurgency as a relatively minor event.

In the cases examined, the national leadership mistakenly focused on foreign actors or powers as the primary cause of insurgency. France blamed the Egyptian government of Abdul Nasser for the insurgency in Algeria. This misconception led the French to invade Egypt in 1956 in a failed attempt to unseat Nasser. The British government of Anthony Eden blamed Greece for the trouble in Cyprus and focused its efforts in a futile attempt to settle the internal problems of Cyprus through foreign negotiations. The result was a messy solution that led to more than five decades of internal and international tension over Cyprus. As the decision was made to intervene in Vietnam, the U.S. government focused on North Vietnam as the driving force behind the NLF insurgency in South Vietnam. This drove the United States to carry out a bombing campaign against North Vietnam and initiate a conventional war against North Vietnam's regular army. In the meantime, the fundamental problems in South Vietnam were ignored for years. In Iraq, the United States focused on the foreign terrorists in the country as the main problem. In the meantime, the Shiite militias, a much greater threat to the long-term stability of the country, consolidated their forces and power bases.

One consistent feature in each case was the tendency of senior leaders to search out and latch on to the views and suggestions of a small group of staunch loyalist indigenous people. This group could be counted on to support the views and prejudices of the counterinsurgent power. In Algeria the miniscule group of Algerians appointed to government councils—derided as "Beni Oui-Ouis" by the vast majority of Algerians—advised the French leadership. This small group, which lacked credibility even among Frenchmen who knew Algeria, reassured the government that Algerians were basically loyal to France. The common people were being misled by a small band of fanatics. It was a comforting view for a French government that desperately wanted to maintain the status quo and avoid the kind of political battles that a major reform program would require.

In Cyprus, early in the insurgency, Greek Cypriots in the British civil service told their bosses exactly what they wanted to hear: that support for enosis was not strong among the population. The British leadership wanted to believe that the cause of the unrest was Archbishop Makarios, and if he were removed the insurgency would die out as a moderate Greek leadership took over. Harding easily fell for this advice and decided on the simple expedient of exiling Makarios. The reality was that Makarios was one of the more moderate of the Cypriot leaders. Without Makarios on the scene, much more radical leaders took over the insurgent leaderships and quickly escalated the violence.

Starting with the Diem regime in Vietnam, the American leadership became enamored of, and inevitably disillusioned with, a succession of highly westernized Vietnamese leaders. Leaders like Diem came from the elite classes and spoke good English, or at least an educated French, and they readily convinced American political and military leaders that they were the legitimate voice of the Vietnamese. Americans, few of whom understood Vietnamese history or society, usually needed little convincing. The Vietnamese elites quickly convinced American leaders that with generous U.S. support they could lead their nation and make it a bulwark against international communism.

Prior to the Iraq War, many in the Washington political establishment came to see the situation in Iraq through the eyes of a small group of elite

Iraqi exiles. Through the 1990s the Iraqi National Congress (INC) ran one of the most effective lobbying campaigns in Washington DC. The INC, a small group of highly westernized Iraqi exiles, could routinely be found at Washington's receptions and political meetings. For years the INC pushed for U.S. military action against Saddam Hussein and convinced Washington insiders like Paul Wolfowitz and Douglas Feith that Ahmed Chalabi, an exile wanted for bank fraud in Jordan who had lived outside of Iraq for forty years, was the logical choice to be president of a post–Saddam Hussein Iraq. Chalabi, with his Western style, Shiite ethnicity, and superb connections, cleverly cultivated the people who came to power under George Bush. The Bush administration and the Defense Department leadership were repeatedly warned by army planners, the Defense Intelligence Agency, the CIA, and State Department experts that Chalabi had little real following inside Iraq. In fact, the real conditions in Iraq were far different than those described by the Iraqi National Congress, and plenty of U.S. experts were aware of this. But neocons were so taken with Chalabi and the INC that all the warnings about him were ignored. Chalabi was easy to deal with, and he represented a simple solution to the Iraq problem.

In each case, policy makers and leaders perceived their own appointed indigenous leaders, or fluent and attractive westernized factional leaders, as representing the "authentic voice" of the indigenous majority. This is what I call the "Chalabi effect," and it is used by policy makers to enhance the credibility of their position. After all, who could know the local situation better than a local?

In the counterinsurgencies examined here, the government of each major power had its own experts, usually mid-level soldiers or civilian advisors, who knew the country intimately. They explicitly warned their superiors against accepting the advice of the clever indigenous politicians who enhanced their leadership positions by telling British, French, or American leaders precisely what those leaders wanted to hear. The government's own experts usually offered a far more complex and pessimistic analysis of the country's condition, which went against the grain of the government's preferred strategy. Unfortunately, senior government and military leaders often make sure to hear what they want to hear. In every case there was a successful effort by those at the top in the decision-making process to suppress the analysis and advice of their own experts while preferring the optimistic analysis of power-seeking local figures.

Intelligence Failure

Armed forces and national intelligence agencies tend to be very good at conventional military intelligence tasks such as counting warheads, tanks, and heavy equipment items of enemy nations. Military intelligence analysts generally have a thorough knowledge of the doctrine and procedures of potential enemies, as well as their capabilities. But dealing with insurgencies is not so simple and straightforward, and civilian and military intelligence agencies are often unequal to the task.

All four cases represent major intelligence failures at the national and operational level. The French police and intelligence services failed to spot the start of an insurgency in Algeria for what it was. For the first months of the war, French intelligence believed that it was dealing with the same old Algerian nationalist groups instead of a much younger, and much more radical, new force. French intelligence recovered from its early mistakes and produced excellent intelligence on the FLN that helped break that organization. But it was done at the price of widespread torture and strong-arm tactics, which helped turn the Algerian population and world opinion against the continued French presence in Algeria. Such tactics were unnecessary. There were many French officers and SAS personnel who treated the Algerians with respect and did not tolerate torture and abuse, and they collected excellent intelligence on the FLN.

In Cyprus the British neglected to establish a police intelligence branch until the eve of the insurgency—even though there had been warnings of violence from credible sources for years. Indeed, the local joke was that everyone in Cyprus *but* the British governor knew that the island was about to blow up. Once the insurgency began, British police and intelligence continually fumbled. Throughout the whole insurgency the rebels' top military leader, Colonel Grivas, lived in Nicosia and operated under the nose of the British. They never suspected. As in Algeria, human rights abuses in the name of intelligence gathering helped turn domestic public opinion against the British cause. Unlike Algeria, the British got very little useful information from such methods.

253

In Vietnam the intelligence effort was distorted by directives from Westmoreland that forced accurate intelligence analysis to be revised and made more optimistic. The whole intelligence process in Vietnam was corrupted from the tactical to the strategic level in an effort to provide optimistic figures to the national leadership. In the course of pushing a false intelligence picture through doubtful statistical analysis, senior U.S. commanders also fooled themselves. The Tet offensive of 1968 was a major enemy effort that ought to have been identified beforehand.

The U.S. military and CIA went into Iraq with a superb high-tech conventional war intelligence capability but utterly inadequate human intelligence resources. The United States had faced terrorists and unconventional threats from the Islamic world for a decade before the invasion of Iraq in 2003, but the military and intelligence services had only a handful of people able to speak fluent Arabic. In Iraq the military effort was continually hampered by a shortage of trained and competent human intelligence specialists—which is exactly what is needed when dealing with a civilian population among whom the insurgents are hidden. Despite the obvious shortcomings of U.S. military intelligence, only a small effort has been made to improve the situation and increase the number of human intelligence specialists.

Counterinsurgency and the Military Culture

In Western armed forces, the personalities and thought patterns of those that make it to the top tend to be linear and rigidly systematic. To ensure military coordination and efficiency, standardization is important—including standardization of doctrine. A set formula approach to warfare is preferred, and this approach is governed by the well-known "principles of war." The principles of war are taught in slightly different variations in the officer schools of every major Western military and form the basis for operational thinking. In the American version, the principles of war are: mass, offensive, surprise, security, economy of force, unity of command, objective, and maneuver. In theory, if one adheres carefully to the principles of war, one is assured of a competent battlefield performance. That's how it goes in theory.

However, this systematic approach to war also carries a heavy price. Western staff colleges tend to be training institutions where a rigid application of set principles is emphasized. Careers are made in following the "school solution" and applying doctrine in an exact manner. However, conformity in doctrine and procedure, which are necessary elements of conventional war, can easily become conformity of thought. If a senior officer spends his whole adult life mastering one form of warfare, he might be unable to understand a conflict that lies outside the confines of his training.

The conventional training of Western armies and the formulaic and linear thinking that produces battlefield success in conventional war are largely irrelevant in countering an insurgency. Cyprus, Vietnam, and Iraq are examples of wars in which the conventional war mindset of most military leaders failed to address the unconventional situations they encountered. Many military leaders prove themselves as first-rate leaders in conventional war, a condition where there are more knowns than unknowns. But the same men often fail when confronted by the unknowns of unconventional war. Field Marshal Harding is a good example of a first rate conventional soldier who got it completely wrong when thrown into counterinsurgency operations in Cyprus. Westmoreland earned a solid reputation as a combat soldier in World War II, but failed spectacularly to understand the nature of the war in Vietnam. More than a few knowledgeable commentators have pointed out that General Tommy Franks' campaign to destroy Saddam Hussein's army in March and April 2003 was brilliantly executed. Yet Franks was also at a loss to deal with the disorder of post-Saddam Iraq, and he failed to recognize the conditions of an insurgency that had begun. Indeed, his approach to the war, and that of most other senior American commanders who served in Iraq, failed to consider the nonmilitary tasks and complex political requirements necessary to reach the desired end-state for Iraq.

Senior officers who can function as both good conventional soldiers and counterinsurgency strategists are relatively rare. The conventional generals who muddled through Cyprus, Vietnam, and Iraq did not lack professional competence, but they still failed to adapt the military strategy to the realistic needs on the ground. These conventional commanders lacked two necessary traits of successful generalship in counterinsurgency: imagination and vision. Only a few of the senior officers discussed in this book were able to succeed both as conventional and unconventional soldiers. General Creighton Abrams

255

had the imagination to change the strategy in Vietnam. General Challe was a brilliant commander whose strategy in Algeria handed the advantage to President De Gaulle. Unfortunately, in his participation in the failed 1961 coup, he destroyed the advantage that he had won a year before.

Seeking Political Settlements

Counterinsurgency campaigns, even the most successful ones, usually end with a negotiated solution in which the government makes concessions in order to get the insurgents to stop fighting and to join the political process as a peaceful partner. One of the most important responsibilities of a strategic leader in counterinsurgency is to understand the political conditions and work these to the best advantage. Military success is not an end in itself. It is, rather, an important part of a comprehensive strategy. For example, military operations can buy time for the government to employ other resources to strengthen their position and undermine the insurgents; such a program might be infrastructure development. Military success can also help secure a large proportion of the population and deny whole regions to the insurgents. Most importantly, military success gives the government the advantage at the negotiating table.

When governments agree to negotiate with the insurgents, as they usually do, ultimate success relies largely upon the political and negotiating skills of the civilian and military leaders. It often comes down to doing one's homework. A leader must understand not only the position of the foreign governments, but also of the insurgent factions. At the same time, the government and military leaders must possess a thorough understanding of the insurgent movement, and they need to consider all the factors that might advance or block a peace settlement. In most cases, there are members of the insurgent organizations who are willing to compromise. However, various conditions can also arise that can overwhelm even the best negotiators.

Unfortunately for the British in Cyprus and the French in Algeria, their strategies of negotiating with the insurgents and the countries that supported them were poorly prepared. In the early stages of negotiation with the Algerians, the French government offered positions that some of the Algerian insurgents might have accepted, but these were nonstarters as far as the leadership of the FLN was concerned. At the start of the insurgency, the FLN did not represent the majority view of the Algerians. The French had a window of opportunity to drive a deep wedge between the insurgent leadership and the population but failed to seize the opportunity.

The British strategy in Cyprus took a similar course. The constitutional reforms offered to the Cypriots in 1947 were acceptable to only the tiny minority of Greek Cypriots who supported the British. In fact, the Greek Cypriots took the British proposals as an insult. Instead of building a foundation for a negotiated settlement of British and Cypriot differences, the British intransigence on Cyprus' status encouraged the Greek Cypriot leaders take a stronger line against the British. Even the slightest amount of homework on the issues, coupled with a willingness to sound out mainstream Greek Cypriot opinion, would have informed the British government and Field Marshal Harding that the British proposals were counterproductive to an effective peace process.

In Vietnam the U.S. government and military leadership failed to understand the importance of helping the South Vietnamese government build political support in the countryside, where the majority of the South Vietnamese lived. It may have been beyond the power of the U.S. government to make the South Vietnamese government enact the reforms that were necessary to win the support of the people. However, such a strategy would have had a better chance at success if the American leaders had made more of an effort to understand the political context of Vietnam. In Iraq, the United States began the occupation of that country with a false view of the political conditions. Indeed, State Department and Defense Department experts who understood Iraqi politics were excluded from the strategy process. Years into the insurgency, the U.S. civilian and military leaders still wrongly focused on the foreign fighters as the cause of the violence in Iraq and failed to understand the internal dynamics of Iraqi politics that fueled the conflict.

Civil Military Relations and Strategy

A healthy relationship between the military and the civilian political leaders in a democracy is essential if a nation is to develop a sound strategy. In a democracy, the military serves the government and the nation, and this subservience to civilian control is one of the primary elements of an effective democracy. Civil-military relations are, however, a two-way street. While the military must accept the principle of civilian control, the civilian government must not exhibit contempt or distain for the military, especially when the military is operating in its own professional sphere of operations and military capabilities. A poor relationship between the civilian and military leadership means that bad advice will be offered and good advice not taken. A lack of trust between civilian and military leaders can cripple the strategic process.

In the conflicts examined in this book, one of the primary causes of strategic failure was a poor state of civil-military relations. In the cases of France and Britain, the greatest share of responsibility for poor civil-military relations lay with the military leadership. In France the problem was very deep, as the colonial army had developed a unique culture, doctrine, and worldview that were greatly at odds with the national culture as well as the rest of the French armed forces. Both the British and French military leaders had grown up in an era of empire, and many senior soldiers simply could not adjust to post–World War II realities. This was certainly true in the case of the British military leaders who, for more than a decade after World War II, pushed an imperial worldview on the government that was utterly unrealistic in terms of Britain's financial condition. It was irresponsible for the military leaders to refuse to come to grips with the end of the empire.

During the Algerian War the relations between the armed forces and the national government broke down completely. Indeed, French military commanders in Algeria carried out their own policies in thorough disregard of the national government. The bombing of Sakiet in Tunisia in 1957 set off a major international crisis. The decision to bomb another country seems to have been made by the military high command without informing the prime minister—a clear case of a military operating outside the normal controls of a democratic nation. The colonial army came to identify not only with the *pied noirs*, but with the most radical faction of that group. The culture of the colonial army was so much at odds with the French government and regular armed forces that it mutinied in 1961, an act that crippled French civil-military relations for a decade. Although the mutiny was put down, the colonial army's actions sabotaged the conditions De Gaulle had created for a favorable peace.

258

From Vietnam to Iraq, the problem that the U.S. military has faced dealing with its civilian superiors is very much the opposite problem of the British and French. The U.S. military has long maintained a 1950s corporate culture, in which unthinking obedience to superiors and policy is stressed. In the 1950s corporation, the CEO was the boss who set all policy and insisted that everyone be a "good team player." Pointing out problems with any of the boss' pet ideas was "not playing on the team" or even "disloyal." Confronted with a determined civilian leadership, a careerist military leadership can easily devolve into a "yes man" culture, where the highest good is to please the boss. This was much in evidence during the Vietnam War and has been one of the characteristics of American civil-military relations during the Iraq War. Coupled with the corporate culture is the vast bureaucracy of the U.S. military government in which empire building and departmental infighting are laudable endeavors. In many cases the advancement of one's service or department is the main thing, while answering national concerns is secondary.[3]

It was not always this way. In 1939 when President Roosevelt interviewed General George Marshall as prospective Army chief of staff, Marshall told Roosevelt that, if appointed, there would be times that he would have to tell the president things he did not like to hear. Marshall accepted his appointment on the condition that he could freely offer advice to Roosevelt. And Roosevelt gladly accepted the services of this brilliant leader and strategist. The end result was not without friction and arguments over policy, but it still led to a very successful strategic process. One can scarcely imagine a senior American military officer of today being prepared to act like General Marshall when advising the president or the secretary of defense.

In the 1960s the senior U.S. military leaders found themselves cut out of the strategic process, and they failed to speak up. Yet this unhappy situation has become even more pronounced since the early 1990s. The culture of the senior military leadership is so attuned to following the lead of the civilian leadership that it will readily suppress any discussion of the civilian leaders' ideas, even during the early planning phases when traditionally problems have been frankly discussed. Of course, for the military, once decisions are made, then the debates should be over between those who decide policy and those who execute it. But to suppress critical thinking *before* the policy decisions are made is the exact opposite of a healthy civil-military relationship. Unfortunately, this is precisely the strategic culture that evolved during the Clinton and Bush administrations. Donald Rumsfeld exacerbated the bad traits of the American military leadership by politicizing the senior military leadership positions and suppressing even the limited internal discussion that had previously existed.

In a healthy democracy there should be an atmosphere of frank and open discussion between the civilian and military leaders. The military leaders ought to be free to offer open and candid advice without fear of repercussion. Politicization of the process, that is, punishing military leaders for advice that the politicians do not appreciate, corrupts the process and undermines the relationship. On the other hand, the political leaders who make the decisions are ultimately accountable to the public, and they ought to be free to disregard the military's advice. Indeed, there are often sound reasons for disregarding advice from the military's leaders. But to close out all dialogue completely, or to corrupt the dialogue process, ensures strategic failure. The actions of the Kennedy and Johnson administrations that shut out policy input from the Joint Chiefs of Staff was a severe blow to a sound strategic process. A generation later, the Goldwater-Nichols Act of 1986 was supposed to reform the armed forces. But it also had the unintended consequence of shutting out all but the Chairman of the Joint Chiefs from the strategic process. The result was a civil-military relationship with minimal input by the military. The result in the Iraq War was similar to that of Vietnam—a badly crafted strategy.

The International Aspects of Insurgency

The examples of Algeria, Cyprus, and Iraq show how major powers can fail to think through the international implications of their counterinsurgency strategies. France maintained that the war in Algeria was really just part of a grand campaign against international communism. This explanation failed to even convince the French, much less any of France's allies. For years the French policy in Algeria had a negative effect on France's relations with her NATO partners and the United States. The French military actions, notably the bombing of Sakiet, Tunisia, set off some major international crises and encouraged neighboring states to increase their support for the FLN rebels. The assumption that the Algerian insurgency was directed by Nasser's regime in Egypt helped propel France into the fiasco of the Suez campaign. The latter action further damaged France's international prestige and position.

In dealing with the Cyprus insurgency, Anthony Eden made the fundamental mistake of taking an internal British problem and internationalizing it. By bringing Turkey into the negotiations at the start, the British set up unnecessary obstacles to reaching a peace settlement. When a peace agreement was finally crafted, the Turks were given a blank check to intervene in Cyprus in the future. This led to further crises over the status of the island after independence. Because of the initial strategy of the Eden government in 1955, Cyprus remains a potential crisis point five decades later.

The Kennedy, Johnson, and Nixon administrations considered the international aspects of the Vietnam War. U.S. actions were carefully crafted to ensure that China would not be provoked into interventions as had occurred a decade before in Korea. Care in this regard was good common sense but resulted in strict limits on the use of U.S. force against North Vietnam. These self-imposed limits guaranteed that the bombing strategy, upon which the Johnson administration pinned its hopes, was not likely to have a decisive effect.

The Bush administration did a fairly good job obtaining international support for the invasion of Iraq. From that point on, the international aspects of the war were handled poorly. The assumption that the international community would pour aid into Iraq and take the lead in reconstruction had little basis in reality. When U.S. policies triggered an insurgency in Iraq, the United Nations was driven out and the likelihood of significant international support vanished. The U.S. failure to plan for the occupation or quickly secure Iraqi borders offered foreign Islamic radicals the perfect opportunity to pour into Iraq and further destabilize the country. There is little chance that current proposals will fix the problem. We ought not to expect any results from the bipartisan policy proposal to seek a solution through Syria and Iran. The status quo of insurgency in Iraq perfectly suits the national interest of both those nations. The clumsy manner in which the Iraq War has been handled by the Bush administration has cost the United States a great deal of international prestige. More importantly, it has created a crisis situation in the Middle East that could easily escalate into a regional war. Even under the most optimistic scenarios, the long-term consequences of the Iraq War mean that allied nations will be reluctant to support U.S. military intervention in the future.

Training the Local Forces

One of the fundamental requirements for success in counterinsurgency is enabling the population under threat to effectively defend itself. In Algeria the French were very successful in raising and training local forces, the *harkis*, who made large sections of the Algerian countryside unwelcome to the insurgents. The only major critique of the French program to arm and train the Algerians is that it came too late in the insurgency. The SAS-led program began as a small initiative in 1956, two years into the insurgency. It only became a major effort in 1957–1958. A larger program put in place early in the insurgency would have tamped down the insurgent violence and created more favorable conditions for the civic action side of the French strategy.

In Cyprus the British policy of throwing poorly led and poorly trained Turkish auxiliary forces at the Greek population was incredibly counterproductive. The British failure to keep discipline among the auxiliary police forces triggered communal violence between the Greek and Turkish communities, which had not existed before. This soon became ugly indeed and remains the dominant factor of Cyprus life decades later.

The United States developed some sound programs for training Vietnamese home guards. The combined action platoons of the Marine Corps worked exceptionally well in securing a part of the Vietnamese countryside. However, Westmoreland, with his conventional war fixation, dismissed successful programs like the combined action platoons and the South Vietnamese regional forces as irrelevant. Until 1968, programs to train and support the South Vietnamese Army were an afterthought for the U.S. military. In many respects, the U.S. military culture worked against developing effective programs to train and advise the South Vietnamese. Advancement and recognition in the U.S. military comes from serving with U.S. combat units, not by training and advising foreign troops. In many cases, senior American military commanders did not take the effort seriously or ensure that the officers assigned to advisory and training duties received due recognition.

Throughout the war, the United States failed to push the necessary military and leadership reforms that were necessary for the South Vietnamese to be able to defend their own country. At the end, the South Vietnamese military collapsed because of the generally poor and corrupt leadership of their army. By Americanizing the war so totally in 1965, the United States helped ensure this final result.

In Iraq the U.S. military took on a much tougher mission than training the South Vietnamese Army, but did so with far fewer resources, no planning, and insufficient personnel. The same U.S. military cultural problems that hampered the U.S. training and advisory effort in Vietnam appeared in Iraq. The U.S. military leadership still places a low value on training and advising foreign forces, so much of the mission of training the Iraqi army was given to Reserve and National Guard units that arrived in Iraq unprepared to undertake such complex tasks. The lack of planning and the chaos at the start of the occupation ensured that the U.S. efforts to stand up Iraqi forces were poorly supported and executed. The U.S. military also failed to address the fundamental problem of the Iraqi Army, and of all Arab armies—that of leadership. Instead of a systematic program to build an effective leadership corps for the Iraqi forces, leaders were hastily chosen and trained. This ensured that the same weaknesses of the old regime would be passed on to the new armed forces. Common descriptions of the Iraqi officer corps made by American trainers and advisers mention widespread corruption, favoritism, and politicization. After four years of effort, senior U.S. officers in Iraq still doubt that the Iraqi army can operate effectively in combat. Iraqi desertion and AWOL rates remain extremely high—a good indicator of poor morale and leadership—and units normally show up for operations at half strength. Unless an effective Iraqi army and police force can be established, there can be little hope that the U.S. forces can withdraw and leave behind a stable country.

The Battle for Public Support

Each of the four counterinsurgency campaigns began with overwhelming public support for the government. In each case, public support was lost over time. In France support for the Algerian War started to decline after three years. In the Cyprus campaign, British opinion turned after two and a half years. The U.S. public strongly supported the U.S. military effort in Vietnam for more than three years, up to the Tet offensive. In Iraq, the American public became negative about the war after only eighteen months. The primary factor affecting public support was not the military casualty figures. In each case the public was willing to accept some sacrifice in blood *if* progress was clearly being made. As soon as it became evident that the conflict had reached stalemate and the chance for progress was minimal, then public support faltered.

Successful national leadership in a time of conflict requires that the head of the government be able to communicate effectively to the public. The most important message to communicate is the national interest at stake in prosecuting a counterinsurgency campaign. If the campaign becomes a stalemate, then the problem of winning public support becomes doubly difficult. Casualties are a factor in the level of public support for a war, but not the primary one. Several opinion studies conducted at the time of the Gulf War of 1991 laid to rest the post-Vietnam assumption that the American people would never tolerate high casualties in war. The studies showed that the American public would accept heavy losses *if* they were convinced that war was clearly in the national interest.[4] If the national leadership fails to convince the public on this issue, then public support will collapse.

The Requirements of Strategic Leadership

National leaders carry an enormous burden when they lead democracies in times of conflict. It is difficult for national leaders to coordinate the efforts of the large bureaucracies that they supposedly control, but which contain departments and special interests in a state of constant rivalry. Getting the branches of government to work together to achieve a common goal, what the U.S. government calls "interagency coordination," requires exceptional leadership and management skills. Failure to manage one's own bureaucracy puts a nation fighting an insurgency at a disadvantage. Moreover, national leaders in democracies have to contend with vocal opposition parties in the national legislature. The national leader of a democracy has to craft a strategy that will be supported by a majority of the peoples' representatives, or he will fail.

The major contributing factor to the failure of the four counterinsurgency campaigns examined was poor national leadership. In Algeria the weakness of the

French Fourth Republic was evident. The system was so unstable that no prime minister, no matter how talented, was able to craft a strategy that addressed the fundamental problems of Algeria. By the time France developed an effective system, in the Fifth Republic, and had an outstanding leader in the person of Charles De Gaulle, the passions of the war had progressed too far. De Gaulle established a strategy that would have worked if implemented earlier. But the system of the Fourth Republic blocked the national leadership for years.

The leadership of Anthony Eden was the fundamental cause of the British failure in Cyprus. Every decision made by Eden on the Cyprus issue made the situation on the island worse. There is no doubt that Anthony Eden was a brilliant and talented man, but he had also learned lessons in his younger days that he could not discard decades later when the context had completely changed. One of the characteristics of good leadership is the ability to take advice, and this was one of Eden's weak points. Having studied the Middle East as a student at Oxford before World War I, he was convinced of his own expertise in the region and readily disregarded sound advice from the Colonial Office's experts. Eden's policy on Cyprus was driven more by his pro-Turk and anti-Greek prejudices than by serious analysis. Finally, Eden remained trapped in an imperial worldview that bore little relationship to the realities of the post–World War II world.

Presidents Kennedy and Johnson created a closed strategic decision-making process that failed to identify the core problems in South Vietnam. Those administrations instead focused on simplistic military solutions against North Vietnam—the bombing campaign and conventional ground war. President Johnson and his top advisors practiced a high degree of self-deception in pushing the military commanders and the intelligence agencies for data that supported their strategy. The elaborate system created to generate positive information collapsed during the Tet offensive of 1968. The United States eventually did develop an effective strategy that coordinated the civilian and military efforts and concentrated on securing the population of South Vietnam. But by this time, President Johnson had lost the support of the American public. Johnson, and Presidents Nixon and Ford after him, faced increasing resistance to their strategy in Congress and were thus highly limited in their ability to develop new solutions.

President George Bush took the Kennedy and Johnson mistakes a step further in creating a highly dysfunctional strategic decision-making system. The Bush administration's strategic policy, or lack of it, was the product of a very small and closed inner circle that brooked no discussion or questioning. If the inner circle of the Kennedy and Johnson administrations could be described as men of great hubris, the Bush administration took this trait and magnified it. Where policy debate in the Kennedy and Johnson administrations was restricted, in the Bush administration it was shut down completely. Flawed assumptions were never questioned, and theories with little basis in reality became the cornerstone of the U.S. policy to transform Iraq into a democracy. The order to occupy Iraq without a coherent plan was concocted by a small group—Rumsfeld, Wolfowitz, Feith—that had little to no military experience. Indeed, the one man within the cabinet with extensive experience in military operations and strategy, Colin Powell, was effectively shut out of the strategic process by the inner circle. The resulting Iraq policy went against the unanimous advice of every military planning group and the State Department. Then, after things went badly wrong, the Bush administration failed to quickly adapt to the realities on the ground.

President Bush delegated the responsibility for war policy to a small group of insiders whom he trusted for their unwavering loyalty, and to whom he gave his loyalty. Even when top officials repeatedly demonstrated gross incompetence—CIA Director George Tenet is an excellent example—President Bush stood loyally by them and kept them on his team. Donald Rumsfeld remained in his job as the situation in Iraq progressively deteriorated. He left office as the longest-serving—and probably most unsuccessful—secretary of defense in American history. Although one of the most important jobs of a leader is to hold people accountable, only one person in the top level of government was held accountable for Iraq policy: the president's economic advisor Lawrence Lindsay. He was fired in late 2002 for saying that the projected war in Iraq could cost as much as $100 billion. That estimate was, of course, far too low. But when Lindsay made this statement, the administration's message was that the war would be dirt cheap, a matter of less than twenty billion dollars. In short, the only top official held accountable for Iraq policy between 2002 and 2006 was one of the few top people who gave sound advice.

President Bush's reliance on a small circle of loyal advisors, who repeatedly blundered, will provide generations of psychological historians with a fascinating field of study. Yet understanding the mind of George W. Bush is not within the expertise of this author, and I will gladly leave others to follow this line of analysis. However, one effect of George Bush's leadership that we can assess with some accuracy is his remarkably rapid loss of public support and confidence.

Good strategic leadership requires managing a process that discusses all the reasonable options, as well as their advantages and disadvantages. In this fundamental aspect of leadership the Bush administration failed. Some final questions that one can ask of President Bush's policy in Iraq are: What did the president know? And when did he know it? To all appearances, President Bush surrounded himself with a small circle of loyalists who gave him optimistic reports on Iraq that supported his own highly optimistic view of the world. But optimism is not a foundation for good planning. One possible explanation for the Iraq strategy is that George Bush created a policy system that was so closed that it failed to provide him with a realistic picture of the situation. We will only definitively know the answer when the policy documents of the Bush administration are declassified.

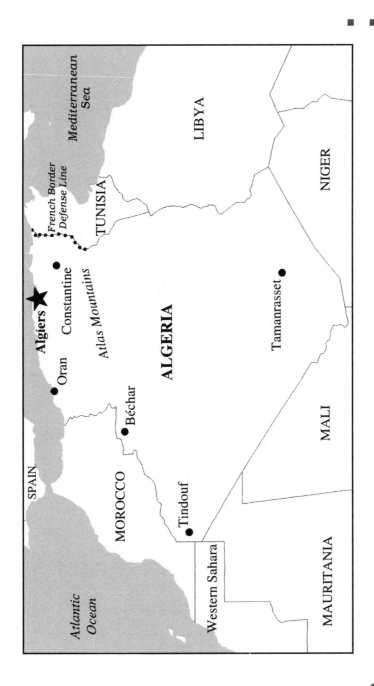

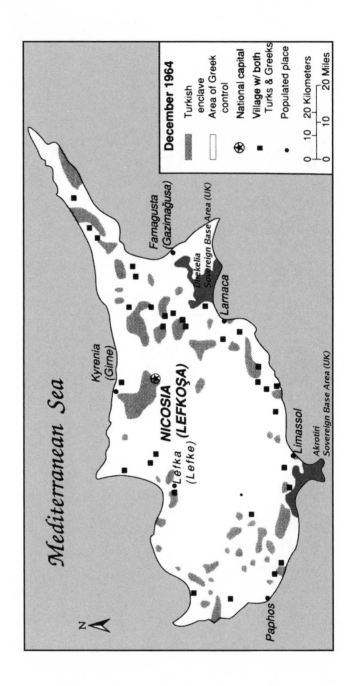

December 1964

Turkish enclave

Area of Greek control

⊛ National capital

■ Village w/ both Turks & Greeks

• Populated place

0   10   20 Kilometers
0   10   20 Miles

Famagusta (Gazimağusa)

Dhekelia Sovereign Base Area (UK)

Larnaca

Kyrenia (Girne)

NICOSIA (LEFKOŞA)

Lefka (Lefke)

Limassol

Akrotiri Sovereign Base Area (UK)

Mediterranean Sea

N

Paphos

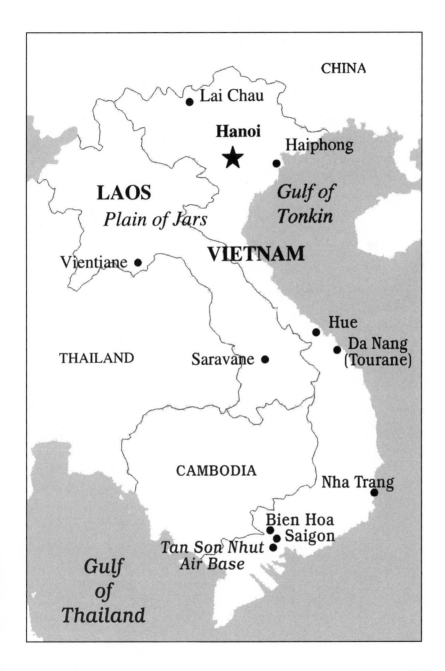

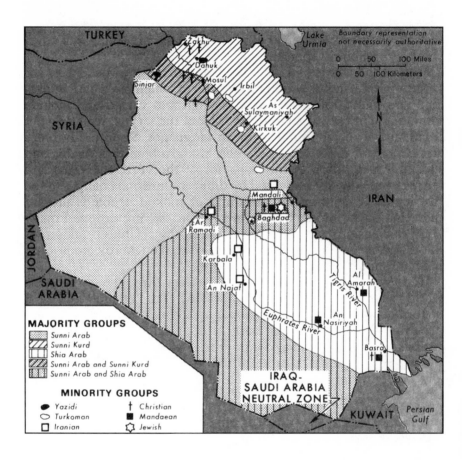

NOTES

■ ■ ■

Introduction

1. Colin Gray, *Modern Strategy* (Oxford: Oxford University Press, 1999), 1.
2. Ibid.
3. Carl von Clausewitz, *On War*, trans. Michael Howard and Peter Paret (Princeton NJ 1976), 128.
4. Colin Gray, *Modern Strategy*, 17.
5. Basil H. Liddell Hart, *Strategy: The Indirect Approach* (London 1967), 335.
6. *U.S. Military Joint Publication 3.0*
7. Within weeks of its publication in December 2006 more than 600,000 copies of the new Army/Marine counterinsurgency doctrine were downloaded. The interest in the doctrine was so great that the University of Chicago has published a copy of the doctrine. I was the primary author of Chapter 6, "Developing Host Nation Security Forces," and Annex F, "Airpower in Counterinsurgency."

Chapter 1

1. The constitution of the Fourth Republic talked of the "French Union" and its preamble stated "France with its overseas peoples creates a Union based on equality of rights

273

and duties without distinction of race or religion." There was no mention in the constitution about different kinds of citizenship. Frank Giles, *The Locust Years: The Story of the Fourth French Republic 1946–1958* (New York: Carroll and Graf Publishers, 1991), 130–132.

2.   An excellent account of America's strategic advice to France concerning North Africa is found in Irwin Wall, *France, the U.S. and the Algerian War* (Berkeley: University of California Press, 2001).

3.   James Corum and Wray Johnson, *Airpower and Small Wars* (Lawrence: University Press of Kansas, 2003), 73–77.

4.   A good account of Grandval's tenure as governor general is found in "Revolt and Revenge," *Time* magazine, 5 September 1955.

5.   Amina Aouchar, "Le disengagement militaire français au maroc au lendemain de l'indépendance," *Revue Historique des Armées* 235 (2004), *Dossier: France-Maroc*, 14–23.

6.   Alexander Werth, *France 1940–1955* (New York: Henry Holt, 1956), 567–568.

7.   Ibid., 571–572.

8.   Giles, 134–135.

9.   For a good overview of the Algerian economy and social system see Rachid Tlemcani, *State and Revolution in Algeria* (Boulder: Westview Press, 1986).

10.   Ibid., 57.

11.   Cited in "Bastille Day Riot," *Time* magazine, 27 July 1953.

12.   The 2006 French film *Les Indigènes* (English title: *Days of Glory*) tells the story of the North African soldiers who fought bravely and competently through the Italian campaign and then in the campaign to liberate France from Nazi occupation. The French army of 1943–1945 was largely composed of Algerians, Moroccans, and Senegalese who faced discrimination from the French military and government. Several of the leaders of the Algerian insurgency were army veterans.

13.   Thierry Godechot, "Prélude aux rebéllions en Afrique du Nord: les mutineries de soldats maghrébins, décembre 1944–mai 1945," *Revue Historiques des Armées* 229 (December 2002), 3–6.

14.   Alistair Horne, *A Savage War for Peace: Algeria 1954–1962* (London: Penguin Books, 1977). See Anthony Clayton, "The Sétif Uprising of May 1945," *Small Wars and Insurgencies* 3 (Spring 1992), 1–21 for a detailed account of the 1945 rebellion and its political effects. Contemporary reports on the Sétif uprising are found in *La Guerre D'Algérie Par Les Documents, Tome Premier*, ed. Jean-Charles Jauffret (Service

Historique de l'Armée de Terre: Vincennes, 1990). This is the first volume of a twelve volume series of primary documents on the Algerian War.

15. General Henry Martin, Report "Situation en Algérie à la date du 7 mars 1946" to the General Staff, Third Bureau, *La Guerre D'Algérie Par Les Documents, Tome Premier*, 495–497.

16. Clayton, "The Sétif Uprising," 16–17.

17. Horne, 69–73.

18. "Bastille Day Riot," *Time* magazine, 27 July 1953.

19. On the growth of Algerian nationalist parties and ideologies see Rachid Tlemcani, *State and Revolution in Algeria* (Boulder: Westview Press, 1986), 59–61.

20. "Suitcase or Coffin?" *Time* magazine, 15 November 1954.

21. The French Institut National de l'Audiovisuel has newsreels of the French operations in Algeria on its website.

22. George Kelly, *Lost Soldiers: The French Army and Empire in Crisis 1947–1962* (Cambridge: M.I.T. Press, 1965), 150–151.

23. Tlemcani, 62–64.

24. A good account of the French strategy in Algeria is found in Peter Paret, *French Revolutionary Warfare from Indochina to Algeria* (London: Pall Mall Press, 1964), 38–39.

25. Martin Windrow and Mike Chappell, *The Algerian War 1954–62* (London: Osprey, 1997), 17.

26. Philippe Vial and Pascal Tanchoux, "Les archives Algérie: De l'Armée de l'Air," *Revue Historique des Armées* 187 (June 1992), 66–75. See 67.

27. Horne, 118–122.

28. Jean Nicot, "Les S.A.S. et la Pacification en Algérie," *Revue Historique des Armées* (4:1992), 26–39.

29. Martin Windrow, Mike Chappell, *The Algerian War 1954–62* (London: Osprey, 1997), 15–16.

30. John Talbot, "The War Without a Name—France in Algeria 1954–1962," *The Chopper Boys: Helicopter Warfare in Africa*, ed. J. Ventner (London: Greenhill Books, 1994), pp. 37–44. See 44.

31. Lt. Col. Claude Carré, "Aspects Opérationnels du Conflit Algérien 1954–1960," *Revue Historique des Armées* 166 (May 1987), 82–91. See 89.

32. For an overview of French military tactics and operations in Algeria see Corum and Johnson, 161–174.

33. Charles Christienne and Pierre Lissarague, *A History of French Military Aviation* (Washington: Smithsonian Institution Press, 1986), 464–465.

34. Windrow and Chappell, 9–10.

35. Ibid.

36. The Gendarmerie played an important role in the Algerian campaign, both in supporting police operations and also in conducting covert operations against guerrilla leaders. By 1961 the French had more than 14,000 Gendarmerie in Algeria. The Gendarmerie also played a central role in the Battle of Algiers. See Jacques Frémeaux, "La gendarmerie en guerre d'Algérie," *Revue Historique des Armées* 229 (December 2002), 7–16.

37. Giles, 301.

38. Cited in Werth, 731–733.

39. See Roger Trinquier, *La Guerre Moderne* (Paris: Éditions de la Table Ronde, 1961). English translation, *Modern Warfare* (London: Pall Mall Press, 1964), 21–22.

40. For an example of a French commander who got results by treating the Algerians with respect (Major Jean Pouget), see Alexander Zervoudakis, "A Case of Successful Pacification: The 584th Battalion du Train at Boudj de l'Agha (1956–1957)," eds. Alexander and Keiger, *France and the Algerian War, 1954–62: Strategy, Operations and Diplomacy* (London and Portland, OR: Frank Cass, 2002).

41. Frédéric Guelton and Geneviève Errera, "Transmissions et Guerre Subversive en Algérie," *Revue Historique des Armées* 178 (March 1990), 74–83.

42. The story of the Battle of Algiers and the intelligence campaign, including frank admissions of torture and summary executions of Algerian detainees, is found in the memoirs of a French intelligence officer. See Paul Aussaresses, *The Battle of the Casbah* (New York: Enigma Books, 2002). See also Horne, 183–207. General Massu also wrote an account of the campaign in his memoirs. See Jacques Massu, *La Vraie Bataille d'Alger* (Paris: Librairie Plon, 1971).

43. On the problem of torture in the French army in Algeria see Lou DiMarco, "Losing the Moral Compass: Torture and the Guerre Révolutionaire in the Algerian War," *Parameters* 36:2 (Summer 2002), 63–76.

44. Giles, 274.

45. On the French view of the Suez Crisis see André Beaufre, *The Suez Expedition, 1956* (New York: Praeger, 1969), 18. General Beaufre was commander of the French land forces during the Suez expedition.

46. For a guide to the politics of the Fourth Republic see William Andrews, *French Politics and Algeria* (New York: Appleton-Century-Crofts, 1962).

47. Philippe Vial, "De L'Impuissance À La Renaissance: le Général Léchères à la tête de l'Armée de l'Air (1948–1953)," *Revue Historique des Armées* 192 (September 1993), 43–51.

48. Giles, 266–267.

49. For an overview of French psychological operations in Algeria see François Pernot, "La Guerre Psychologique en Algérie vue à travers les archives de l'Armée de l'Air," *Revue Historiques des Armées* 190 (March 1993), 90–99.

50. François Pernot, "La Rébellion et la Fait Aérien," 91.

51. George Kelly, *Lost Soldiers: The French Army and Empire in Crisis 1947–1962* (Cambridge: M.I.T. Press, 1965), 173.

52. Kelly, 198.

53. "Acts of Desperation," *Time* magazine, 27 April 1959.

54. Maurice Faivre and Paul Villatoux, "La Guerre d'Algérie, un conflit Surmédiatisé," *War, Military and Media from Gutenberg to Today*, ed. Major General Mihael Ionescu (Bucharest: Institute for Political Studies of Defense and Military History, 2004), 69–79, see 75–76.

55. Ibid.

56. A useful overview of the FLN and its politics is Abder-Ramane Derradji, *The Algerian Guerrilla Campaign: Strategy and Tactics* (Lewiston, New York: Edwin Mellen Press, 1997).

57. Patrick Facon, "L'Algérie et la Politique Générale de L'Armée de L'Air (1954–1958)," *Revue Historiques des Armées* 187 (June 1992), 76–85. See 84.

58. Derradji.

59. Edgar O'Ballance, *The Algerian Insurrection, 1954–62* (Hamden, CT: Archon Books, 1967), 60–61.

60. Giles, 302–303.

61. Horne, 249–250.

62. Kelly, 210–211.

63. David Thompson, *Democracy in France: The Third and Fourth Republics* (London: Oxford University Press, 1958), 253–255.

64. Rachid Tlemcani, 57–58.

65. For a good account of the SAS and *harkis* see Horne, 109, 220–221, 255–256. See also Christophe Cazorla, "*Concept d'emploi et évolution statutaire des suppletifs durant la guerre d'Algérie*," *Revue Historique Des Armées* 4 (2002): 75.

66. On the French civic action programs see Paret, 40–51.

67. On the Challe plan see François-Marie Gougeon, "The Challe Plan: Vain Yet Indispensable Victory," *Small Wars and Insurgencies* 16:3 (December 2006), 293–316.

68. Corum and Johnson, 170–172.

69. "To the Barricades," *Time* magazine, 8 February 1960.

70. Martin S. Alexander and J.F.V. Keiger, *France and the Algerian War*, xiv–xvi.

71. Horne, 480–495.

72. Ibid., 455.

73. Ibid., 490–491.

74. Ibid., 537–538.

75. Ibid.

Chapter 2

1. Epigraphs cited in Alistair Horne, *Harold Macmillan Volume I 1894–1956* (London: Viking Press, 1989), 365; Charles Foley, *Island in Revolt* (London: Longmans, 1962), 228.

2. Anthony Kirk-Greene, *On Crown Service: A History of HM Colonial and Overseas Civil Services 1837–1997* (London: I.B Tauris Publishers, 1999), 14.

3. "British Finish Repaying U.S. Loan to Fight WWII," *Arizona Daily Star*, 29 December 2006.

4. The story of postwar British imperial ambitions and strategic overreach is told in Corelli Barnett, *The Lost Victory: British Dreams, British Realities 1945–1950* (London: Macmillan, 1995), 76–77.

5. L. J. Butler, *Britain and Empire: Adjusting to a Post-Imperial World* (London: I.B. Tauris, 2002), 76.

6. Barnett, see esp. 46–69.

7. Nigel Hamilton, *Monty Volume 3: The Field Marshal 1944–1976* (London: Hodder and Stoughton, 1987), 650–651, 652–653, 660–661, 676–677.

8. Butler, 76.

9. Barnett, 75.

10. R. N. Rosecrance, *Defence of the Realm: British Strategy in the Nuclear Epoch* (Oxford: Oxford University Press, 1968), 37. On the huge budget requirements for a UK bomber force in the 1940s and 1950s see Martin Navias, "Strengthening the Deterrent? The British Medium Bomber Force Debate, 1955–56," *The Journal of Strategic Studies* 11:2 (June 1988), 203–219.

11. Rosecrance, 138–139, 156.

12. On Britain's military strategy in the Middle East see Michael Cohen, *Fighting World War Three from the Middle East: Allied Contingency Plans 1945–1954* (London: Frank Cass, 1977) and Behçet Kemal Yeşilbursa, *The Baghdad Pact: Anglo-American Defence Policies in the Middle East 1950–1959* (Abingdon, Oxon: Frank Cass, 2005).

13. Simon Ball, "Bomber Bases and British Strategy in the Middle East, 1945–1949," *Journal of Strategic Studies* 14 (1991), 515–533, see especially 519–520, 526.

14. Barnett, 97.

15. Barnett, 65–67.

16. Air Chief Marshal David Lee, *Wings in the Sun: A History of the RAF in the Mediterranean 1945–1986* (London, 1989), 45–47.

17. Cited in Butler, 98.

18. Butler, 66.

19. For details of Eden's life and views see Anthony Eden, *The Eden Memoirs: Facing Two Dictators* (London: Cassells, 1962).

20. Butler, 99.

21. An example of the overblown rhetoric about Nasser common among the British leaders is found in Harold Macmillan's diary entry for 18 August 1956: "If Nasser 'gets away with it', we are done for . . . it may be the end of British influence and strength for ever. So, in the last resort, we must use force and defy opinion, here and overseas." Cited in Alistair Horne, *Harold Macmillan Vol. 1 1894–1956*, 393.

22. Anthony Nutting (Foreign Office Parliamentary Under-Secretary), secret memorandum, 8 February 1955, doc. 128a, *The End of Empire: Dependencies Since 1948 Part 1*, ed. Frederick Madden (Westport: Greenwood Press, 2000), 424–425. In his memoirs, Anthony Eden is far more critical of the Greeks than the Turks. See Anthony Eden, *Full Circle* (London: Cassells, 1960), pages 395–413 deal with Cyprus.

23. John Newsinger, *British Counterinsurgency From Palestine to Northern Ireland* (London: Palgrave, 2002), 88.

24. Anthony Nutting, parliamentary secretary in the foreign office (1951–1954) and minister of state (1954–1956), secret memorandum, 8 February 1955, F.O. 371/117625, ed. Frederick Madden, *The End of Empire*, 424–426.

25. Foreign Office memo, 8 February 1955, F.O. 371/117625, ed. Frederick Madden, *The End of Empire*, 426.

26. Foreign Office memo, 8 Feb 1955, Madden, 427–429.

27. Horne, 365.

28. Ibid., 364.

29. For a biography of Grivas see Doros Alastos, *Cyprus Guerrilla: Grivas, Makarios and the British* (London: Heinemann, 1960), 18–25.

30. Alastos, 32.

31. Ed. Madden, *The End of Empire: Dependencies Since 1948 Part I*, 424.

32. Alastos, 32.

33. *The Memoirs of General Grivas*, ed. Charles Foley (New York: Praeger, 1965), 204–207. See also George Grivas, *Guerrilla Warfare* (Athens: Longmans, 1964), 5–10.

34. For a good view of the campaign from the insurgent viewpoint see *The Memoirs of General Grivas*. Grivas provides considerable detail on how he subverted the police force. On EOKA's infiltration of the police see Anderson, "Policing and Communal Conflict," 184–185; Foley and Scobie, 104–105.

35. Cited in Robert Holland, "Never, Never Land: British Colonial Policy and the Roots of Violence in Cyprus, 1950–1954," *The Journal of Imperial and Commonwealth History* XXI (September 1993, no. 3), 148–176. See 148.

36. Holland, "Never, Never Land," 149–150.

37. One Colonial Office legal advisor noted that it was "far and away the most extreme demand put up by any (colonial) territory so far as my experience extends." Holland, "Never, Never Land," 149.

38. Ibid., 151.

39. Ibid., 152.

40. Colin Baker, *Retreat from Empire: Sir Robert Armitage in Africa and Cyprus* (London: I.B. Tauris, 1998), 104–106.

41. Alastos, *Cyprus Guerrilla*, 47.

42. Anthony Eden, *Full Circle*, 395. "Early in 1955, the British authorities in Cyprus began to have to deal not with demonstrations by crowds, but with terrorism led by a few."

43. Robert Holland, *Britain and the Revolt in Cyprus 1954–1959* (Oxford: Clarendon Press, 1998), 60.

44. David Anderson, "Policing and Communal Conflict: The Cyprus Emergency, 1954–1960," *The Journal of Imperial and Commonwealth History* (September 1993), 177–207. See especially 182–183.

45. *Cyprus Police Commission Report*, March 1956, doc. NA 378, Rhodes House, Oxford University, para 114.

46. Cyprus Police Commission, para. 114.

47. Cyprus Police Commission, para. 10.

48. Cyprus Police Commission, para. 29.

49. Anderson, "Policing and Communal Conflict," 185.

50. Ibid., 191.

51. Ibid., 194–197. The UK Police unit in Cyprus also developed a reputation for poor discipline. The first commander of the UK Police Unit maintained that some of the British county police forces had dumped their unwanted personnel on Cyprus.

52. Holland, *Britain and the Revolt in Cyprus*, 80.

53. Ibid., 100.

54. The standard biography of Field Marshal Harding is Michael Carver, *Harding of Petherton: Field Marshal* (London: Weidenfeld and Nicolson, 1978).

55. James S. Corum, *Training Indigenous Forces in Counter-Insurgency* (Strategic Studies Institute: Carlisle Barracks PA, March 2006), 35.

56. Nancy Cranshaw, 153.

57. Holland, *Britain and the Revolt in Cyprus*, 101.

58. For comments on the futile tactics of the British forces on Cyprus see Charles Allen, *The Savage Wars of Peace: Soldiers' Voices 1945–1989* (London: Michael Joseph, 1990), 140–142. A good description of Harding's counterinsurgency campaign is described in John Newsinger, *British Counterinsurgency From Palestine to Northern Ireland* (London: Palgrave, 2002), 84–107. On British regulations and heavy fines see Leontios Iorodiakonou, *The Cyprus Question* (Stockholm: Almqvist and Wiksell, 1971), 109–110.

59. Newsinger, 99.

60. Newsinger, 98.

61. Grivas' memoirs include his numerous objections to Makarios' orders to restrain EOKA actions in the hope of starting negotiations with the British. See *The Memoirs of General Grivas*, ed. Charles Foley (New York: Praeger, 1965).

62. An excellent overview of the Cyprus insurgency is found in Nancy Cranshaw, *The Cyprus Revolt* (London: George Allen and Unwin, 1978).

63. Holland, *Britain and the Revolt in Cyprus*, 60.

64. Anderson, 190.

65. Ibid., 187.

66. *Cyprus Police Commission Report*, para 197.

67. *Cyprus Police Commission Report*, paras 198–200.

68. Anderson, 190.

69. Anderson, 193.

70. W. Byford-Jones, *Grivas and the Story of EOKA* (London: Robert Hale Limited, 1959), 159–160.

71. Ibid., 54, 58.

72. Charles Foley, *Island in Revolt* (London: Longmans, 1962), 228–229.

73. William Jackson, *Withdrawal From Empire: A Military View* (New York: St. Martin's Press, 1986), 170.

74. Thomas Ehrlich, *Cyprus 1958–1967: International Crises and the Role of Law* (Oxford: Oxford University Press, 1974), 20–21.

75. Baker, 161.

76. John Newsinger, 97, 101; Allen, 148–149; Foley, *Island in Revolt*, 130–132.

77. Foley, *Island in Revolt*, 132.

78. Foley, *Island in Revolt*, 131. On strong-arm tactics by the British army in Cyprus see Charles Allen, *The Savage Wars of Peace: Soldiers' Voices 1945–1989* (London: Michael Joseph, 1990), 147–150. The book contains descriptions of the constant patrols in villages, searches, cordons, sweeps, roadblocks, and other operations among a population that was clearly hostile.

79. Charles Foley, *Legacy of Strife: Cyprus from Rebellion to Civil War* (London: Penguin Books, 1964), 96.

80. Ehrlich, 16–17.

81. David Anderson, "Policing and Communal Conflict: The Cyprus Emergency, 1954–60," 187–217 in *Policing and Decolonisation: Politics, Nationalism and the Police, 1917–65*, eds. David Anderson and David Killingray (Manchester: Manchester University Press, 1992), 204.

82. Ehrlich, 16–17.

83. Brian Lapping, *End of Empire* (New York: St. Martin's Press, 1985), 333–334.

84. Anderson, 193.

85. Foley, *Island in Revolt*, 140–141.

86. Cited in Ehrlich, 20. Statement of the Labour Party: "The people of Cyprus, like all other peoples, have a right to determine their own future."

87. Robert Holland, *Britain and the Revolt in Cyprus 1954–1959* (Oxford: Clarendon Press, 1998), 210.

88. Cranshaw, Appendix 6.

Chapter 3

1. Troung Nhu Tang, *A Viet Cong Memoir* (New York: Vintage Books, 1985), 56.

2. On the U.S. aid to the French in Indochina see James Corum and Wray Johnson, *Airpower in Small Wars* (Lawrence: University Press of Kansas, 2003), 151–159.

3. For a superb account of the Dien Bien Phu campaign see Bernard Fall, *Hell in a Very Small Place: The Siege of Dien Bien Phu* (New York: De Capo Press, 1966).

4. Tran Van Don, *Our Endless War* (Novato: Presidio Press, 1978), 27.

5. Ibid. Tran Van Don, *Our Endless War*; Truong Nhu Tang, *A Viet Cong Memoir* (New York: Vintage Books, 1985).

6. Tran Van Don, 1; Troung Nhu Tang, 30–31.

7. On Diem's background see Tran Van Don, 47–57.

8. Tran Van Don, 60–62.

9. Robert Brigham, *ARVN: Life and Death in the South Vietnamese Army* (Lawrence: University Press of Kansas, 2006), 4–7. See also Cao Van Vien and Dong Van Khuyen, *Reflections on the Vietnam War* (Washington, D.C.: U.S. Army Center for Military History, 1980), 2. The authors were former South Vietnamese general officers. They contended that the American emphasis on preparing the South Vietnamese Army to face North Vietnamese invasion succeeded in preventing a repeat of the Korean War; however, communist leaders simply resorted to aiding the insurgency in the South. But had "popular forces" been emphasized from the outset, the Viet Cong could have been managed if not defeated outright. Nevertheless, the American Advisory Group did not appreciate the importance of countering the insurgents and the role played by paramilitary forces until 1961, but by then six years had been irretrievably lost and the insurgency alone threatened to overthrow the government of South Vietnam.

10. Jeffrey Clarke, *The U.S. Army in Vietnam: Advice and Support. The Final Years, 1965–1973* (Washington, DC: U.S. Army Center for Military History, 1988), 514.

11. The best general history of the ARVN (Army of the Republic of Vietnam) and its leadership and combat experience is Robert Brigham, *ARVN: Life and Death in the South Vietnamese Army* (Lawrence: University Press of Kansas, 2006).

12. Brigham, 27–29.

13. On the U.S. Army counterinsurgency efforts of the late 1950s see Andrew Birtle, *U.S. Army Counterinsurgency and Contingency Operations Doctrine 1942–1976* (Washington, DC: U.S. Army Center for Military History, 2006), 158–171.

14. Military History Institute of Vietnam, *Victory in Vietnam: The Official History of the People's Army of Vietnam*, 1954–1975, trans. Merle Pribbenow (Lawrence: University Press of Kansas, 2002), 20–42.

15. *Victory in Vietnam*, 42–44.

16. Ibid., 46–54.

17. See James S. Corum, "Building the Malayan Army and Police—Britain's Experience During the Malayan Emergency 1948–1960," *Security Assistance: U.S. and International Historical Perspectives*, ed. Randall Gott (Leavenworth: Combat Studies Institute Press, 2006), 291–314.

18. Gen J. Lawton Collins, sent to observe the situation in Vietnam by Eisenhower, sent a report in April 1955 with a frank assessment that Diem was incorruptible, intelligent and a devoted nationalist—but would fail because he had no grasp of politics and no willingness to deal with those who disagreed with him. On the U.S. and Diem see Philip Catton, *Diem's Final Failure* (Lawrence: University Press of Kansas, 2002), 10.

19. McNamara, *In Retrospect*, 41–43.

20. See Catton for a good account of the collapse of the Diem regime and the aftermath.

21. For an account of the international anti-communist propaganda war waged by the Eisenhower administration see Kenneth Osgood, *Total Cold War: Eisenhower's Secret Propaganda Battle at Home and Abroad* (Lawrence: University Press of Kansas, 2006).

22. David Halberstam, *The Best and the Brightest* (New York: Ballantine Books, 1972). This book has certainly stood the test of time as an insightful and accurate analysis of the major personalities who developed the failed strategies of the Kennedy and Johnson administrations.

23. See H.R. McMaster, *Dereliction of Duty* (New York, Harper Perennial, 1997), 4–31.

24. For one of the best accounts of strategic decision making within the Kennedy administration see Lawrence Freedman, *Kennedy's Wars: Berlin, Cuba, Laos and Vietnam* (New York: Oxford University Press, 2000), especially 40–41. H.R. McMaster also provides a superb analysis of the policy process in the Kennedy and Johnson administrations.

25. *Victory in Vietnam*, 182.

26. Rostow has been described by David Milne as "capable of sycophancy and flattery of the highest order." See David Milne, "Our Equivalent of Guerrilla Warfare: Walt Rostow and the Bombing of North Vietnam, 1961–1968," *Journal of Military History* 71:1, 169–203. See 183.

27. Ibid., 169.

28. Stephen Budiansky, *Air Power* (New York: Viking Books, 2003), 378–379.

29. After the decision was made to bomb North Vietnam, Johnson told McNamara, "I don't think that anything is going to be as bad as losing, and I don't see any way of winning." Cited in Milne, 187.

30. H.R. McMaster, *Dereliction of Duty*, 314–315.

31. Ibid., 317–318.

32. Ibid., 319–320.

33. Ronald Spector, *After Tet* (New York: The Free Press, 1993), 8.

34. Ibid.

35. Fredric Smith, "Posture of the U.S.A.F.: Statement to the Committee on Armed Services, House of Representatives," *The Airman* (May 1962), 20, 22. See also Frederic Smith, "Nuclear Weapons and Limited War," *Air University Quarterly Review* (Spring 1960), 3–27.

36. A good overview of the early years of the U.S. advisory mission to the Vietnamese forces is Robert Futrell, *The U.S. Air Force in Southeast Asia: The Advisory Years to 1965* (Washington, D.C.: Office of Air Force History, 1981).

37. General William Westmoreland, directive no. 525-4, 17 September 1065, "Tactics and Techniques for the Employment of U.S. Forces in the Republic of Vietnam." The document is reproduced in full in John Garland, ed., "Winning the Vietnam War: Westmoreland's Approach in Two Documents," *Journal of Military History* 68:2 (April 2004), 554–574.

38. Spector, 8–9.

39. *Victory in Vietnam*, 182.

40. Ibid., 183.

41. Ibid., 115–116.

42. Budiansky, 380–381.

43. Wayne Thompson, *To Hanoi and Back: The U.S. Air Force and North Vietnam, 1966–1973* (Washington: Smithsonian Institution Press, 2000), 26.

44. The memoirs of Admiral U. S. Grant Sharp are a long argument for the idea that more bombing would have won the Vietnam War. See U. S. Grant Sharp, *Strategy for Defeat* (Novato: Presidio Press, 1968). Much more convincing is Mark Clodfelter, *The Limits of Airpower: The American Bombing of North Vietnam* (New York: The Free Press, 1989). Clodfelter argues that the various bombing campaigns against North Vietnam never had a realistic chance to be decisive.

45. Budiansky, 381.

46. Wayne Thompson, 153–154.

47. Spector, 188.

48. McNamara, *In Retrospect*, 238.

49. Spector, 24–25.

50. James Arnold, *Tet Offensive 1968: Turning Point in Vietnam* (London: Osprey, 1990), 27–28, 87.

51. Ibid., 16.

52. See Arnold, 16, for an assessment of each of the South Vietnamese Army divisions.

53. Arnold, 65–67.

54. James Warren, *American Spartans* (New York: The Free Press, 2005), 261.

55. Wayne Thompson, 131.

56. Graham Cosmas, *MACV: The Joint Command in the Years of Escalation 1962–1967* (Washington DC: U.S. Army Center for Military History, 2006), 360–363.

57. On the success of the CORDS program and pacification effort see Andrew Birtle, *U.S. Army Counterinsurgency and Contingency Operations Doctrine, 1942–1976* (Washington DC: Army Center for Military History, 2006), 324–326.

58. Stephen Hoadley, *Soldiers and Politics in Southeast Asia* (Cambridge: Schenkman Publishing, 1975), 72–81. This book provides a useful analysis of the politics of the South Vietnamese officer corps.

59. Anthony James Joes, *Resisting Rebellion: The History and Politics of Counterinsurgency* (University Press of Kentucky, 2004), 114–115.

60. On the U.S. experience in Vietnam and the failure to employ a coherent counterinsurgency campaign see eds. W. Scott Thompson and Donaldson D. Frizzell, *The Lessons of Vietnam* (New York: Russak and Co., 1977). In it are articles by Maj. Gen Edward Lansdale on counterinsurgency and an article on the small but successful U.S. program to train local self-defense forces by Col. Robert Rheault, "The Special Forces and the CIDG Program," 246–255. See also Thomas Thayer, "Territorial Forces," 256–262. Sir Robert Thompson, who had served in Malaya and understood Southeast Asian conditions, was brought in as a special advisor to the U.S. high command in Vietnam. He told the U.S. military commanders in 1969 that the U.S. conventional war strategy was "a failure" and argued that the U.S. should have concentrated on building up the South Vietnamese Army from the start along with supporting political and economic reforms. See Robert Thompson, *No Exit From Vietnam* (London: Chatto and

Windus, 1969), 122–144. However, Thompson also pointed out that some potentially effective counterinsurgency programs were weak because the effort was too thin and spread out and that programs to build the economic and social infrastructure lacked coherence. See 152–155.

61. James Willbanks, *Abandoning Vietnam* (Lawrence: University Press of Kansas, 2004).

62. Col. G.H. Turley, *The Easter Offensive: Vietnam 1972* (New York: Warner Books, 1985), 22.

63. Ibid., 164–176.

64. Turley, 302–306.

65. James Wilbanks, *Thiet Giap! The Battle of An Loc, April 1972* (Ft. Leavenworth: Combat Studies Institute, 1993). On U.S. air see 57–60. On the VNAF and the role it played in 1972 see 153.

66. On the South Vietnamese view of the Paris negotiations and the final act of the U.S.–South Vietnamese relationship see Tran Van Don, 213–239.

67. Catton, *Diem's Final Failure*, 179–180.

68. See Robert S. McNamara, *In Retrospect: The Tragedy and Lessons of Vietnam* (New York: Times Books Random House, 1995), 46–47.

69. This assessment of the hamlet evaluation report system and the demands for favorable intelligence made by higher headquarters comes from my brother, then Lt. Michael Corum, who served as an intelligence officer in Muc Hua Province in South Vietnam from 1967 to 1968.

70. Cosmas, 446–450.

71. Cosmas, 445.

72. Cosmas, 451–454.

73. Harry Summers Jr., *On Strategy; A Critical Analysis of the Vietnam War* (New York: Dell, 1982,) 48–52.

74. Cosmas, 442.

75. Cosmas, 442.

76. Cosmas, 442–443.

77. Cosmas, 444.

78. After Tet public opinion polls showed that 25 percent of the public favored "broadening and intensifying our military operations" and just 24 percent wanted to "pull out of Vietnam in the near future." However, in August 1968 the Gallup Poll showed that 50 percent of the public viewed the Vietnam War as a mistake. See Linda Feldman, "Why Iraq war support fell so fast," *Christian Science Monitor*, 21 November 2005.

79. In March 1952 more than 50 percent of the U.S. public surveyed in the Gallup Poll believed that the Korean War had been a U.S. mistake. See Feldman.

80. Susan Page, "Poll: American attitudes on Iraq similar to Vietnam era," *USA Today*, 15 November 2005.

81. James Corum and Wray Johnson, *Airpower and Small Wars*, 230–233. For a thorough study of the Vietnamese approach to revolutionary war doctrine see Wray Johnson, *Vietnam and the American Doctrine for Small Wars* (Bangkok: White Lotus Press, 2001).

82. On *dich van* see Mark Woodruff, *Unheralded Victory* (London: Harper Collins, 1999), 197–199.

83. Ibid., 199–207.

84. Ibid., 198–199.

85. On the Chinese commitment to North Vietnam see Xiaoming Zhang, "The Vietnam War: A Chinese Perspective," *Journal of Military History* 60:4 (October 1996), 731–762.

86. Robert W. Komer, *Bureaucracy Does its Thing: Institutional Constraints on U.S.-GVN Performance in Vietnam* (Santa Monica: Rand Study, August 1972).

87. An excellent study of the U.S. Army's intellectual response to Vietnam is Conrad Crane, *Avoiding Vietnam: The U.S. Army's Response to Defeat in Southeast Asia* (Carlisle PA: Army War College, Strategic Studies Institute, September 2002).

88. Shelby Stanton, *The Rise and Fall of an American Army: U.S. Ground Forces in Vietnam, 1965–1973* (New York: Dell Books, 1985), see 26–27, 349–350.

89. James Warren, *American Spartans* (New York: The Free Press, 2005), 271.

90. Allan R. Millett, *Semper Fidelis: The History of the United States Marine Corps*, rev. ed. (New York: The Free Press), 603.

91. Warren, 280.

Chapter 4

1. The process of strategic decision making early in the Bush administration is presented in great detail in Bob Woodward, *Bush at War* (New York: Simon and Schuster, 2002).

2. In the mid-1990s, the army troop levels fell to the lowest point in 50 years, with only 475,000 troops to carry out a set of broad, worldwide missions. By 1999, the Army Secretary and staff were lobbying the Defense Department for 20,000–50,000 more troops, but the Defense Department turned down the request. See "Cohen Dashes Services' Hopes for More Troops," *Army Times*, 2 August 1999.

3. DOD News Service, transcript, Town Hall Meeting in Kuwait, 8 December 2004.

4. Paul Wolfowitz and Zalmay Khalilzad, "Overthrow Him," *Weekly Standard*, 1 December 1997, 14.

5. A good overview of the neocon views is found in James Mann, *Rise of the Vulcans* (New York: Penguin, 2004).

6. Cited in "Even with Moves, Military's Ranks Thin," *Atlanta Journal Constitution*, 19 August 2004.

7. Max Boot, *The Savage Wars of Peace: Small Wars and the Rise of American Power* (New York: Perseus Books, 2002).

8. Ibid., 343–346.

9. Max Boot, "The New American Way of War," *Foreign Affairs* 82:4 (July/August 2003), 42.

10. In the Army Command and General Staff College in the mid-1990s an elective course on counterinsurgency was cancelled due to lack of interest. The situation was the same at the other service staff colleges where the subject of counterinsurgency was virtually nonexistent. Only in the Special Forces schools was the subject taken seriously.

11. For an insightful critique of U.S. military doctrine and thinking in the post Gulf War period see Jeffrey Record, *Hollow Victory* (Washington: Brassey's, 2003).

12. James Corum, *Fighting the War on Terror* (St. Paul: Zenith Press, 2007), 51–82.

13. Cited in Thomas Keaney and Eliot Cohen, *Revolution in Warfare?* (Annapolis: Naval Institute Press, 1995), 188.

14. For some examples of the statements common in the 1990s, see Barry Watts, *Clausewitzian Friction and Future War* (Collingdale, PA: Diane Publishing Co.), 1996.

15. General John Shalikashvili, Chairman of the Joint Chiefs, *Joint Vision 2010*, 1996. See 17, 19, 25.

16. In 2001 and 2002, defense leaders floated proposals to actually cut the army from the current ten to eight divisions. Army officers privately complained about Stephen Cambone, the undersecretary of defense for intelligence and a key Pentagon insider, who reportedly favored increasing space funding and support for the national missile defense at the expense of ground forces. "Army Officials Fear More Cuts," *Washington Times*, 4 June 2002.

17. See Mann, 179–194.

18. See Richard Kohn, "Out of Control: The Crisis in Civil-Military Relations," *The National Interest* 35 (Spring 1994), 3–17; Andrew Bacevich and Richard Kohn, "Grand Army of the Republicans," *New Republic*, 8 December 1997, 22–25; Richard Kohn,

"The Erosion of Civilian Control in the U.S. Today," *The Harmon Memorial Lectures in Military History* 42 (U.S.AF Academy: Colorado, 1999).

19. Peter Feaver, *Armed Servants: Agency Oversight and Civil-Military Relations* (Cambridge: Harvard University Press, 2003), 271.

20. The comment about General Shalikashvili was made to me at the time by a colonel on the Joint Staff. It seemed at the time, and still today, to be a fair evaluation.

21. Michael Desch, "Bush and the Generals," *Foreign Affairs* 86:3 (May/June 2007), 97–108. See 102.

22. Cited in Vago Muradian, "Grading Rumsfeld," *Defense News*, 13 November 2006, 4.

23. W. Shane Story, "Transformation or Troop Strength? Early Accounts of the Invasion of Iraq," *Army History* (Winter 2006), 21–29. See 25.

24. Michael Gordon and Bernard Trainor, Cobra II (New York: Pantheon, 2006), 46.

25. Rowan Scarborough, "Wolfowitz criticizes 'suspect' estimate of occupation force," *Washington Times*, 28 February 2003. Testifying before Congress, Wolfowitz asserted that Shinseki's estimate of troops required for the occupation of Iraq was "wildly off the mark" and also argued that the U.S. would not likely have to foot the bill for the occupation and reconstruction of Iraq thanks to Iraq's oil reserves and frozen assets. As Wolfowitz noted, "There's a lot of money there, and to assume we're going to pay for it is wrong."

26. See Gen. Barry McCaffrey, "We Need More Troops," *Wall Street Journal*, 29 July 2003; *Washington Times*, "Increasing Our Ground Forces," 26 January 2005, 18. In 2004 Major General Robert Scales (Ret.), a brigade commander in the First Gulf War, proposed a ground force hike of 150,000, increasing the number of Army brigades to fifty from the current thirty-three. In November 2003 a bipartisan group of 128 house members—including 54 of the 61 members of the House Armed Services Committee—asked the Bush administration to approve 30,000 more troops. Retired General Theodore Stroup said the army should be expanded by 40,000–50,000 men. David Brownfeld, "Debate Over Size, Shape of Army," Fox News Online, August 30, 2004; Frederick Kagan of the Hoover Institute pointed out that even if the army committed itself to no further operations it would still need 14 divisions (4 more than present) to conduct current operations efficiently. See Frederick Kagan, "War and Aftermath," *Policy Review Online* 102 (August/September 2003). One of the most eloquent calls for increasing the army's size came from Medal of Honor winner journalist Joe Galloway, who compared Secretary Rumsfeld with Secretary McNamara and argued that the army leaders were

"in denial" about the manpower problem. See Joseph Galloway, "How to Ruin a Great Army in a Short Time," *Miami Herald*, 28 September 2003.

27. "The Pentagon Wants Bigger Army, Marine Corps," *Washington Times*, 11 January 2007.

28. Alistair Finlan, "Trapped in Dead Ground: U.S. Counterinsurgency Strategy in Iraq," *Small Wars and Insurgencies* 16:1 (March 2005), 1–21. See 5.

29. Story, 24–25.

30. The author was briefed on the army plan for Iraq in November 2002, and the colonel who presented the brief made it absolutely clear that the 250,000 troop number was to control Iraq after the regime fell. One Air Force Colonel, a Rumsfeld fan who had just come from the Pentagon staff, ridiculed the army plan after the briefing, calling the army "dinosaurs" for thinking that more than 80,000 men were necessary.

31. For an account of interagency infighting in the 1990s see Major Vicki Rast, *Interagency Fratricide: Policy Failures in the Persian Gulf and Bosnia* (Maxwell AFB: Air University Press, 2004).

32. The process of strategic decision making early in the Bush administration is presented in great detail in Bob Woodward, *Bush at War*.

33. *The National Security Strategy of the U.S. of America*, 1 March 2006.

34. Ibid.

35. Although the U.S. maintains that the end of all tyranny is the national strategic objective, the U.S. provides considerable aid and assistance to countries such as Pakistan, Egypt, Uzbekistan, and so on. None of these countries can be honestly described as anything other than dictatorships.

36. For an overview of the Bush administration National Security Strategies see Lawrence Korb, "A Critique of the Bush Administration's National Security Strategy," The Stanley Foundation, policy analysis brief, June 2006.

37. *National Security Strategy for Victory in Iraq*, National Security Council, November 2005. See especially 10, 14–26.

38. Rast, 42–73.

39. One of the committee members present at the meeting told me of this in June, 2007.

40. In 2001 Cheney drew up the policy decision to detain foreign terrorism suspects indefinitely and took it straight to President Bush for approval. Secretary of State Powell and National Security Advisor Condoleeza Rice were not even consulted before the policy was endorsed by the president. On Cheney's role in wartime decision making see Barton Gellman, Jo Becker, "A Different Understanding with the President," *Washington Post*, 24 June 2007.

41. For a good analysis of the cultural and bureaucratic barriers that prevented effective State Department and Defense Department planning for the occupation of Iraq see Donald R. Drechsler, "Reconstructing the Interagency Process After Iraq," *Journal of Strategic Studies* (February 2005), 3–30.

42. There were various efforts for prewar planning that included a group at the Army War College and the National Defense University. These groups coordinated their efforts in conferences in November and December 2002. ORHA was officially formed on 20 January 2003, with some of the personnel from the planning groups becoming part of the initial cadre.

43. James Fallows, "Blind into Baghdad," *Atlantic Monthly* (January/February 2004). The Army War College Planning group doubted that Iraq's oil wealth could pay for the cost of reconstruction. They estimated the cost of rebuilding Iraq to be between $30 to $100 billion—not including the cost of occupation troops. See Conrad C. Crane, W. Andrew Terrill, *Reconstructing Iraq: Insights, Challenges, and Missions for Military Forces in a Post-Conflict Scenario*, U.S. Army War College, Strategic Studies Institute, February 2003, 41–42.

44. *Reconstructing Iraq*, 31. According to former CIA analyst Judith Yaphe, "Iraqi exile leader Ahmad Chalabi and the INC (Iraqi National Congress) are known quantities and extremely unpopular in Iraq."

45. *Reconstructing Iraq*, 18–20, 34–39.

46. Woodward, *Bush at War*, 48–49, 84–85.

47. This information is from an army Intelligence Corps major who worked in the Intelligence Center during the Gulf War and who personally briefed General McKiernan on the Iraqi forces and Fedayeen several times before and during the combat operations.

48. Lt. Col. Antulio Echevarria, *On the American Way of War*, U.S. Army War College Strategic Studies Institute Paper (Army War College SSI: Carlisle Barracks PA, May 2004).

49. Rowan Scarborough, "Post-Saddam resistance unforeseen, U.S. officials say," *Washington Times*, Sept. 1–7, 2003, 17.

50. Letter to the author by Colonel Paul Hughes, U.S. Army Ret., Nov. 2004. Colonel Hughes was involved with the prewar planning for the Iraq occupation and served as an army strategist with ORHA during the 2003 invasion of Iraq.

51. Ibid.

52. A good picture of the CPA and its employees is Rajiv Chandrasekaran, *Imperial Life in the Emerald City: Inside Iraq's Green Zone* (New York: Knopf, 2006).

53. For an Iraqi view of the CPA and the competence of the American administrators in Iraq see Ali Allawi, *The Occupation of Iraq: Winning the War, Losing the Peace* (New Haven: Yale University Press, 2007), 101–111. Allawi argues that ORHA and CPA were overwhelmed by the job of administration in Iraq. He speaks disparagingly of the "neocon warriors" of the Bush administration and rates Bremer as "not in the first rank of diplomats."

54. Ali Allawi, who served for a time as defense minister and later president in the interim Iraqi government, argues that the American de-Baathification program and disbanding the Iraqi army triggered the insurgency. Allawi points out that even the majority of the Shiites were against the move. See Allawi, 155–159.

55. One senior CPA official on Bremer's staff said the decision to disband the Iraqi army came from Washington and "was a done deal." Official to author, December 2003.

56. On the early development of the insurgency see Ahmed Hashim, "The Insurgency in Iraq," *Small Wars and Insurgencies* 14:3 (Autumn 2003), 1–22. See 8–9.

57. Hashim, "The Insurgency in Iraq," *Small Wars and Insurgencies* 5.

58. Rowan Scarborough, "U.S. Miscalculates Security for Iraq," *Washington Times*, 23 August 2003, 1.

59. Mark Mazzetti and Solomon Moore, "Insurgents Flourish in Iraq's Wild West," *Los Angeles Times*, 24 May 2005. See also Tom Lasseter, "Officers Say Army Lacks Troops To Protect Gains," *Miami Herald*, 1 June 2005, p. 1.

60. On U.S. forces and adapting to war in Iraq see Greg Jafe, "On the Ground in Iraq: Captain Ayers writes his own playbook," *Wall Street Journal*, 22 September 2004, A-1.

61. Between 2003 and 2006 the Pentagon spent $250 billion in Iraq. In 2006 there were only two Pentagon Inspector General Office investigators in Iraq and six auditors to track contract performance. In 2005 there had been none. See Griff White, "Contractors Rarely held Responsible for Misdeeds in Iraq," *Washington Post*, 4 November 2006, A-12.

62. Anthony Schwarz, "Iraq's Militias: The True Threat to Coalition Success in Iraq," *Parameters* 37:1 (Spring 2007), 55–71. See 64.

63. Tom Lasseter, "Al-Sadr Militia, Warriors and Traffic Cops," *Detroit Free Press*, 14 July 2004.

64. Deputy Secretary Paul Wolfowitz testified to Congress on June 22, 2004, that he had underestimated the strength of the insurgency—expecting that once Saddam had been captured it would die away. But he continued to argue that U.S. didn't need more troops and "getting Iraqi forces up and fighting for their country is the answer." See Rowan Scarborough, "Iraq insurgency surprised Pentagon," *Washington Times*, June 28– July 4, 2004, p. 3.

65. On training the Iraqi military see James S. Corum, *Fighting the War on Terror* (St. Paul: Zenith Press, 2007), 222–231.

66. See Mark Bowden, "When Officers Aren't Gentlemen," *Wall Street Journal*, 8 February 2005, A-18.

67. Christine Spoler, "Iraqi Soldiers Deserting New Army", *Chicago Tribune*, 9 December 2003.

68. Tom Squitieri, "Long Way to go Before Iraqis Take Over Security," *USA Today*, 14 Dec. 2004. When the police in Mosul came under attack in November 2004, three quarters of the 4,000 member force ran away. Most of the ICDC battalion in Mosul also ran, but not before looting their base of weapons and equipment.

69. Eric Schmitt, "Iraqis Not Ready to Fight Rebels on Their Own, U.S. Says", *New York Times*, July 21, 2005.

70. Eric Schmitt, "General Seeking Faster Training of Iraqi Soldiers," *New York Times*, 23 January 2005.

71. James Fallows, "Why Iraq has no Army," *Atlantic Monthly* (December 2005), 67–70.

72. Ahmed Hashim, *Insurgency and Counterinsurgency in Iraq* (Ithaca: Cornell University Press, 2006), 110–122, 197.

73. Ned Parker, "Christians Forced Out of Baghdad District," *Los Angeles Times*, 27 June 2007.

74. Sundarsan Raghaven, "War's toll on Iraqis put at 22,950 in '06," *Washington Post*, 8 June 2007.

75. Alissa Rubin, "U.S. Generals Doubt Ability of Iraqi Army to Hold Gains," *New York Times*, 25 June 2007, 10.

76. L. Paul Bremer, *My Year in Iraq* (New York, Simon and Schuster, 2006), 61–66.

77. Scarborough, 17.

78. Kenneth Pollack, *Arabs at War: Military Effectiveness, 1948–1991* (Lincoln: University of Nebraska Press, 2002).

79. For a good summary of the problems see Kenneth Pollack's introduction and conclusion, 1–13, 552–583.

80. Norvell De Atkine, "Why Arabs Lose Wars," *Middle East Quarterly* (December 1999).

81. Thomas Ricks, "Intelligence problems in Iraq are detailed," *Washington Post*, 25 October 2003, A-1. A report from the Army Center for Lessons Learned noted junior intelligence officers and NCOs were poorly prepared to carry out human intelligence operations and that many had "very little or no analytical skills." On the shortage of

qualified intelligence personnel for the Iraq War see Anthony Cordesman, "The Current Military Situation in Iraq," Washington DC: Center for Strategic and International Studies Paper, 14 November 2003, 13–14.

82. Linda Feldmann, "Why Iraq War Support Fell So Fast," *Christian Science Monitor*, 21 November 2005.

83. In May 2007 only 22 percent of Americans accepted President Bush's view that keeping U.S. forces in Iraq are preventing terror attacks in the United States. "Gallup Poll," *USA Today*, 9 May 2007, A-8.

84. "Bush: 'Bring on' attackers of U.S. Troops," *USA Today*, 3 July 2003.

85. Heard by the author at a military briefing. Quote is by a U.S. army general.

86. One example of the tough journalism that the Bush administration faced is the work of Thomas Ricks. Ricks, a former editor of *Army Times*, is one of the most knowledgeable and respected of the U.S. journalists. His 2006 book, *Fiasco*, is a devastating critique of the Bush administration's lack of planning and bad decisions on the occupation of Iraq.

87. Michael Moss, "Many Actions Tied to Delay in Armor for Troops in Iraq," *New York Times*, 7 March 2005, p. 1. The author was in Iraq in January 2005 when the Pentagon publicly announced that all the troops deployed to Iraq now had the new body armor. This was not correct. Not all the members of my army team deployed to Iraq at that time had it.

88. *Jefferson City News Tribune*, "Despite U.S. promise, soldiers in Iraq still buying their own body armor," 4 April 2004. Senator Susan Collins of Maine of the Senate Armed Service Committee stated, "We lagged far behind in making sure that our soldiers who are performing very difficult and dangerous missions had protective equipment."

89. Thomas Ricks, Ann Tyson, "Defense Secretary Sends Message About Accountability," *Washington Post*, 3 March 2007, A-8.

90. Greg Zoroya, "At U.S. Military Hospitals Everybody is Overworked," *USA Today*, 5 June 2007.

91. Conrad Crane and W. Andrew Terrill, *Reconstructing Iraq*, U.S. Army War College, SSI Study, February 2003, 65.

92. Special Study, James S. Corum, "Lessons on Occupying an Enemy Country," Section 2. Sent to Planning Cell September 2002. Author's files.

93. Ibid., 4. See also Tina-Marie O'Neill, "Commission Seeks to Regulate Iraqi Media Sector," *Sunday Business Post*, 4 July 2004. "Unregulated media allowed scores of local and foreign stations to lay siege to its airwaves."

94. The Governing Council in Iraq only issued a temporary code of media ethics to regulate the media in July 2004.

95. The first budget of the Iraqi government in 2004 allocating only $1.57 million to press and media operations, probably less than some of the violent factions in Iraq.

96. General Franks, interview, *Parade Magazine*, New York, 30 July 2004.

97. *The Iraq Study Group Report*, James Baker and Lee Hamilton co-chairs, (Washington: November, 2006). On recommendations for the Iraqi government see 45–48.

98. ' Center for Strategic and International Studies, *Report of the Independent Commission on the Security Forces of Iraq* (CSIS: Washington DC, September 2007), 20.

99. U.S. Congress, General Accounting Office, *Report: Securing, Stabilizing and Rebuilding Iraq* (Washington DC: September 2007).

100. For a good overview of the state of the U.S. military in 2007 see Mark Thompson, "America's Broken Down Army," *Time* magazine, 5 April 2007; "Air Force General: 'Air Fleet Wearing Down'," *USA Today*, 8 May 2007, 1; Peter Spiegel, "Guard Equipment Levels Lowest Since 9/11," *Los Angeles Times*, 10 May 2007. Spiegel notes some states are down to 56 percent of their equipment and are unready in case of homeland emergencies; Gordon Lubold, "Key U.S. Army ranks begin to thin," *Christian Science Monitor*, 2 May 2007.

101. Byan Bender, "Army is Worn Too Thin, says General," *Boston Globe*, 27 September 2007, 1.

Chapter Five

1. In 1946 a crushing 15 percent of the British GNP went to defense spending. See L. J. Butler, *Britain and Empire* (London: I.B. Tauris, 2002), p.66.

2. Butler, 100.

3. Officers who have served in the Pentagon have told me that the army remains reluctant to ask for more manpower, even in 2006 when the manpower crunch was extreme: The army leadership is afraid to add force structure that Congress will be unwilling to finance, which would mean that any improvements in equipment would have to be shelved and the army turned into a "hollow force" much like in the 1970s. So the army remains wedded to the concept of somehow making do with a force that was considered by most to be far too small even for the relative peacetime requirements of the 1990s.

4. See John Mueller, *Policy and Opinion in the Gulf War* (Chicago: University of Chicago Press, 1994).

INDEX

■ ■ ■

Index